A SYSTEM OF PRAGMATIC IDEALISM

VOLUME II

THE VALIDITY OF VALUES

A Normative Theory of Evaluative Rationality

Nicholas Rescher

PRINCETON UNIVERSITY PRESS   PRINCETON, NEW JERSEY

Copyright © 1993 by Princeton University Press
Published by Princeton University Press, 41 William Street,
Princeton, New Jersey 08540
In the United Kingdom: Princeton University Press, Oxford
All Rights Reserved

Library of Congress Cataloging-in-Publication Data

(Revised for volume 2)
Rescher, Nicholas.
A system of pragmatic idealism
Includes bibliographical references and index.
ISBN 0-691-07391-0 (v. 1)
ISBN 0-691-07393-7 (v. 2)
Contents: v. 1. Human knowledge in idealistic perspective —
v. 2. The validity of values.
1. Idealism. 2. Pragmatism. I. Title.
B823.R44   1991
141   91-15122

This book has been composed in Linotron Caledonia

Several sections of this book have appeared elsewhere in slightly
different form. Grateful acknowledgment is made for permission to
reprint from the following works by Nicholas Rescher: Chapter 6
of *Ethical Idealism: An Inquiry into the Nature and Function of
Ideas* (Berkeley and Los Angeles: University of California Press,
1987), copyright © 1987 The Regents of the University of California;
"How Wide Is the Gap between Facts and Values?" *Philosophy
and Phenomenological Research* 50 (Fall 1990): 297–319
(Supplement); chapter 2 of *Human Interests* (Stanford, Calif.:
Stanford University Press, 1990), © 1990 by the Board of Trustees
of the Leland Stanford Junior University; and chapter 3 of *Moral
Absolutes* (New York: Peter Lang Publishing Co., 1989).

Princeton University Press books are printed
on acid-free paper and meet the guidelines
for permanence and durability of the Committee
on Production Guidelines for Book Longevity
of the Council on Library Resources

Printed in the United States of America

10 9 8 7 6 5 4 3 2 1

To the Memory of My Parents

Eleven
Moral Values as Immune to Relativism   187

Twelve
Moral Rationality: Why Be Moral?   206

PART V: VALUES AND RATIONALITY

Thirteen
Rationality and Happiness   233

Fourteen
Values, Pragmatism, and Idealism   246

Bibliography   255

Name Index   261

Subject Index   263

List of Displays

1.1   Stratification Levels of the Norms of Rationality   8

4.1   The Cognitive Parallelism of Inquiry and Evaluation   83

9.1   A Hypothetical Course of Change   158

9.2   The Spectrum of Positions Regarding Value in Nature   170

11.1   Illustrations of the Implementation Hierarchy for Moral
       Norms   192

Preface _____

THIS BOOK is the second volume of my "Pragmatic Idealism" trilogy. It is preceded by *Human Knowledge in Idealistic Perspective*, which deals with issues of epistemology and philosophy of science, and it will be followed by *Metaphilosophical Inquiries*, which deals with the nature and methodology of philosophizing. Taken in combination, these books weave together a fabric of ideas, arguments, and positions that present the principal features of the philosophical system that I have developed over a long period of time—a system that combines and extends ideas at work in various classical philosophical positions (pragmatism and idealism above all) into a new and, as I hope, illuminating perspective on major philosophical themes.

Drawing extensively on work I have produced over the past twenty-five years, the present book was written during the 1989–91 biennium. For me, this project of synthesis was an enlightening labor of self-education, because it has helped me to bring into clearer, more sharply articulated focus the general tenor of the idealistic position elaborated in the more limited versions and specific investigations that have conveyed my thought and work over the recent decades.

Walter Sinnott Armstrong read the manuscript with care and offered many useful comments and criticisms. Jon Mandle helped with the editing process, and Marian Kowatch and Annamarie Morrow with the preparation of a printable typescript. Ann Himmelberger Wald and her associates at Princeton University Press have been unfailingly helpful and cooperative. I am very grateful to all concerned for their assistance.

Pittsburgh, Pennsylvania
March 1991

Introduction _____

THE SIGNIFICANCE of values and evaluation is a central theme of philosophical idealism. And the utility of values for a proper understanding of ourselves and the world we live in is also the leitmotiv of the present book, whose general tenor could accordingly be characterized as that of an axiological idealism. Its central theme is the important role of values in understanding ourselves, the environing world, and our place within it.

In the endeavor to expound this position, the book sets out a normative theory of rationality. Its key thesis—which is argued pragmatically from various angles and points of departure—is that rationality as such and in general is bound up with the theory and practice of rational evaluation. A rational being must view in the light of this rationality not only its beliefs but its values as well. Valuation is an inherent part of the life of reason—moral evaluation included.

For such a perspective to make sense it must show that value is not merely a matter of taste, like the preference of one flavor of food over another. Evaluation must be acknowledged in its objective, rational mode as dealing with facts of the matter (albeit evaluative rather than descriptive facts). And this too is a central theme of the book.

In addition to these more abstract deliberations about the nature and role of values, the book also deliberates about the prospect of a conflict between natural science and human values, about the role of values as guides to life, and about the evaluative aspects of our ethical and moral convictions. Its aim overall is to clarify how values play an important and appropriate role in the proper understanding of the human condition. Our value commitments are a crucial part of what makes us into the creatures we are, so that a just appreciation of their role is indispensable to a proper understanding of a salient sector of the world's realities.

Part I

VALUES AND REASONS

One

The Reach of Reason

The Universality of Reason

Rationality is a matter of the intelligent pursuit of appropriate objectives—of proceeding in what we do in line with cogent reasons. Whether in cognitive, practical, or evaluative matters, rationality accordingly has two distinguishable although inseparable aspects: the one personal, private, and particular; the other impersonal, public, and universal. The private (particularized) aspect turns on what is advisable *for the agent*, duly considering his or her own personal situation and circumstances—the agent's idiosyncratic information, experience, opportunities, capabilities, talents, objectives, aspirations, needs, and wants. (Note that we here construe "circumstances" very broadly, including not only the outer and situational but also the inner conditions that relate to a person's physical and psychological condition and makeup.) The universal aspect of rationality turns on its being advisable by standards that are person indifferent and objectively cogent *for anyone in those circumstances* to proceed in a "rationally appropriate" way in the matters at issue. The standards of rational cogency are unrestricted and general, in the sense that what is rational for one person will also be rational for anyone else who is in the same condition. Both aspects, the situational and the universal, are inseparable facets of rationality as standardly conceived.

For a belief, action, or evaluation to qualify as rational, the agent must (in theory at least) be in a position to "give an account" of it on whose basis others can see that "it is only right and proper" to resolve the issue in that way. An intelligent, detached observer, apprised of the facts of the case, must be in a position to say: "While I myself do not happen to believe or pursue or value these things, I can see that it is appropriate that someone in the agent's circumstances should do so and in consequence realize that it was altogether sensible for the agent to have proceeded in that way." People's circumstances differ, but the *standards* of rationality that govern their comportment are universal. It lies in the very meaning of the concept of rationality as such that if something is indeed "the rational thing to do," then it must be possible in principle for anyone to recognize the rational sense of it once enough information is secured.

To be sure, considerations of rationality may not constrain to uniqueness. We speak of *the* rational resolution of an issue when there indeed is only one, but also of *a* rational resolution when there are various alternatives that are inherently no less acceptable. Moreover, while it is indeed irrational to make rationally suboptimal judgments, this is capable of degrees where there are ever more serious deviations. Departures from rationality are certainly not of a piece in point of severity.

Rational belief, action, and evaluation are possible only in situations where there are cogent grounds (and not just compelling personal motives) for what one does. The idea of rationality is in principle inapplicable where one is at liberty to make up one's rules as one goes along—to have no settled and predetermined norms or standards at all. The dictates of rationality proceed under the aegis of objective and impersonal standards. This matter of good reasons and cogent grounds is not something subjective or idiosyncratic; that good reasons indeed are good reasons is something that is objective and lies in the public domain.[1] Both the appropriateness of ends (for a person of particular makeup, talents, tastes, and the like) and the suitability of particular means for pursuing those particular ends pose objective issues that are open to others every bit as much as to the agents themselves. Indeed, with respect both to someone's needs and to their best interests, other informed people (one's doctor, one's lawyer, one's tax adviser, and so on) may well be in a position to make better and wiser—that is, more rational—judgments than the individual can. An isolated Robinson Crusoe may well act in a perfectly rational way, but he can do so only by doing what hypothetically would make sense for others in similar circumstances. He must in principle be in a position to persuade other people to endorse his course of action by an appeal to impersonal general principles to show them that his actions were appropriate in the circumstances, either uniquely or no less so than the alternatives. Rationality is thus something inherently universal in its operations.

The circumstantiality of reason reflects an unavoidable element of person relativity. Our concrete rational commitments are indeed universal, but only *circumstantially* universal in a way that makes room for the variation of times, places, and the thousands of details of each individual and situation. What it was rational for Galen to believe in his day, given the cognitive state of the art in antiquity regarding medical matters, is in general no longer rational for us to believe today. The routines of training and practice that a young man who is a "natural athlete" can appropriately set for himself may not make sense for a young cripple or an active septuagenarian. Obviously, what it is rational for someone to do or to think hinges

---

[1] Which is not to say that people cannot be blind to good reasons—they can be blind to anything!

on the particular details of how one is circumstanced—and the prevailing circumstances differ from person to person and group to group. The rulings of rationality are indeed subject to person relativity, but one that proceeds in an impersonal way in taking personal conditions and circumstances into account.

Consider an example. I am hungry; I go to a restaurant; I order a meal. Have I acted rationally? Of course. But why exactly? Because a long story can correctly be told about what I have done, a story in which all of the following play a significant role: my well-evidentiated beliefs that eating food alleviates hunger pangs and nourishes the body; my appropriate conviction that restaurants provide food; my sensible preference for physical health and for the comfort of satiation over the discomfort of hunger; my custom of doing what I effectively can to alleviate discomfort and promote well-being, and the like. The whole chain—alleviate discomfort, proceed to secure food, go to a food supplier, order food—is part and parcel of the rationality-dictated rationale of my action. If the chain were severed at any point (if, for example, I realized that the restaurant had run out of food last week), then my action in proceeding to the restaurant to order that meal would cease to be rational in the circumstances.

One proceeds rationally only when one's actions can be subsumed under a universal principle of rationality that holds good generally and for everyone. In the restaurant I study the menu and order steak. Was it *rational* of me to do so? Of course—because I was hungry, came to eat something at the restaurant, and found steak to be the most appealing entry on the menu, thus proceeding on the principle "Presented with various options for food (and other things being equal), select that which one deems the tastiest." (To be sure, other things may not be equal—my choice of beef might deeply offend my dinner guest, who deems cattle sacred.) Here we have a strictly universal principle, one that it makes perfectly good rational sense for anyone to act on. Though clearly not every sensible person would order steak, nevertheless, under the aegis of the indicated principle, I could be said to have acted rationally only when I have done what any sensible person would. Similarly, any rational choice must be "covered" by a universally valid desideratum. It must implement, in its particular context, a principle that is of strictly universal validity—although, to be sure, one that is of a conditional nature.

Again, some things we desire for ourselves ("Mary as a wife"); others we see as universal desiderata that hold generally and for everyone ("having a good spouse if married"). Now, the crucial fact is that a personal want or preference qualifies as rational only insofar as it can be subordinated to something that is an unrestrictedly universal desideratum (all else being equal). Only insofar as I am convinced that Mary will prove to be an instance of something that everyone can acknowledge as desirable at a sufficiently high level of generality (having one's marriage partner be "a good spouse," "a caring helpmeet," "a desirable mate," "a delightful companion," or some such) will my own personal desire to have her for a wife be a rational one. Only those acts that instantiate in this way something that deserves the rather pompous title of a "universal principle of reason" can qualify as rational. It is not "being the last to cross the bridge safely" that would be rationally advisable for anyone and everyone to opt for in relevant circumstances but only something like "gaining one's way to safety from a dangerous situation." Only those acts whose *salient* characterization is universally rational at some level of abstraction are rational at all.

The ground of the universality of reason is not far to seek. It is rooted in the nature of interests. Something can be in my (real) interests only by being an item of a generic type that is in everyone's (real) interests. It is in my interest to take a particular medicine because it is generally in anyone's and everyone's interest to care for their health. Any valid interest— any that merits the acknowledgment of reason—must inhere in a universal interest (as the validity of an interest in tennis rooted in a generic need for exercise or skill development). And the very raison d'être of reason is as a servant of our interests, in being both the ultimate arbiter of what those interests are and the appropriate guide to their realization.

The contention "What's rational for you need not be so for me" is certainly correct—within limits. Consider the medical analogy. You might do well to eat chocolate to provide the calories needed for the strenuous outdoor life you lead; for me, with my diabetes, it would be a very bad thing indeed. And so, low-level recommendations like "Eat chocolate" indeed fall into the range of the just-stated dictum. But with "Eat the foods conducive to maintaining your health" the matter stands very differently, and we have moved to a much higher level of generality. And finally with "Do what best furthers the realization of your real best interests" we have reached a level where there is no variability. What is right and proper here in point of rationality is right and proper for everybody. Similarly, at the higher level of governing principles, rationality is increasingly compelling and universal. The uniformity of overarching rational principles transcends the variability of their particular cultural implementations. Different cultures do indeed implement a rational principle like "Be in a position to substantiate your claims" very differently. (For one thing, there are culturally or historically different standards as to what constitutes a proper "substantiation" for claims.) But they cannot simply abandon it. If they convert to "It's all right to maintain anything that suits your fancy," they do not have a *different* mode of cognitive rationality; rather, in this respect at any rate, they are simply *deficient* in cognitive rationality. The characteristic nature of the cognitive enterprise as such imposes limits in its appropriate pursuit.

To be sure, the question "What is the rational thing to believe or to do?" must receive the indecisive answer: "That depends." It depends on context and situation, on conditions and circumstances. At the level of the question "What is rational; what should properly be believed or done?" a many-sided and pluralistic response is called for. The way in which people proceed to give a rational justification of something—whether a belief, an action, or an evaluation—is unquestionably variable and culture relative. We mortals cannot speak with the tongues of angels. The means by which we actually pursue our ends in the setting of any major project—whether rationality, morality, communication, or nourishment—are "culture dependent" and "context variable." Nevertheless, those projects themselves—in terms of the objectives and ideals that define them and of the basic principles that implement these objectives, aims, and ideals—have a uniform and universal validity. Greek medicine is something very different from modern medicine. But the aims of the enterprise—"the maintenance of health," "the relief of distressing symptoms," "the prolongation of life," and the like—are similar throughout. These aims, after all, define the issue, indicating that it is medicine we are talking about rather than, say, basket weaving. This is so with rationality itself as well. Rationality is, after all, a definite sort of enterprise with a characteristic goal structure of its own—the pursuit of appropriately adopted ends by intelligently selected means. The defining principles that determine rationality's particular nature as the sort of thing it is make for an inevitable uniformity.

Cultivation Hierarchies

But how can the absolutistic universality of the defining principles of rationality—themselves rooted in the monolithic uniformity of "what rationality is"—be reconciled with the pluralistic diversity of appropriate answers to the question "What is it rational to do?"

The answer lies in the fact that various intermediate levels, or strata, of consideration separate the "basic principles of rationality" from concrete decisions about what it is rational to do in the various particular conditions that prevail. The tabulation of display 1.1 depicts this descending hierarchy of principles, norms and standards, rules, and (finally) rulings, which composes the structure of rationale development. There is a distinctive hierarchical continuum of levels throughout. At the top of the hierarchy, the defining principles of rationality specify the characterizing aims of the enterprise. They explicate what is at issue: the giving of good reasons for what we do, the provision of a reasonable account, the telling of a sensible story (*logon didonai, rationem reddere*). The characteristic mission of rationality is that of providing an account of our dealings, of committing

Display 1.1 Stratification Levels of the Norms of Rationality

1. *Characterizing aims of rationality.* Rationality calls for the intelligent pursuit of appropriate objectives.

2. *Defining principles of rationality.* The basic principles that delineate and specify rationality's requirements. (For cognitive rationality, for example, the project at issue turns on the pursuit of truth and the achievement of correct answers to our questions. It seeks "the truth, the whole truth, and nothing but the truth.") These principles provide our criteria for assessing the acceptability and adequacy of rational norms and standards of rational procedure.

3. *Governing norms and standards of rationality.* Standards for appraising the "rules of the game" governing the rational transaction of affairs. (For cognitive rationality these norms are afforded by desiderata such as coherence, consistency, and simplicity.) These norms provide our criteria for assessing the acceptability and adequacy of our rules of rational procedure.

4. *Rules of rational procedure.* Rules for the rational resolution of choices. (In the cognitive case, rules like *modus ponens* in deductive inference or trend extrapolation in inductive inference.) These rules constitute our criteria for assessing the rational acceptability and adequacy of particular resolutions.

5. *Rationally warranted rulings.* Resolutions with respect to particular issues arising in particular concrete cases, such as: "Do (or accept) X in the existing circumstances."

---

ourselves in the context of our affairs to "making sense," of rendering our dealings intelligible, of conducting our affairs intelligently. At the next level down, the governing norms and standards are our yardsticks of rational procedure: basic principles of logic, canons of inductive reasoning, standards of evidence, and the like, which already admit of some variation. Then, descending further, we encounter the "rules of the game" that specify the procedures through which we implement ends and objectives of the enterprise in the concrete context of particular cases. Finally, at the bottom level, come the specific resolutions for particular cases achieved through the subsumption of concrete cases under the rules. (It is clearly these last that vary most of all.) Such a "cultivation hierarchy" (as we shall call it) characterizes any purposively oriented human endeavor. It takes the format:

1. governing "finalities": the characterizing aims of the enterprise (governing principles);

2. implementing policies (guiding norms and standards; basic values and desiderata);

3. methods of procedure (operating rules);

4. specific rulings.

The top-level purpose is itself "ultimate" for its own domain: it defines and specifies what is at issue in the venture under consideration, the concerns that make it the sort of project it is (whether science or horticulture). The subsequent descending levels each address the matter of implementing the previously fixed aims and objectives. Justification at each subordinate level is thus purposive and turns on questions of efficiency and effectiveness in serving the needs of the next, superordinated higher level. There is a step-by-step descent from finalities (the characteristic aims inherent in the very definition of valid, need-meeting enterprises) through norms to rules and eventually to specific rulings. And it should be stressed that all of these stages of rationale development appertain equally to rational belief, action, and evaluation.

It is helpful to consider an analogy, turning from cognitive rationality to medicine.

1. *Finalities (defining principles).* "Maintaining health," "curing illness and disease," "restoring and maintaining normal bodily functioning," "removing painful symptoms." (Note that if these things are not at issue, then medicine is not at issue. An enterprise not concerned with any of these, whatever it may be, is not medicine.)

2. *Implementing norms, standards, and criteria.* "How is one to assess 'health'?" "How is one to construe a satisfactory 'normality'?" "How is one to identify a 'symptom'?" "Just what constitutes an 'illness'?" (Note that for the Greeks, unlike ourselves, the idea of an illness without subject-experienced symptoms was scarcely conceivable. At this level there is already some room for variation.)

3. *Rules or procedures.* The modus operandi of medical practices—surgery or chiropractic treatment, drugs or psychotherapy, and the like. (These of course differ drastically from age to age and culture to culture.)

4. *Rationally warranted rulings.* The specific interventions, prescriptions, and medical measures adopted in particular cases. ("Take two aspirin and get some rest.")

At the top level there is a fixity and uniformity based in conceptual constraints inherent in the very definition of the nature of the enterprise. But uniformity is achieved here at the price of an abstractness and generality that endows the principles at issue with a conditional or hypothetical character. As we move downward toward the level of particular cases, the situation is increasingly one of concrete detail, and this detail brings increasing scope for variation in its wake. Thus, while the top level is itself absolute and constant, there is "slack" at each step down the ladder, leaving (appropriate) room for an increasingly large element of variability and differentiation. At each successive step in the process of subordination, there is some degree of underdetermination, with scope for diversity and some degree of contextual variability. (In the cognitive case, variability arises with such issues as: What sorts of rules best implement the demands for cogent deductive and inductive reasoning? What sorts of solutions do schematic rules like "Adapt theories to the data as well as possible" lead to?) As we move down this hierarchical ladder, there emerges an increasing looseness of fit that provides for the differential adaptation of general principles to the specific characteristics of particular settings and circumstances.

However, if there is not a filiation of continuity—if a particular measure is not part of a long story that leads from our concrete choices all the way up to that fixed and stable top level of the principles that define, in the present case, "the aims of the medical enterprise"—then it is really not a genuine medical measure that is in question. Throughout, justification of one's proceedings at lower levels involves an appeal to the higher. But the highest level is final in its defining role for the overall enterprise at issue. (After all, medicine—or cognition—is a definite sort of enterprise, different in its teleological nature from ventures like astronomy or butterfly collecting.)

The bearing of that fixed, topmost, and universally valid desideratum transmits itself all down the line, albeit with ever-increasing qualifications as the situation gains in concrete particularity. In the medical case, for example, we get:

1. maintaining health;
2. maintaining health through nourishment (eating);
3. getting nourishment by eating healthy foods that one also happens to like.

Observe, however, that all of these are also universally appropriate modes of operation: doing the things involved is rational for *everybody*. But this universality becomes increasingly qualified in its conditions of application when one proceeds down the ladder by appropriate steps.[2] (Clearly, not everyone happens to like meat in general or steak in particular.) And so, there is much room for variation in the concrete implementation of universals. As regards (2), different things are nourishing for different people, given their particular biomedical makeup. And as regards (3), it is clear that different people like different things.

Such a hierarchy of rationale-furnishing levels always plays a crucial role in providing for the rational legitimation of what we do. At its pinnacle there is some rationally valid (appropriately interest-serving) desideratum like health (or rationality itself) to furnish the "ultimate" pivot point, but in moving down the line, we encounter the increasingly more concrete factors of rationalization, until ultimately we arrive at specific determinations about concrete items. Here, there is increasing room for context-supplied variation and dissensus.

---

[2] Note that it is not homogeneously a means-end hierarchy. (Steak is not a *means* to food; it is a *kind* of food.)

For a particular resolution to qualify as rationally valid, the entire ascending chain of subordination that links it to those topmost determinative principles of reason must thus be appropriately validated. The whole rationale developed in terms of such an implementation hierarchy must be cogent "all the way up" for the ruling itself to be rationally cogent.

In being rational, we pursue universal desiderata in person-differential ways that we have good reason to deem effective in the peculiar conditions of our particular case. Not all of us eat what Tom does. But we can, all of us, (1) explain and understand his eating kumquats once we realize that he happens to like them and (responsibly) believes them to be both hunger removing and healthful, and (2) agree that the modus operandi involved in his case ("eating what one likes and responsibly believes to be nourishing") is one to which we ourselves do (and should) subscribe. Rationality is a matter of pursuing valid (and universally appropriate) desiderata as ends by appropriate means (but means that are *individually* appropriate and adjusted to the circumstances of one's personal situation).[3] And so, while we pursue common projects, we do so by person-differential means. But there can be no rationality without universality. The overall account (or "rationale") that establishes the rationality of what we do (in action, belief, or evaluation) must be one in which strictly universal needs and totally universalizable standards play the ultimate determinative role.

This perspective makes it clear that a uniformitarian absolutism at the top level of "what rationality is"[4] is perfectly consonant with a pluralism and relativism at the ground level of concrete resolutions regarding "what is rational" in particular cases. The ruling principles of rationality never uniquely constrain their more specific implementations; their application to concrete circumstances always permits some degree of "slack." At each step along the way we repeat the same basic situation: delimitation, yes; determination, no. Resolutions can, in principle, always be accomplished in distinct yet still appropriate ways. The sought-for reconciliation between the universalistic absoluteness of rationality and the variability and relativity of its particular rulings is thus provided by the consideration that the absolutism of principles operates at the highest level of the hierarchy of rationale development, while there is ever more "slack" and variability as one moves toward the lowest level of concrete determinations. The variability and relativity of good reasons at the level of our actual operations can indeed be reconciled with the absolutism of rationality itself by taking a hierarchical view of the process through which the absolutistic

---

[3] It sounds circular to say that rationality consists in pursuing valid ends by appropriate means, seeing that rationality itself will have to be the arbiter of validity and appropriateness. The nature of this circularity and the problem of its putative viciousness will be dealt with below.

[4] Note that this comes to "what rationality *as we understand it* is."

conception of ideal rationality is brought to bear on the resolution of concrete cases and particular situations.[5]

Accordingly, an indifferentism of "it just doesn't matter what your principles of 'rationality' are" simply does not follow from a pluralism of concrete rational resolutions. It may be a contingent matter that it is English that is at my disposal, rather than Polish. But that does not make it irrelevant how I go about using that language. It does not mean that there are no norms and standards—that I can throw words together any way I please. And similarly with rationality; such pluralism as there is in this domain certainly does not mean that there are no higher, determinative, time- and place-indifferent principles that define and delineate the process of communication as such.

Irrationalism does not follow either. The fact that one can implement the call to rationality only in the particular way that one's historical context puts at one's disposal does not mean that rationality as such is something so protean and variable as to lose any meaningful identity altogether. People must feed themselves and shelter themselves—what is at issue here are universal human needs. But of course nature does not dictate any one single process for meeting them; we must proceed to make the best we can of the materials that the conditions of place and time put at our disposal. And the same holds good for reason. We need to build a cognitive home for ourselves in this world—to create a viable thought structure for our beliefs, choices, and evaluations. Here too one must simply do the best one can. Neither the project nor its implementation is irrelevant, immaterial, or indifferent. A sensible relativism of situational variability is certainly not at odds with the fundamental and altogether absolute demand of rationality: that we pursue our ends intelligently, doing the best we can with the limited means at our disposal in the restrictive circumstances in which we labor.

Practical Reason Requires Cognitive and Evaluative Reason

The three major contexts for rationality are belief, action, and evaluation; it is in these three spheres that success or failure to act rationally standardly manifests itself. Correspondingly, there are three modes of reasoning: the theoretical or *cognitive* (reasoning about matters of information),

---

[5] Note, too, that different top-level finalities can lead to priority conflicts through competing demands on resources. Health and knowledge, or family life and professional life, for example, may certainly conflict—not, to be sure, as abstract desiderata but in the competing demands that arise in the course of their practical implementation. Insofar as such conflicts are rationally resolvable at all, still other finalities must be involved as arbiters. Even at the highest levels, our valid aims are not really "ultimate"—except for their own domain.

the *practical* (reasoning about actions), and the *evaluative* (reasoning about values, ends, priorities, and preferabilities). It is a noteworthy fact, however, that these three modes of rationality overlap in so intertwined a manner that they just cannot be strictly separated. This, clearly, is a conclusion that must be argued in stages, and so we shall proceed step by step, beginning with the involvements of practical reason.

Practical rationality requires that our actions and their objectives be duly validated and coordinated under the aegis of intelligence. In its generic structure, practical reasoning about particular actions takes the following generic form:

1. All things considered, my attaining the result X would be to the good.
2. Of the various alternative actions (or courses of action) available to me, it is A which, on the available information, is optimally conducive (overall) to my attaining the result X.
3. Doing A meets the condition of optimality in relation to the whole spectrum of my appropriately operative ends. It involves no X-irrelevant side effects that would offset its X-connected benefits.
4. *Therefore*: A is the rational thing to do in the circumstances at hand: I am rationally well advised to do A.

If any one of those three premises fail, then a claim on the basis of its X-connection that A is the rational thing to do becomes problematic. Now that first premise patently involves a reference to values, while the second premise makes a strictly factual claim about how things work in the world. (The third premise is of mixed character.) As this sort of example indicates, cogent practical reasoning in the context of particular decisions accordingly involves reference both to matters of fact and to matters of value.

One cannot effect a rational choice among alternative courses of action without determinate beliefs about the consequences of these actions—beliefs in which both factual and evaluative matters will have to figure. Even if performing an action is in fact conducive to realizing someone's appropriate ends (if, say, ingesting yonder chemical substance will actually cure one's illness), it is nevertheless not rational so to act if the agent has no knowledge of this circumstance (and all the more so if such information as the agent possesses actually points the other way). Even when we happen by luck or chance to do that which is, in the circumstances, the best thing to do, we have not acted rationally if we have proceeded without having any good reason to think that our actions would prove appropriate—let alone if we had good reason to think that they would be inappropriate. Agents who have no good reason to think that what they do conduces to their appropriate ends are not acting rationally. Such deficiency as regards rationality is not redeemed by unmerited good fortune, by luck's having it that things turn out all right. Rationality in action is not simply a matter of acting *effectively* toward our ends but one of acting *intelligently*; given the role of the fortuitous in the world's events, these are not necessarily the same.

Practical rationality thus pivots on a proper cognitive backing by duly exploited information. If someone's action is to qualify as fully rational, then (1) the agent must be in a position to recognize his or her *actual* reasons for doing it (there must be no self-deception here), and (2) the agent must be able to evaluate his or her reasons as *appropriate* ones. A misunderstanding either about the character or about the merit of one's reasons for action is a defect of rationality. Practical rationality accordingly requires cognitive rationality, seeing that rational action is a matter of doing what we have good reason to think to be effective on the basis of the information that is available to us. For practical rationality, it is not belief as such but sensible (i.e., rational) belief that counts. Rationally warranted action must be intelligently guided by rationally warranted information.

The issue of rational cognition is therefore critical for practical rationality as well. If we have no idea how things work in the world, we remain impotent to act intelligently in the effective pursuit of our goals. Lapses from cognitive rationality would also involve us in lapses from pragmatic rationality, seeing that they involve an avoidable risk of frustrating our own purposes and interests. (We are in sad straits when, for instance, we cannot tell foods from poisons.) Rational action within the world must be predicated upon rationally warranted beliefs about it; we cannot expect to succeed with a praxis that is not underwritten by knowledge.

A similar account holds on the side of values. If our practical decisions are directed at "unsuitable" ends—ends that are at odds with the indications of appropriate evaluative reasoning—then we are not conducting our business of practical reasoning aright. Evaluative rationality is an integral component of rationality at large. If our evaluations conflict with what it makes good sense for us to value—if they are at odds with our best interests and the best interests of those with whom our interests are interconnected—then this dissonance renders them irrational. Actions aimed at inappropriate objectives or geared to mistaken priorities are thereby automatically flawed from the rational point of view. Practical activity in the pursuit of an objective is rational on our part only insofar as we have sound reason for deeming the realization of this objective to be a good. Accordingly, evaluation too is an essential resource for practice. Practical action makes sound rational sense only when it proceeds with a view to an end of some sort, and ends are appropriate only insofar as they can secure the legitimatizing authorization of values. Practical rationality accordingly stands correlative with valuation. All of our rational choices necessarily proceed, as such, from what qualifies as being (on balance) preferable with reference to the relevantly operative goals and values. All of our rational endeavors proceed within the setting of a governing teleology. Exactly this feature marks a choice (or issue resolution of any sort) as rational— that it duly fosters the realization of a goal or value of some appropriate sort. Intelligent action cannot proceed without evaluative knowledge, in whose absence we would no longer be able to select those acts that afford us warranted hopes for optimal results.

When the adoption of one or another of a set of alternatives is under consideration, rationality requires that two sorts of issues must be addressed: their relative feasibility (costs), and their relative desirability (benefits). Without evaluative as well as cognitive reason, the issues of practical, action-oriented rationality cannot be addressed effectively. The pursuit of inappropriate goals—however cleverly coordinated—is still unintelligent and thus contrary to reason.

Cognitive Reason Has both Practical and Evaluative Dimensions

Not only does practical rationality require cognitive rationality (since we cannot sensibly identify practically promising steps in the absence of factual information), but the converse holds as well: cognitive rationality also requires practical rationality. Even in the sphere of our specifically cognitive concerns, praxis and action are not external, supplemental afterthoughts. For inquiry and the acquisition of information is itself a practical activity on the same footing with any other—a process that must be governed by the standard justificatory ground rules of practical reason. In falling afoul of practical reason, we would compromise our claims to cognitive rationality as well, because rational belief about this world can emerge only from a rationally effective praxis, that is, from an appropriate process of information acquisition. Inquiry too is an activity that, properly conducted, must be governed by the principles of practical rationality.

Consider just one aspect of this. Clearly if experience cannot validate our factual information regarding the world, then nothing can. Yet, how is experience to be exploited to secure information about objective facts? Experience is inevitably episodic, personalized, and subjective. It operates at the level of appearances. I am under the impression that yonder object looks roselike; I judge that it emits a rosy fragrance; it feels like a rose to my touch. But this sort of thing is all I get at the level of actual experience. In describing my experiences, I must use such autobiographical-sounding reports about how things strike me. Experience as such goes no further than to place me in a situation where *I take something to be a rose*. And the move from this merely subjective circumstance to the objective fact that *it actually is a rose before me* traverses a substantial distance. (As skeptics have always been ready to point out, there is—in theory—a lot that can conceivably go wrong.) However, the following complex piece of practical reasoning provides our only practicable way of validating the inference from subjectively experiential indications to objective fact:

1. On present indications, P.
2. In the prevailing circumstances, we can do no better (epistemically) than to go by present indications. We (ex hypothesi) cannot now do better than the best we can manage in the prevailing circumstances.
3. Accepting P is our best available option in the prevailing circumstances (from 1 and 2).
4. Let us adopt the best available option (a matter of "practical policy").
5. Let us accept P (from 3 and 4).
6. P (from 5).

As this perspective indicates, arriving at objective judgments on an experiential basis is not a matter of reasoning in the purely theoretical order of deliberation at all, but one of reasoning in the practical order of deliberation. We do not—nay, cannot—move from step 1 to step 6 directly, but only via the practical policy of acceptance represented by item 4. What is thus at issue when we move from "on present indications, P" to P itself is not a matter of any duly consolidated *inference* at all; it is a matter of *practical* procedure. As such, this policy does indeed have a backing of rational warrant, but this policy-supportive warrant itself lies in the practical rather than the purely cognitive sector.

We have no alternative but to proceed to cross the evidential gap from our inevitably personal experience to objective factual claims (from phenomenal evidence to actual fact, from putative to real truth, from subjective data to objective claims) by what is, to all intents and purposes, a strictly practical inference whose ultimate foundation lies not in the sphere of information but in that of practical policy. Our rational procedure in the accession of substantive information about the world is part and parcel of our cognitive praxis under the aegis of interests. That basic demand for information and understanding presses in upon us, and we must do (and are pragmatically justified in doing) what is needed for its satisfaction. (On one reading, this is the lesson Hume himself drew from his critique of "induction.")

Cognitive reason as such has two sides: the hypothetical and the categorical. The hypothetical proceeds by way of: *"If* you accept P, *then* you must (or, alternatively, cannot) in due consistency also accept Q." Its conditionalized, if-then aspect does not involve us in any substantive commitments whatever. But of course it also provides no substantive information.

Only through the unconditionally committal use of cognitive reason can we obtain outright information—effective answers to our questions. And this categorical dimension of cognitive reason has an ineliminably practical basis. For we cannot get answers to our questions about the world without taking action. But to accept a thesis is to *do* something—to *take* it as true. And even mental action is itself a kind of action, and belief formation a kind of praxis.

The following objection arises:

> You maintain that cognitive reason involves practical reason through construing *acceptance* as an act—an "act of acceptance." But you also hold that practical reasonings always require premises that can be secured only through cognitive reason. Do these together not make for a skeptical regress that blocks all prospect of cognition via the vitiating consequence that every valid practical argument presupposes others?

A negative answer to this question is in order. For one must observe: "Requires, yes, but not *pre*-requires; demands, yes, but not *pre*-supposes in the literal sense of something that must be before." Requirements and requisites are not necessarily preliminaries. If I endorse "We must leave the house," I am also required to endorse the claims "We must not remain in the living room," "We must not remain in the dining room," and so forth. But I need not preestablish these other requisites en route to validating that initial claim. The later claims stand coordinate with the earlier: they form part of the overall fabric of concomitant claims, but we do not have to validate them in advance as prerequisites. It is quite enough that they can eventually be validated, though perhaps only "with the wisdom of hindsight." And that holds for the present case as well. Those concomitant contentions must hold good and be available in the overall scheme of things, but we need not secure them in advance. The structure of rationality is a matter of system, not of sequence. The mutual involvement at issue is reciprocal and harmless rather than presuppositional and vitiating. It does no more than illustrate the systemic unity of reason, the cohesive conjunction of its several components.

It is exactly because cognitive reason and practical reason are intertwined that cognitive reason has *evaluative* involvements as well. Once one has certain facts at one's disposal, one can, of course, proceed to derive others from them by logical inference. But one must somewhere make a start at the inferential venture by accepting some facts not on the basis of other facts but on the basis of outright indications. We cannot proceed in factual matters without making *some* noninferential judgments of fact, and such unconditional "acts of acceptance" must be guided by evaluative processes. A contention that "the indications are indeed strong enough to warrant acceptance in the particular case at hand" presupposes judgments along the lines of "This issue is important enough for us to chance a resolution on present evidence, notwithstanding an inherent risk of error." Without these judgments regarding issues of cognitive value, there is no sensible basis for holding that the prevailing conditions justify running the risks involved in the acceptance of something that could, in the end, turn out to be incorrect. Thus, evaluation is also bound to enter into our cognitive deliberations.

What deserves particular emphasis, however, is the close interconnection between cognitive and practical reasoning. On the one hand, we need cognitive inputs to *operate* practical reasoning; on the other, practical considerations must be invoked to *validate* the processes of our cognitive operations.

Evaluative Reason Has Factual and Practical Dimensions

Even as cognitive rationality demands both practical and evaluative rationality, so evaluative reason has both cognitive and practical involvements.

Evaluative judgments often take the generalized form "Items of a certain kind (e.g., of type T) have positive (or negative) value of such-and-such a sort, and to such-and-such an extent." ("Acts of stealing are morally just plain wrong.") But of course such a general rule remains unproductively ineffectual, spinning inoperatively like a disengaged gear, until it is connected up with concrete situations (until, in the example, we can determine a particular act to be one of stealing). If we are ever to make actual use of such a generalization, we must bring it to bear on a specific case.

> The existing situation S actually represents an instance of an item of the type at issue (type T).

We can move from the premise "Type T things have value V" to the conclusion "X has value V" only via the linking premise "X is of type T"— moving from "Theft is wrong" to "X has done something wrong" via the premise "X has played the thief (has taken something that actually did not belong to X)." And this last item is clearly something that involves factual information. Only on the basis of factual inputs are we able to apply or implement our values; in the absence of factual information, our value generalizations are no more than bloodless abstractions.

Moreover, the preceding consideration indicates that evaluative rationality demands practical rationality as well. For it follows from its cognitive involvement through the consideration, already examined above, that evaluation's demand for factual information will require a practically grounded leap across the gap from subjective evidence to objective conclusions.

The Systemic Unity of Reason

Rationality, then, is a matter of the intelligent pursuit of appropriate ends. Here "intelligent" bespeaks knowledge, "pursuit" indicates action, and "appropriate ends" calls for evaluation. All sectors of reason must be invoked and coordinated in any formula that adequately characterizes the overall nature of rationality.

To serve its function as a guide to human actions and interactions, reason must eliminate disorder and dissonance and similar impediments to well-coordinated thought; accordingly, reason strives, always and everywhere, for consistency, uniformity, generality, and orderly harmony of all sorts. Rationality demands that our beliefs, evaluations, and actions should "make sense," which means that the whole fabric of rationality must be seamless—cognition, evaluation, and action must form a cohesive unit. People have questions and demand answers. And we require that these answers fit, in mutual coherence, attuned to one another in systemic unity, forming a body that we are willing to implement in practice and use as a guide to action. Accordingly, we must be (cognitively) confident that—as best we can tell—such (practical) action will eventuate in (evaluatively) good effects. Where an agent's beliefs, values, and actions are not in themselves appropriate in a mutually concordant way, then the preconditions for rationality remain unsatisfied. Reason is an organic unity, an indivisible whole.

To be sure, philosophers sometimes envision a bifurcation of reason into two separate domains with altogether different ground rules, distinguishing sharply between theoretical and practical matters, between *theōria* and *praxis*. In theoretical matters, they maintain, there is no urgency to make up our minds—we can always postpone a decision until further evidence comes to view, simply suspending judgment until all requisite returns are in. In practical matters, in contrast, there is an urgency to resolve issues through making up our minds—we must act in one way or another (since even inaction is a mode of action), and so must reach a decision of some sort.

In this light, theoretical and practical reason are not disparate domains but interconnected sectors of one comprehensively unified whole. A single, uniform governing principle obtains throughout: "Proceed everywhere on the basis of the best available reasons to do what is appropriate in the situation at hand." The division between the practical and the theoretical does not bifurcate reason, it simply illustrates the fundamental uniformity of the rational through a diversity of situations. Our factual judgments (beliefs) and our evaluative judgments (appraisals) are both validated by rational processes whose fundamental structure is one and the same—and on both sides ultimately rest on considerations of *praxis*.

As these considerations indicate, reason is an organic unity, an indivisible whole. Each of its sectors interpenetrates the rest, seeing that rational persons must, in a duly coordinated way:

1. strive to secure information adequate for the effective management of their affairs;
2. endeavor to assure the appropriateness of their values and goals;
3. act (in the absence of putative impediments) in ways that, given their beliefs, are circumstantially optimal for the implementation of their values and goals.

The fabric of rationality is seamless; its several departments are inseparably interconnected.

Rationality calls for harmony within (and between) the spheres of action and belief in the interests of the efficient pursuit of legitimate ends. Its characteristic demand is for good reasons for what we believe, for what we do, and for what we value. Under the aegis of rationality, these three domains form part of a single, uniform, and coordinated whole. If our acts are based on inappropriate beliefs, they lack rational justification; if our beliefs do not admit of implementation in practice, they too suffer a defect of rationality; if our values are inappropriate, they clearly go against reason. In no such case would a *rational* agent be able to muster the confidence necessary for effectual thought and action.

This holistic unity of reason serves to secure our analysis against a change of circularity. For someone might object, "How can you say that A presupposes B and C, and yet that B presupposes A and C?" The response is that that is *not* what has been said. We have spoken in terms of involvement, not *pre*-supposition; of mutual connection, not of preliminary requirement. What is at issue in relating the three modes of rationality is a matter not of sequential priority but of systematic coordination.

Rationality as a Duty: The Ontological Obligation to Rationality

Does rationality issue commands or counsels? Thomas Aquinas sensibly observed that "a commitment implies obligation, whereas a counsel is left to the option of the one to whom it is given."[6] A command is imperative and definitely binding—its demands are framed in the compelling language of "you must." A counsel, by contrast, is advisory and offers a recommendation governed by the formula "You are well advised to do it"—its demands are framed in the recommending language of "you should." Which is at issue with the declaration of reason?

---

[6] Thomas Aquinas, *Summa Theologica*, I of II, q. 14, art. 1.

Those who violate the standards of rationality simply manage their affairs in a way that is less than fully intelligent and thereby (in general) damage no one but themselves by frustrating the realization of their own best interests. To all appearances the voice of reason accordingly recommends rather than commands, and advises rather than obliges, so that rationality is a matter of discovering and choosing that which, as best we can tell, optimally conduces to the realization of our overall interests. Now doing what reason instructs is mostly not a matter of duty, of some sort of obligation, but rather a matter of prudential advisability. Thus, rationality's injuctions are seemingly matters of recommendation rather than obligation, of counsel rather than requirement.

But while this may be how things are situated in the first instance, ultimately the matter stands otherwise. For we have not only an opportunity but even a duty to be rational. The most fundamental injunction of reason is, "Be rational—act in line with reason's recommendations!" This fundamental imperative is a command rather than a counsel. But whence does the advice of rationality obtain the imperatival force, in virtue of which we *ought* to do what it indicates? How is it that the advice of reason obtains to deontic force—that one is somehow *obliged* to do what reason recommends? What is the basis of this "obligation" to be rational?

The answer here lies in the consideration of ontology. The pivot point is the situation of the individual and of the species in the world's scheme of things. The deontic impetus to rationality inheres in our very nature. It is rooted ultimately in the fact that rationality is part and parcel of the capacities that define man as an intelligent agent. Our capacity for reason is a fact, a given. To be sure, we have many capacities—some for good, some for evil. So the crux is that our rationality is part of our capacity for the good, and indeed is a capacity whose exercise facilitates the pursuit of all other positive capacities. The consideration that we should exploit and cultivate it is something normative—a duty of sorts. The alignment of given opportunity with self-developed reality is mediated by an ontological imperative to duty—that we ought to develop our given potential for the realization of value. The deontic impetus to rationality lies in the basic ontological imperative to make the best of our given opportunites for the good. The binding obligation to be rational inheres in the "metaphysical" consideration that we "owe it to reality at large" to realize ourselves as the sort of being we are, to take our proper place in the world's scheme of things. The factors of self-interest and of self-realization contrive to thrust the rationality project upon us as one in which we both self-interestedly *should* be and deontologically *ought* to be involved.

We ought to comport ourselves rationally because rationality is an essential part of our self-definition as human persons. Rationality thus represents a crucial aspect of our deepest self-interest—our being able to maintain a proper sense of legitimacy and self-worth by being able to see ourselves as the sorts of creatures we claim to be. Our very identity as beings of the sort we can and should want to be is at stake.[7]

We have to do here with an injunction issued by one part of our self to the whole. The crucial point is not that we have a *propensity* for rationality but that we have a *capacity* for it and that this capacity is a preeminently positive one. Our claim to be rational, free agents of itself establishes our position in the world's scheme of things, with the result that rationality becomes a matter of duty for us, of ontological obligation. Through this fundamental ontological imperative mere "counsels of reason" are transmuted into commands issued by one side of our nature (the rational) to ourselves in general.

An ontological or metaphysical imperative to rationality is thus at work. A creature endowed with the capacity for rational agency *ought* to realize this potential—it ought to act so as to develop itself as a rational being. To lose out on such an opportunity to realize the good is simply unintelligent and thus contrary to the impetus of reason. The obligation to be rational is an ontological obligation that inheres in our capacity for self-development and self-realization—it is a commitment to the full development of our human potentialities. The imperative to rationality is a matter of the fundamental impetus to self-optimization, to making good use of our opportunities for self-development, to doing the very best we can with ourselves under the conditions in which we labor. We have here a rationale that grounds obligation in axiology—in the consideration that a being endowed with the capacity for value realization ought to exercise it. We here cross the boundary from an *is* of sorts (albeit of evaluative sorts) to an *ought*.

Rational agents have a fundamental duty to make good use of the opportunities that come their way to realize themselves as fully as possible—the *fundamental duty of self-realization*. Insofar as one "owes" it to anyone at all, one owes this duty to oneself and to "the world at large," or at any rate to the community of conscious intelligences within it. The duty at issue is a duty at once to oneself and to the general scheme of things that brought one forth to develop one's highest potential as the kind of creature one is. It roots in the imperatives "Realize your highest potential as the sort of being you are!" and "Develop yourself for the best as best you can!" This "fundamental ontological duty of self-realization" appertains to any rational agent whatsoever. Any such agent is in a position—insofar as it actu-

---

[7] To be sure, a skeptic can say: "Well and good, so we have a capacity for intelligence and rationality. But why should we *exercise* that capacity?" The answer is simply—and circularly—that its exercise is the rational and intelligent thing to do. And this circularity is benign rather than vicious, since if we intend to pose the issue in a serious and responsible way, it is clearly our intelligent and rational answer that we wish to obtain.

ally is an agent—to realize its potentialities for providing good (for enhancing value). Self-realization is the point of confluence where self-interest and obligation flow together.

Human rationality is the product of a prolonged process of evolution. There are many ways for an animal species to make its way in the world; many diverse alternative routes for coping within nature present themselves to biological organisms: the routes of multiplicity, toughness, flexibility, isolation, and others. But one particularly important pathway is afforded by the route of *intelligence*, of adapting by the use of brain rather than brawn, of cleverness rather than force, of flexibility rather than specialization. In a competitive, Darwinian world a creature that can understand how things work in its environment and exploit this understanding in action has an evolutionary edge, as the master himself already stressed. There is a promising ecological niche for a creature that makes its way in the world not by sheer tenacity or by tooth and claw but by intelligence— by coordinating its own doings and the world's ways through cognitive foresight. We live and breathe and have our being in a natural environment that is not originally of our making and in which, at any rate, we must forge our own way by the use of our wits. For it is the route of mind, and not the route of tooth and claw, that is our evolutionary destiny.

Accordingly, there is yet another explanation for reason's centrality in human affairs. As members of the genus *Homo sapiens*, we are creatures that have a capacity for at least partial self-construction, for making ourselves in a certain way. In substantial part, we are what we are because of what we claim to be. Persons become persons through their capacity to see themselves as such. In particular, we value ourselves as members of a certain category (species, society, group). We have a sense of belonging, a preparedness to recognize others as instances of "our type" accompanied by a sense that we ourselves deserve to be so recognized by them in turn. We see ourselves as bearers of value in a community of mutual recognition, as members along with others of an affinity community of "people like us."

It is a crucial part of our interests to maintain a proper sense of self-worth in such a setting of reciprocity. An injury to this sense of self-worth is one of the very worst things that can happen to a person. We are then deprived of the self-esteem that goes with membership in a group of which we are pleased and proud to be a part. In eroding one's sense of legitimacy, such an injury undermines one's sense of worth by degrading one where it counts the most—in one's own eyes. After all, we are in crucial part what we are because of what we claim ourselves to be in determining an identity for ourselves as members of a wider community. (The "I" one takes oneself to be is crucially conditioned by the "we" of its associates.) The first-person-plural ideal of "we" and "us" that projects one's own identity into a wider affinity-community is a crucial basis for our sense of worth and self-esteem. A feeling of self-worth is essential to one's sense of legitimacy, or one's ability to feel at home in the world. (It is this threat, rather than a fear of its superior weaponry, that makes the idea of contact with a "superior" civilization so intimidating.)

An Idealistic Vista

The basis of our obligation to rationality lies in the region of axiology; its roots are in the *value* that rationality has for us. And if rationality were merely a matter of (true) prudence and self-interest (however much it is our real interests that are at stake), then the value of rationality would be less than it is. We do—and must—value our rationality not just because it helps to feather our nest but because it is the pivotal component of our very nature as the sort of beings we are—or at any rate see ourselves as being. The crux of our deontic commitment to personhood thus lies in the region of axiology—in the value that it has for us as the salient feature that determines our place in the world's scheme of things.

Accordingly, the present line of consideration takes an emphatically normative approach to rationality. Neither is it viewed as a simply de-scriptive aspect of the human condition (so that one cannot properly speak of an obligation to be rational), nor is its validation simply a matter of self-centered advantage (so that its significance for us is wholly pruden-tial). An additional and more powerful instrument of normativity comes upon the scene in the conception of ontological obligation, which serves as the crucial hallmark of our value-grounded commitment to the pivotal role of reason in the human scheme of things.

The centrality of values in human affairs has always been a leading theme of philosophical idealism. As the present deliberations indicate, evaluation is an integral component of both cognitive and practical ration-ality. In particular, our cognitive values canalize the ways in which we answer our questions about the world. For "the-world-*as-we-see-it*" is a conceptual artifact that unites and synthesizes our putative knowledge of things, and this artifact comprises what we deem it warranted (fitting, appropriate, etc.) to accept—which is invariably an evaluative matter that hinges on standards and criteria of rational assessment. Accordingly, cognition is and must be guided by values: our worldview is, and cannot but be, an artifact, shaped and delineated by our evaluative standards of cognitive assessment. The values that determine those acceptances thereby serve to shape and condition a cognitive acceptor's resultant world picture. This view of the pivotal role of evaluation in constituting—and thus also in determining the constitution—of our thought-contrived picture of the world and our place within it is an aspect of the present perspective that reflects the central themes of traditional idealism.

It is exactly because we can, do, and ought to see ourselves as being intelligent, mind-equipped creatures that mind and its operations come to play such a central part in our conception of the world's scheme of things. Here, then, we approach the central thesis of idealism—that our descriptive and evaluative instrumentalities of self-understanding are thereby also crucial for our understanding of reality. This idealistic theme runs as a unifying thread throughout these pages.

Two

Maximization, Optimization, and Rationality

Rationality and Maximization

Rationality demands a due care for the realization of values. But this is not a matter of *maximization*. Rather, what it demands is *optimization*, which is, in fact, something quite different. Yet the issue is complex and demands closer scrutiny.

There is a widespread tendency to view rationality as committed to maximization, taking rational choice to consist in maximizing something called "utility." Practitioners of economics, social-choice theory, game theory, management science, and other exponents of "the theory of rational decision" are virtually unanimous in endorsing this approach of construing rationality in terms of utility maximization.[1] They commonly hold that the rational agent always aims at some kind of measurable good (the "utility" measure of "satisfaction" or "well-being" or some such) and accordingly chooses among alternatives for action in such a way as to maximize the expectation of its realization, endeavoring to "maximize expected utility," as the economists' cliché has it.[2] Then, too, philosophers of widely different ethical orientations also take this same general line. Utilitarians identify rationality with utility maximization outright.[3] And contractarians too see rational persons impelled to a consensus regarding the ground rules of social interaction in an endeavor to maximize their satisfaction.[4] Is this sort of position tenable?

[1] See, for example, D. M. Winch, *Analytical Welfare Economics* (Harmondsworth: Penguin Books, 1971): "We assume that individuals balance rationality and endeavor to maximize utility" (p. 25); cf. Kenneth J. Arrow, *Social Choice and Individual Values*, 2d ed. (New York: Cowles Comission Monographs, 1963), pp. 3, 21. Some, to be sure, take exception to this line. For example, it has received a sophisticated critique in Herbert Simon's well-known proposal of a shift from maximizing to "satisficing."

[2] As one discussion puts it: "The theory of games is a valuable tool in making more determinate our understanding of rational self-interest. For the solutions it provides . . . [enable people] to maximize their expected utilities, or in other words, their expected well-being" (R. D. Luce and H. Raiffa, *Games and Decisions* [New York: John Wiley & Sons, 1957], p. 200).

[3] See John Stuart Mill, *Utilitarianism*, chap. 3.

[4] Cf. Kurt Baier, *The Moral Point of View* (Ithaca, N.Y.: Cornell University Press, 1958), pp. 308–15.

One issue must be put aside straightaway. There is, of course, a perfectly trivial sense in which rational agents are maximizers. For presumably they endeavor—by hypothesis—to maximize the extent to which they behave rationally. This truism is not in question—and not to the point. Of course, rationality is a matter of doing what is most appropriate and most intelligent. But the question that matters is: *What sort of thing is that?* Does this intelligence and appropriateness itself call for maximizing something of a particular sort? Can all our ends be amalgamated, fused together into a single all-embracing measurable good, one all-inclusive mode of merit?

To be sure, members of an achievement-oriented society who strive for the most performance and the greatest success are card-carrying maximizers. But then so are those lazybones who always try to get by with the very least that will meet the requirements of the situation. They are simply maximizing something else—say, energy conservation. One can be a maximizer no matter what one does—namely, someone who maximally conforms to the behavior pattern of a person who acts like *that*. There is not all that much glamour in the abstract idea of maximization as such; the interest lies in the crucial issue of just what is to be maximized.

Here we come to the elusive commodity of "utility" that, so we are told, provides the fuel that runs the engine of rationality. But this view that rational agents are utility maximizers has deep problems. If taken seriously to apply to rational agents in the real world, rather than as characterizing that useful fiction the "economic man," then this conception of rationality in terms of utility maximization runs into difficulties.

Incommensurable Goods

The conception of rationality as utility maximization is predicated on the plausible idea that the quintessentially rational thing to do for individuals and groups is to promote their own good—to enhance human well-being. But, sensible though this may seem, it does not validate a recourse to "utility." For human goods and satisfactions are often complex and variegated. They not only come in different *sizes* (as measurable in terms of volume or of realization likelihood) but also come in different *kinds* as well. The sphere of human values is a complex and pluralistically diversified realm.[5] And this raises difficulties.

[5] As one recent writer sensibly puts it: "Value has fundamentally different kinds of sources, and they are reflected in the classification of values into types. Not all values represent the pursuit of some single good in a variety of settings" (Thomas Nagel, "The Fragmentation of Values," in his *Mortal Questions* [Cambridge: Cambridge University Press, 1979], pp. 131–32).

The idea of maximizing the good rests on the presupposition that all of the different items of value at issue can be evaluated by a common, uniform measure. After all, it makes no sense to think of literally maximizing the good when we cannot measure goods by a common standard. *Commensurability* is basic to the project of value maximization. And thereby hangs a problem.

Goods are commensurable only if, despite their evident seeming to be of different kinds, they can all be assessed in terms of a "common denominator," a yardstick of some sort that applies to all of them alike. Different shares of them thereby differ as to value only in point of different quantities of one common measure—in exactly the way in which baskets of apples and of oranges differ in (monetary) value only in terms of their price. Commensurability presupposes a common unit in which all evaluative comparisons can be effected in terms of a neutral and pervasive common-denominator unit of appraisal .

This requirement poses problems. Different kinds of desiderata are not necessarily convertible. Consider some of the points of merit of a car: maximum speed, starting reliability, operating reliability (freedom from breakdown), passenger safety, and economy of operation. If the top speed of a car is 1.75 MPH, no augmentation in passenger safety or operating reliability makes up for this shortcoming. Again, if the car is eminently unsafe, an increase in its other virtues cannot offset this defect. Where the various merits of a car are concerned, there simply is no free exchange among the relevant parameters, but only complicated (nonlinear) trade-offs over a very limited range.

This example illustrates a general situation. There are very different ingredients to goodness, qualitatively different value aspects, different sorts of good-making factors. Just how is one to go about the prospect of combining these value parameters into an overall result—a single, every-thing-taken-into-account, synoptic "bottom line"? In general, things have many different value aspects V_i, and we have no function of combination V to extract a single, all-embracing measure of overall value from them. We have to deal with a plurality of distinct "parameters of value." Even if we assume (perhaps rashly) that measurability is possible within each of these parameter dimensions, there need be no way of making quantitative comparisions across different value parameters by way of weighing them off against each other in a common scale. (Interthematic comparisons of "utility" are just as problematic as interpersonal ones.)

But perhaps one can move automatically from preferability to mensuration by making much capital from the fact that we just about always have preferences in situations of choice. Confronted with alternatives and constrained to choose among them, we will almost invariably come up with *something*. Can one not therefore effect a shift from mere ordinal preferences to actually measurable utilities by suitably ingenious mathematical contrivances to operate with more preferences? Some economists think one can. They invoke the machinery of probabilities to effect this transition and propose to construct a person's utility rate-of-exchange between diverse items A and B from that person's answer to questions of the form:

> Would you prefer an *x* percent probability of obtaining A to a *y* percent probability of obtaining B?

Following the lead of John von Neumann, these theorists hope to exploit such probabilistic preferences to extract outright utilities.[6] But this approach to utility extraction rests on an "indifference condition" of probabilistic commensurability that for any two desired items A and B, there are probabilities *a* and *b* so proportioned that there is indifference between an *a* percent chance of A and a *b* percent chance of B. And just this supposition is unrealistic. For the commensurability of goods presupposes their exchangeability or convertibility. But goods are not always convertible. The good of man is fundamentally multiform, composed of radically diverse components—comfort, affection, security, understanding, and so forth. People want and need different kinds of goods, and no overflow of one can make up for a shortfall of the other. If here and now it is information I really need and want, I will not trade a library for "all the tea in China."

To be sure, economists are accustomed to the assumption of a *market* that establishes exchangeability and underwrites a price mechanism to provide a general standard of comparision. For them, it is normal and natural to suppose that different goods can be evaluated in terms of a common unit—money. They can equate the value of *x* apples with that of *y* oranges because the price mechanism yields a rate of exchange to establish convertibility between them. In sum, they exploit exchangeability to provide for commensurability. But this envisions a very special set of conditions.

For many of significantly valuable human "goods," there is no market. Consider, for example, life, liberty, and happiness. Once slavery is outlawed, life and liberty are no longer marketable. Only up to a certain (inherently limited) point is health purchasable. It is proverbial that "money can't buy happiness." And there are many other important things it cannot buy, such as true friendship or the affection and respect of those

---

[6] See John von Neumann and Oskar Morgenstern, *Theory of Games and Economic Behavior*, 2d ed. (Princeton: Princeton University Press, 1947).

about us. Walpole to the contrary notwithstanding, it is doubtful that "every man has his price." Again, it is important to us that our children be capable and hardworking, that our neighbors be neighborly, and that our colleagues be cooperative. But none of these desiderata is marketable. It is easy to forget how special a case is at issue with the exchangeability of goods. Sensible people are simply not prepared to put all of their eggs into the basket of some single sort of goods. (As wiser theoreticians have always realized, the dispositions of "economic man" do not pervade the whole spectrum of human life.)

Economists, decision theorists, and their congeners are powerfully attracted to the thesis:

> Value is homogeneous; there is at bottom but one single kind of value—"utility." All other modes of value are ultimately reducible to this.

Now if value really were homogeneous, then rationality would indeed be a matter of maximization—of simply maximizing "utility." But that is just not the way it is. We must reject the dogma of the homogeneity of value.

Of course, life would be much simpler if all goods were in fact commensurable. I would not have to fret about my choices in difficult cases, would not feel "in a dilemma" about them, if everything could be measured in a common unit that provides for automatic comparability. But that just is not the way it is in the real world.

Economists themselves have long seen that it is deeply problematic to try to combine the several ordinal preferences of a group's individual members into an overall collective ranking of utility for this group.[7] But they have been somewhat slower to recognize the (closely analogous) point that it is just as problematic to combine the utility values (or preferability indices) of the several diverse facets of a single object into a synoptic measure of its overall utility (or preferability). All of those notorious difficulties about the comparability of the cardinal utility (or the comparative preferences) of diverse individuals recur quite analogously in the case of the comparability of the measurable value (or the comparative preferability) of an object's diverse value facets.[8]

Even if we grant that one alternative of a spectrum is generally preferable to its rivals, this still does not mean that its being so is a matter of possessing more or less of some mysterious something called "utility." To think of utility in that sort of way is to engage in an illicit reification

---

[7] See Arrow, *Social Choice and Individual Values*; cf. Otto Neurath, "Das Problem des Lustmaximums," *Jahrbücher der Philosophischen Gesellschaft der Universität Wien* 18 (1912): 182–96.

[8] Cf. the attempt to develop a "multiple-attribute utility theory" in Ralph L. Keeney and Howard Raiffa, *Decisions with Multiple Objectives: Preferences and Value Tradeoffs* (New York: Macmillan, 1976).

or hypostatization. The economists' idea of pervasive "utility" is about an order of magnitude more problematic than the IQ testers' idea of a pervasive "intelligence." There just is no monolithic sort of something of such a sort that something preferable is ipso facto equipped with more of *that*—"more X-affording" with respect to some one, single, homogeneous, ubiquitous desideratum. The idea of a generalized utility in whose terms preferability is always embedded is a mere fiction—sometimes useful (for example, where a "market" exists), but by no means universally applicable.

One recent writer says: "The identification of rationality with maximizing activity requires . . . [that] we suppose that there is a single measure of a man's ends, which can be applied to evaluate the contribution of each of the actions possible to him."[9] Just so! But this means that people should put a measurable value on any possible object of choice in terms of a single common yardstick of appraisal, that the good should be seen as ultimately homogeneous. This demand is unreasonable and unrealistic.

Many forms of evaluation—of assessing the comparative merit of goods—cannot be reduced to measurement. We cannot measure the quality of a dramatic performance or of a meal. We can, of course, measure what people are prepared to pay for such things, but this carries us back to the special conditions of a market.

Man does not live for knowledge alone—nor for pleasure, power, or any other single factor. The catalog of appropriate human values has many entries. Happiness and pleasure are of course on the list (so far the utilitarians are right), but so also are justice, knowledge, wisdom, affection, aesthetic satisfaction, and many others. None of these rules the roost by itself. We want justice, but not at all costs (not *fiat justitia, ruat caelum*). And there are certainly also limits to the extent to which one could (reasonably) opt for happiness—say, at the cost of self-respect. We confront a variety of desiderata of limited and circumscribed interchangeability.

The economists' utilitarian idea of the homogeneity of the good is ultimately untenable. The idea of a single, all-governing standard of value, even one so seemingly protean as "utility" or "satisfaction," is too simplified and undiscriminating in its vision of the good as something internally so uniform in composition as to admit of the commensurability of its constituent components. There simply is no common measure, no single, common medium of interchange for diverse aspects of value.

[9] David Gauthier, "Reason and Maximization," *Canadian Journal of Philosophy* 4 (1975): 415. As I see it, Gauthier's painstaking defense of the thesis that rationality consists in the maximization of a utility that reflects "degree of satisfaction" is essentially circular, since it is predicated on a definitional construction of "rationality" that is manipulated to lead to this result. (For analogous criticisms of this line of approach, see Max Black, "Making Intelligent Choices: How Useful Is Decision Theory?" *Dialectica* 30 [1985]: 19–34.)

Utility Maximizing Is Not Generally Feasible

Let us now conjoin the preceding points in interactive juxtaposition:

1. The commensurability of goods—their lending themselves to a literal measurement in terms of a common unit of worth—is a precondition for any meaningful maximization.

2. The commensurability of goods presupposes their mutual convertibility (whether in volumetric or in probabilistic terms).

3. The "goods" at issue with many significant human values are of substantially different qualitative kinds. They lack the common denominator needed for interchangeability and consequently just are not mutually convertible.

When these three points are conjoined, the thesis that the rational pursuit of "the good of man" is a matter of *maximization* comes to grief. The rational choice among items of value (or disvalue) cannot be conceived of in terms of maximizing some single universal mode of value reflected in an omnipresent "utility."

Maximizing is inevitably a matter of "getting as much as one can" of something. The maximization idea has no bearing otherwise. Only where the goods at issue can be compared through appraisal in terms of one single homogeneous value does it make sense to pursue ends by way of maximization. When we lack a common standard and confront a plurality of distinct and nonexchangeable values, none of which simply predominates over the rest, the idea of maximization is of little avail.

In general, the convenient resource of maximization is accordingly denied us. Where there is no quantitative measure, the idea of maximizing based on the comparison of more or less has no application. It makes little sense to ask, "Who is the better athlete, a world-class discus thrower or a world-class high-jumper?" or "Who is the better musician, a good cellist or a good trombonist?" We can, of course, compare them in point of quickness, dexterity, steadiness, and other such particular physical skills and talents. But these are mere prerequisites for excellence at athletics or musical performance, not components thereof. When measuring them, we do not measure the end product in whose realization they cooperate.

The characteristics of the general case are as follows:

1. There are various substantially distinct parameters of value—various distinct *kinds* of goods.

2. They are not mutually convertible.

3. We require them in contextually varying amounts and combinations. Every value parameter must be present to some extent in any acceptable situation. A minimum threshold obtains with respect to these value dimensions. (With a car, for example, some minimal threshold of speed, reliability, safety,

etc. must presumably be assured before we would be prepared even to consider the item as acceptable.)

4. Within the range of "acceptable" cases, in the sense of point (3), comparative preferability is a complex matter of coordinating pro and con considerations in a way that is *not* a matter of maximization of some sort. Everything depends on contexts and combinations.

In sum, "the good" at large is multidimensional, not homogeneous. Enhancing it is a matter of optimizing a profile, not of maximizing a quantity.

To be sure, we can have (perfectly sensible) preferences in such matters. But there is no particular something of such a sort that "preferable" or "better" comes down to having more of this something so that preferability is somehow geared in this way to maximization. We can have *standards* in such cases, but not *measures*. We can have criteria of preferability, but not criteria that proceed by quantitative measurements of some sort (any more than do our standards of "good literature"). And where there is no measure, there can be no maximization either. The rational choice among alternatives of value (or disvalue) cannot be conceived of in terms of maximizing some single, all-pervasive, and universal mode of goodness.

The kingdom of interests is large and diversified. No one type of good and no single preponderant value rules the realm of appropriate ends. Their character is diversified, their bearing variegated, their character heterogeneous, their weight incommensurable. We must recognize the reality of a diversified spectrum of legitimate ends. No one, all-predominant summum bonum is in operation. No single, uniform good-making factor is uniformly present throughout all goods in a way that leads them to differ merely in degree rather than in kind.

Utility maximization is accordingly a special-purpose instrument of significant but substantially limited application. To construe rational choice in terms of maximization is entirely inappropriate in its supposition that the special case of general exchangeability among parameters of value is somehow typical (or even universal). The theoreticians' "utility" is a problematic hypostatization that is useful in some limited contexts—say, when exchangeability is feasible—but has no unrestricted validity.

Diversity is the name of the game where human interests are concerned. The goods and qualities required to sustain a satisfying human life are numerous and varied: food, shelter, liberty and justice, companionship and self-development. Our needs and wants are numerous, diversified—and definitely not interchangeable. No one desideratum reigns supreme.

People constantly make rational decisions in driving their cars, investing their assets, choosing their careers, tidying up their closets, purchasing their food, and so on. Throughout, they are doing all sorts of well-advised and intelligent things—saving money, prolonging longevity, enhancing comfort, enlarging their friendships, enhancing their knowledge, and so forth. But to say that they are throughout doing exactly the same sort of thing—promoting "utility"—is an eminently problematic contention. The idea of a single, all-enhancing good is an oversimplification, a heritage of the monolithic summum-bonum thinking of bygone days.

Realistically viewed, rational choice is a matter not of unidimensional maximization but of multidimensional optimization. It remains a matter of determining what is preferable. But here the preferability at issue need not necessarily reflect itself in some quantitative way through the operation of some measure of value (V) such that

(M) A pref A' if and only if $V(A) > V(A')$.

Once we realize that there are different modes or aspects ("dimensions") of value, and that they bear differentially on different ranges of comparison, we can no longer be confident that preferential valuation can be reduced to mensuration.

If condition (M) held, preferability would invariably be transitive. But it just is not. Consider a (micro)range of objects of comparison A, B, and C. If we compare A and B, within this (micro)range, the apposite standard is a. Then we shall (so let us suppose) arrive at the assessment that A is preferable to B:

$$a\text{: } A \text{ pref } B.$$

However, when we compare B and C, the standard that is appropriate to this particular comparison range may be b, and we will then have (so let us suppose):

$$b\text{: } B \text{ pref } C.$$

But if we now turn to A and C, the appropriate standard will be c, and we may well have:

$$c\text{: } C \text{ pref } A.$$

But there is now no possible way to provide for these three assessments in terms of one single overall measure. For any value measure over the range A, B, and C would have to yield a transitive order of preference, whereas the given preferences are clearly not transitive. And this sort of thing is not just a theoretical possibility but something that can perfectly well happen.

Think of the game "scissor, stone, paper." If you were to choose stone, I would prefer paper to scissor; if you choose scissor, I would prefer stone to paper; but if you choose paper, I would prefer scissor to stone. That is just how preferability works. It varies constantly with context and circumstances; which item is preferable turns on the microdetail of the prevailing situation. But genuine measurement is not like that: it has to be substantially context independent. (It just does not matter whether we measure the duration of a lecture on an odd- or an even-numbered day, a workday or a holiday.) And by assessing these relational and interactional aspects of things, we are certainly not carrying out measurements.

Consider another, more instructive example:

1. I am asked: "Do you prefer butter or olive oil?" I respond: "Butter." For I reason that in contexts where this sort of choice makes sense—namely, in cooking or frying—I prefer butter.

2. Next I am asked: "Do you prefer butter or mayonnaise?" I respond: "Mayonnaise." For I reason that in contexts where this sort of choice makes sense—namely, in sandwich making—I prefer mayonnaise.

3. Now I am asked: "Do you prefer mayonnaise or olive oil?" I respond: "Olive oil." For I reason that in contexts where this sort of choice makes sense—namely, in dressing salads—I prefer olive oil.

It is clear that this sort of nontransitivity can always be expected in cases when different "perspectives of consideration" cast their independent ballot,[10] so that preferability is dependent on context and point of view. This is pretty well *always* the case. Thus suppose that someone had objected at the first step: "You really should not have said that you prefer butter to olive oil if you don't so prefer it in *all* cases." This invites the reply: "But that's just foolish. It gears preference to a condition of things that effectively never obtains." For our preferences among objects of choice are never unqualifiedly universal and situation independent, holding in all kinds of circumstances that go beyond the given level of specificity.[11] I may strongly prefer butter to margarine. But if *A* says to me, "I'll give you a fortune if you give me a bit of margarine here and now," and *B* stands by offering me the free choice between a pat of butter and a pat of margarine, I'm obviously not going to choose the butter! Whenever preference is something situation dependent (and it always is!), we cannot expect our

---

[10] The considerations at issue here run parallel to those involved in M. S. A. de Condorcet's "Voting Paradox" in the theory of rational decision. Condorcet's paradox occurs when we obtain cycles in a group preference determined on the basis of majority-rule voting with respect to pairwise comparisons. An example of this occurs when three voters indicate the following preferences among any items a, b, c: (1) $a > b > c$, (2) $b > c > a$, and (3) $c > a > b$. Note that two (i.e., a majority) prefer a to b, two prefer b to c, and two prefer c to a. See the Marquis de Condorcet's *Essai sur l'application de l'analyse à la probabilité des décisions rendus à la pluralité des voix* (Paris, 1785; reprint, New York: Barnes & Noble, 1973). Cf. Isaac Todhunter, *A History of the Mathematical Theory of Probability* (London, 1865; reprint, New York: Chelsea Publishing, 1949), pp. 374–75, as well as Duncan Black, *The Theory of Committees and Elections* (Cambridge: Cambridge University Press, 1958).

[11] "Yet surely this would not be so if the description of the case was fully specific—i.e., complete." But it never is, and never can be.

preferences to be transitive in the way that their numerical measurements would demand.

In general, then, preferability determination just does not hinge on measuring anything. The measurable is context invariant (at any rate, within limits), but the preferable is not. And so it is infeasible, in general, to reduce questions of preferability to matters of measurement.

Value stands coordinate with *evaluating*—with the reactions and reflections of an evaluator who is capable of thought. And these reactions are complex, diversified, and circumstantial. They are not to be captured in one single number depicted as a measurement of some sort.

The idea of utility maximization is thus caught in a vitiating dilemma. Either utility represents a limited set of determinate goods—in which case we cannot set utility maximization up as a be-all and end-all. Or utility is to amount to "the good at large and as a whole"—in which case we cannot measure it and thus cannot make use of the idea of "utility maximization." Either way, the project comes to grief.

The problem with utility maximization lies at the door of utility itself as a universal index of worth or value that can be applied to make assessments "across the board." To be sure, where maximization of the good is possible, it is clearly sensible and rational to strive for it, other things being equal. That is not in question. The point is simply that the prospect of maximization is *not* always there, and this absence nowise impedes the prospects of rationality.

Practical rationality is thus no more a matter of maximization than is cognitive rationality. In matters of agency we can "measure the value" of alternatives no more than in matters of belief we can "measure the weight of evidence." In each case, preferability is a matter of standards rather than yardsticks, of analysis rather than measurement. We are well advised to resist replacing deliberation by calculation in an ill-fated indulgence of the "yearning for convenience."

Can Utility Theory Abandon the Idea of Measuring Value?

Science has succeeded in mathematicizing the realm of our *knowledge* to such an extent that we tend to lose sight of the fact that the realm of our *experience* is not all that congenial to measurement. It is full of colors, odors, tastes, likes and dislikes, apprehensions and expectations, and loves and hates that are not particularly amenable to measurement. We readily forget how very special a situation measurability is—even in contexts of seeming precision.

But, surely economists will tell us, if you have a preference of A over B, we can assess its strength by asking: "How much will you pay to ensure having *A* instead of *B*?" And they may well be right in holding that this question can always be asked and often answered. But it does not follow that by providing an answer here, one is measuring anything—that some independently preexisting quantitative parameter is being measured when we spend hypothetical money to indulge our hypothetical "preferences." A hypothetical market is no more a market than a stuffed owl is an owl. Not everything quantitative is a measure. "How many of those girls remind you of your mother?" you ask me. "Two," I respond. A lovely quantity, that! But what in heaven's name am I *measuring*? Quantification is not necessarily measurement.

But whenever one chooses, one indicates a preference, and is not the "strength" of such a preference something measurable? By no means! One frown is severer than another, but I cannot quantify by how much. One performance is better than another, but I can put no number to it.

Someone might object as follows: "You grant that quantification can be possible without mensuration—that we can assign meaningful numbers in circumstances where we are not measuring anything. Is this not really all that utilitarians and their economist congeners want and need?" The answer in the context of our present deliberations with respect to rationality is simply no. That "How much would you pay?" question is pointless in a world of impulse buyers. Its answers, however splendidly precise, are fruitless for the issue of measurement because they do not represent any sort of independent value parameter—that is, precisely because they do not *measure* anything. And if one cannot see utility as a measure of value of some sort (of something like goodness, acceptability, or desirability), then the linkage between rationality and maximization is broken.

Exactly here is where the approach of most current decision-theoretic utilitarians runs into trouble. They maintain, in effect, something like the following:

> The idea that utility literally *measures* something is hopelessly old fashioned. Utility is not a measurement at all. It is simply an index of preference. It simply assigns weights to the relative preferences of a person. It does not measure intrinsic preferability but merely expresses the strength of a like or dislike.

This abandonment of a commitment to utility measurement would indeed enable utilitarians to bypass many of the difficulties surveyed in the preceding discussion. But it purchases this advantage at a substantial cost. For in taking this line, these "mere-preference utilitarians" (as we may call them) abandon all claims upon rationality. One person prefers Shakespeare, another the Birdman comics; one man gets his pleasure from gardening, another from incinerating moths. Preference as such is simply inclination with no pretense to appraisal and evaluation in the framework of a rational life plan. Any pretense of a linkage between utility and rationality is thus broken.

Clearly, if preference evaluations are to have a bearing on judgments of rationality, then preference must reflect preferability, and there is no basis and indeed no justification for seeing wants and preferences as something final—something outside the pale of appropriate examination and evaluation. Efficiency in the pursuit of preferred ends is an aspect of *rationality* only if reason can also adjudge those ends as worthy of pursuit.

For Bentham and the early utilitarians, utility was a measure of value. And so for them the injunction "maximize utility!" was a perfectly sensible answer to the question "What would it be rational for me to do?" But if we join the latter-day economists and decision theorists in disjoining utility from value, in setting up a "value-free" utility theory based on mere preference alone, then utility maximization as such becomes disconnected from rationality. For the question whether it is rational for people to strive to implement their preferences crucially depends on what those preferences are—whether, for example, they prefer self-inflicted pain or the suffering of others. (The man who prefers that people should think of him as a flowerpot is scarcely rational, no matter how cogently he may labor in this direction.)

The utility-maximization approach to rationality is thus caught in a dilemma:

   1. When utility is approached in the manner of the old-fashioned value utilitarians, then rationality could indeed be construed as calling for utility maximization—if only this utility were a well-defined quantity (which it is not).
   2. When utility is approached in the manner of the latter-day preference utilitarians, then utility is indeed a feasibly maximizable quantity, but the bearing of utility maximization on rationality is now abrogated.

Either way, the view of rationality as utility maximization comes to grief as an account that qualifies as satisfactory overall.

Unless utility can be construed as a measure of *value*, there is no earthly reason to question the rationality of someone who does not bother all that much about utility. But if the quantity at issue is something adventitious—something as inherently insignificant and potentially unreasonable as mere preference or desire as such—then it is simply irrelevant to matters of rationality. Once the link between utility and value is broken, the link between utility maximization and rational choice is also severed. When utility no longer reflects what is in someone's real interest, then there is no longer any good reason to maintain that maximizing it is "the rational thing to do." Rationality is inherently value oriented. But its commitment is of a kind that eludes any facile recasting into a matter of "utility maximization."

From Maximization to Optimization

Rationality consists in the intelligent pursuit of appropriate ends. Now this is unquestionably a matter of selecting "the best option" among alternatives: it calls for so comporting oneself in matters of belief and action as to prefer what is preferable—what *deserves* to be preferred. But when this preferability cannot be quantified, when its determination is a matter of qualitative judgment rather than quantitative measurement, then rationality ceases to be a matter of maximization.

Maximization has no monopoly on rationality. Different situations call for different procedures; different processes for the rational resolution of choices are appropriate in different contexts. No doubt, rationality is a matter of opting for the best available alternative. But there is simply no way of transmuting this "best" into "the most of something." (To be sure, we may adopt the trivializing formula of "the most preferable." But what is at issue here is a *façon de parler* that we must not allow to delude us into thinking that preferability is some sort of measurable something.)

Rationality calls for promoting a person's real interests, a person's own welfare specifically included. But improving the quality of one's life or the condition of one's well-being is like improving the taste of a particular sort of cake. This cannot be done by simply adding more of this or that ingredient. Central to the whole issue is the problem of blending a plurality of diversified goods into an overall configuration. Rational choice hinges on rational evaluation, and this requires arriving at a suitable profile of diverse elements. Rational choice is not a matter of maximization; rather, it calls for the harmonization of a plurality of goods.

Writers who approach the subject from the angle of decision theory often say things like: "Rationality in the pursuit of goals consists in maximizing the chances of success." But that is nonsense. If X is a goal of mine (making a million, say, or landing a certain job), I shall no doubt maximize my chances of its attainment by dropping everything else and concentrating on it alone—to the exclusion of friendship, health, and so forth. But it is madness, not rationality, that lies down this road. Sensible people do not want to achieve their objectives come what may. (Think of the classic short story "The Monkey's Paw," by W. W. Jacobs.) They want success in goal attainment but in a reasonable balance or combination. At most they are willing to prespecify some particular level of commitment and to maximize their choices within the limits set by this level.

At this point, then, one comes up against the shortcomings of the concept of economic man and the economists' traditional conception of rationality in terms of the efficient pursuit of prudential self-interest. What the moral philosopher finds particularly objectionable in the proceedings of his colleagues in economics and decision theory is the way they appropriate to their own use the honorific rubric "rationality." They enumerate some fundamentally selfish principles of assessment—roughly those of atomistically self-interested prudence—and canonize these as axioms of rational decision-making. Such theses are put before us as principles of rationality by fiat or definition or some comparably high-handed act of preemption. We are told with little ado or argument that conformity to a narrowly self-interested modus operandi in choice situations is what necessarily characterizes the choices of the rational man. And in place of justificatory argumentation, one finds these principles presented as effectively self-evident axioms whose status is virtually definitional—as though such contentions belong to the very meaning of rationality!

When economists, decision theorists, and social choice theoreticians speak so casually of what the rational man does, they manage to conceal under the sheep's clothing of a seemingly descriptive rubric the wolf of a deeply normative commitment, one that is highly dubious and debatable. They arrogate the proud title of rationality for the convenient predilections of their own inherently debatable standpoint.

Economists and decision theorists often talk as though *all* of a person's wants and preferences were equally rational, as though any end whatsoever were automatically valid (appropriate, legitimate) simply by virtue of its mere adoption. But this rides roughshod over the crucial differences between real and apparent interests.

Consider the sequence:

1. what I want (here and now);
2. what I will want when the time comes;
3. what I would want if:
   a. I knew more (through ampler information);
   b. I deliberated more carefully (on the basis of the existing information base);
   c. I managed to make certain (putatively desirable) changes in myself (i.e., made myself over more fully in the direction of my own ideals);
   d. I managed to make myself over into a really good person.

The further we work our way down this list, the more fully do we effect the transition from actual (or apparent) toward real (or legitimate) interests. The various distinctions operative here (short run vs. long run, well informed vs. ill informed, naive vs. reflective, actual vs. ideal) are all crucial for the determination of real as opposed to merely apparent interests. And it is real interests rather than mere wants as such that are central to rationality—not *desiderata* but *desideranda*, not desired things but warrantedly desirable ones. The ultimate pivot point for people's interests is not what people *do* desire or prefer but what they *should* desire and prefer. The distinction between wants we do have and wants we reflectively feel that it is appropriate for us to have is crucial.

In particular, there is nothing in any way inherently unreasonable or irrational about a selfless concern for others. Indeed, there is no adequate reason for calling people unreasonable if their actions militate against their own advantage, for there is no earthly reason why they cannot have perfectly legitimate values that transcend their own condition. To be sure, people will be unreasonable, indeed irrational, if their actions *systemically* impede their own objectives. But there is no adequate ground for holding that their *only* rationally legitimate objectives are of the selfish or self-interested sort. It is a travesty upon this concept to construe rationality in terms of prudential self-advantage. To take this stance is to have too narrow a sense of appropriate value. Neither for individuals nor for societies is "the pursuit of happiness" the sole and legitimate guide to action; its dictates must be counterbalanced by recognizing the importance of doing those things upon which in afteryears we can look back with justifiable pride.

The intelligent pursuit of one's ends is not simply a question of efficiency. For the matter is also one of balance, subject to the consideration that we must not impede or destroy the prospects of achieving our other coordinate objectives.

The diversity of human goods and values has consequences of great importance. One of these is that there are very different structures of rationality because different emphases, different priorities, among diverse goods and values are possible and legitimate. We confront a pluralistic situation. For instance, the rationality of the cognitive life is not the same as the rationality of the artistic life. Formal or "pure" rationality may be the same for everyone, but the diversity of legitimate goals for individuals ensures that material or substantive rationality is not.

The rationality of ends is an important and pressing issue precisely because of the diversity of ends. If there were only a single genus of value, the question of the rationality of ends—of adjudging the proper role of each in contexts where the others too are operative—would not arise. It is because there are various alternatives that the question of their harmonization becomes pressing.

Rational agency requires optimization overall, not solving this problem in the locally best possible way (of buying the best car I can pay for), but in the globally best possible way that takes other commitments and opportunities into account. (Even though the purchase of that car per se is within my resources, its opportunity cost in terms of forgone alternatives may yet be too high.) Rationality is holistic; it is collective optimization rather than distributive maximization that matters.

Rationality, then, pivots on "doing the best we can" in a way that is only loosely connected with what is ordinarily understood by "maximization." It is a grave mistake to think that there is some monolithic sort of "goodness" out there for us to maximize. The realm of value is simply too complex for that.

Yet if rationality is not a project of maximization, then what is it? It is a matter of *optimization* in the pursuit of ends, of doing the sensible thing, of resolving our choices in the most intelligent way realizable in the prevailing circumstances. Rationality consists in the intelligent pursuit of appropriate ends—it looks to the *best*, not to the *most*. And this calls for the effective harmonization of a diversified profile of goods in the endeavor to produce an optimal result. But this is not in general a matter of maximizing some quantity. (Doing something "in the most intelligent way possible" may sound like maximization, but there is in fact no measurable quantity that is being maximized.)

Is the good one or many, homogeneous or heterogeneous? The insight of Plato's *Philebus* holds true here. The good must be construed as a mixture—a matter of blend and proportion, of combining and harmonizing. We return to the root idea of Pythagoreanism that the good is a *harmony* of a certain sort, a suitable balance of diversified factors. The difference between good music and cacophony does not reside in the fact that the former provides more of something that the latter lacks. "The good" at large is multidimensional, not homogeneous; enhancing it is a matter of optimizing a complex profile, not of maximizing a determinable quantity. Its rational cultivation is a holistic matter of organic harmony rather than a mechanical matter of monolithic maximization.

In a rational choice among (mutually exclusive) alternatives, we begin by determining for each the particular mixture of costs and benefits involved. Comparing these mixtures with one another, we use "judgment" to (try to) find one that is preferable, overall, to all the rest—a process that may well involve procedures over and above calculation. (There may be "weighing" at issue, but it is of a purely figurative sort.) To choose the overall preferable result—or at any rate to choose one to which no other is preferable overall—is what reason enjoins, and *all* that reason enjoins. But we may well (and generally do) have to do with a preferability determination in which measurement and maximization as such need play no role whatsoever.

Aristotle was emphatic in insisting that there is no deliberating about valued ends that are ultimate (nonmediate). To deliberate about the appropriateness of an end is to subordinate it to some other end, and this is by hypothesis infeasible in the case of an ultimate end—an ultimate goal or value. But this doctrine of Aristotle's is simply not correct. For it overlooks the fact that ends can be related to each other in appropriateness-relevant ways that are different from *subordination*. We can deliberate about an end not only on the basis of whether its adoption and pursuit facilitate the realization of some other superordinated end, but also on the basis of its *coordination,* by asking how well it fits into the overall economy of other, associated ends. We can ask about the extent to which their conjoint adoption allows for mutual adjustment and supportiveness. And so we can deliberate about ends not only in the light of other higher ends toward which they are means but also in the light of value criteria applied to our "economy of ends" at large—criteria of coordination like coherence and consonance, relative weight or importance (say in the competition for limited resources in the course of their implementation), and the like.

Such issues regarding the formulation of a "rational economy of ends"—issues of compatibility, coherence, consonance, centrality, balance (in point of "weight"), and so forth—are not in themselves yet further, different, and "higher" ends. They operate in a different sphere altogether, being values that we import ab extra in appraising our ends at large. They are not ends but value criteria that we deploy to achieve a rational coordination of ends, adjusting them to one another in the light of the fact that rational optimization requires the harmonization of a diversified variety of goods.

Optimization is thus a matter of harmonizing means and ends in the best way, everything considered—of finding the best overall means to the most appropriate relevant ends. It is a matter at once of efficiency and of teleology. And we must recognize that to optimize—to produce the best overall result—is not necessarily a matter of maximizing anything. As with baking a palatable cake, optimization is not a matter of identifying some particular ingredient or complex of ingredients and then injecting a maximum of that. In general, there just is no identifiable factor or complex of factors such that "better" can be identified with "more of *that.*" The good life, for example, does not consist in a single factor but involves a blended plurality of goods, such as health, happiness, freedom, companionship, and love. Some are irreducible to the rest in that additions of one are incapable of fully offsetting deficiencies of the others. The elements of a good journey are not interchangeable: adding more spectacular scenery cannot make up for bad food. Adding more salt (no matter how much) will not compensate for a cake's lack of sugar. The evaluative aspects of the goal are not interchangeable. We must harmonize rather than maximize. In general, when we have to appraise a profile or gestalt of desirabilities, preferability becomes a matter of a contextually determined structural harmonization rather than of mensurational maximization. (As the Greeks already realized, the theory of *structure* is just as important as the theory of *quantity.*)

But just how is one to determine the best overall combination of goods in cases of a plurality where no trade-offs are possible? No hard-and-fast rule can be laid down. Different contexts call for different optimizing procedures. To give just one hightly schematic example, suppose that for realizing an optimal effect three (individually measurable) goods are needed in the specific proportion 1:1:2. Then if we had to determine whether the combination of 5, 5, and 8 units respectively or 7, 7, and 7 units is preferable, we would sensibly pick the former over the latter, its aggregate "inferiority" notwithstanding.

In sum, then, given the inner complexity of the domain of human values in their interactive interrelation, we are constrained to portray the mechanism of rational choice in terms of judgmental *optimization* (of doing "the best"), rather than mensurational *maximization* (of doing "the most"). Optimization is a matter not of "bigger is better," as with maximization, but of balancing, coordinating, and harmonizing goods in one or another of conceivably alternative ways.

The overall lesson of these considerations is clear. The appropriate way of addressing the issue of rationality in the context of value management is not in terms of maximization but rather in terms of optimization, which is complicated and in itself an issue that is unavoidably evaluative. There is far more to rational evaluation than is dreamed of in utilitarian philosophy. [12]

---

[12] Some themes of the present discussion are treated more fully in the author's *Ethical Idealism* (Berkeley and Los Angeles: University of California Press, 1987).

Three

The Rationality of Values and Evaluations

Rationality and Appropriate Ends: Against the Humean Conception of Reason

In an oft-cited passage in book 3 of the *Nicomachean Ethics*, Aristotle wrote:

> We deliberate not about ends but about means. For a doctor does not deliberate whether he shall heal, nor an orator whether he shall persuade, nor a statesman whether he shall produce law and order, nor does any one else deliberate about his end. They assume the end and consider how and by what means it is to be attained; and if it seems to be produced by several means they consider by which it is most easily and best produced, while if it is achieved by one only they consider how it will be achieved by this and by what means *this* will be achieved, till they come to the first cause, which in the order of discovery is last.[1]

The sort of thinking that Aristotle has in view here—deliberation about efficient means for realizing preestablished ends—is unquestionably important in human affairs. "I need a bed; to make a bed I need a hammer and saw; I can borrow a hammer; so I shall go and buy a saw." Aristotle's own examples of practical reasoning are exactly of this common and familiar sort, and are plausible enough in their way.[2] However, not all deliberative reasoning is means-end reasoning. Admittedly, the doctor does not deliberate about treating illness—that choice is already settled, included as part of one's decision to become a doctor. But a young woman may well deliberate about whether to become a doctor in the first place, reflecting on whether this would be something good for her, given her abilities, skills, interests, options, and so on. And this sort of deliberation is not a question of means to preestablished ends at all. The long and short of it is that there are two very different sorts of deliberations: cognitive deliberations regarding matters of *information* (encompassing the issue of the efficiency of means), and evaluative deliberations regarding matters of *value* (encompassing the issue of the merit of ends). Whether certain means are

---

[1] *Nicomachean Ethics* 1112b12–20.

[2] *Metaphysics* 1032b17–22; *De Motu Animalium* 701a18–20. A helpful guide to Aristotle's theory of practical reasoning is Norman O. Dahl, *Practical Reason, Aristotle, and Weakness of the Will* (Minneapolis: University of Minnesota Press, 1984).

appropriate to given ends is a question whose resolution must be addressed in the former, informational order of deliberation. But whether the ends we have are appropriate as such, whether they merit adoption, is an issue that can and must be addressed in the latter, evaluative order of deliberation.

Rationality plays a crucial role here. A rational agent certainly cannot say: "I adopt G as a goal of mine but am indifferent regarding the efficiency and effectiveness of means toward this goal." But no more can a rational person say: "I adopt G as a goal of mine but am indifferent regarding its validity; I just don't care about the larger issue of its appropriateness as such." Both matters—the efficacy of means and the validity of goals—are essential aspects of practical rationality. Specifically, the question of the rationality of freely adopted ends cannot justifiably be avoided by anyone concerned for the demands of rationality as such.[3]

David Hume drew a sharp contrast between a (narrowly construed) "reason" that is concerned only with means and a reason-detached faculty of motivation that concerns itself with ends—namely, the passions. And he considered these motivating passions as autonomous forces to operate outside the rule of reason proper. He regarded an impetus toward or away from some object—a desire or aversion—as simply the wrong sort of thing to be rational or sensible, as lying outside the rational domain altogether.

As Hume saw it, the formal issues of logic and mathematics apart, reason merely deals in descriptive information about the world's states of affairs and relationships of cause and effect. Accordingly, reason is strictly instrumental: it can inform me about what I must do *if* I wish to arrive at a certain destination, but only "passion"—desire or aversion—can make something into a destination for me. When one asks what is to be done, reason as such has no instructions—it is wholly a matter of what one happens to want. Reason is thus "a slave of the passions." Its modus operandi is strictly conditional: it dictates hypothetically that if one accepts this, then one cannot (in all consistency) fail to accept that. But all this is a matter of the hypothetical if-then. The categorical "accept this!" is never a mandate of reason, but of that extrarational faculty of "the passions," which dictates the bestowal of one's unconditional allegiances. Reason it-

---

[3] On the rationality of ends, see Stephen Nathanson, *The Ideal of Rationality* (Atlantic Highlands, N.J.: Humanities Press, 1985). Social-science aspects of the issue are treated in S. I. Benn and G. W. Mortimore, *Rationality and the Social Sciences* (London: Routledge & Kegan Paul, 1976), esp. pt. 2, "Rationality in Action." As these authors point out, social scientists are caught in a dilemma between the impetus of Max Weber's influential contention that social science must be value-free and the idea that the social scientist should be able to proceed prescriptively and render policy advice. It is clearly one thing to inform clients about how to get what they want and another to counsel them about where their real interests lie.

self is inherently conditionalized. It says not what one must (or must not) opt for, but only what one is consequentially committed to if one *already* stands committed to something else.

Hume insisted: "It is not contrary to reason to prefer the destruction of the whole world to the scratching of my finger. It is not contrary to reason for me to choose my total ruin. . . . It is as little contrary to reason to refer even my own acknowledged lesser good to my greater, and to have a more ardent affection for the former than the latter."[4] But this is clearly strange stuff. On any plausible view of the matter, reason cannot simply beg off from considering the validity of ends. Our motivating "passions" can surely themselves be rational or otherwise: those that impel us toward things that are bad for us or away from things that are good for us go against reason; those that impel us away from things that are bad for us and toward things that are good for us are altogether rational. We cannot divorce rationality from a concern for people's best (i.e., "real" or "true") interests. Reason can and should deliberate not only about what it is ill advised to believe (because it is probably at odds with the truth) but also about what it is ill advised to esteem (because it is probably at odds with our interests). Like various beliefs, various evaluations are palpably crazy.[5] Reason, after all, is not just a matter of the compatability or consistency of pregiven commitments, but of the warrant that there is for undertaking certain commitments in the first place. An *evaluative* rationality that informs us that certain preferences are absurd—preferences that wantonly violate our nature, impair our being, or diminish our opportunities—fortunately lies within the human repertoire.

To be sure, philosophers even now often follow Hume in saying things of the following sort: "Reason is wholly instrumental. It cannot tell us where to go; at best it can tell us how to get there. It is a gun for hire that can be employed in the service of any goals we have, good or bad."[6] On such a view, reason has no concern with goals as such—all it can do is to inform us about the efficiency of means to ends. It can neither guide us in setting ends nor advise us about priorities, about how conflicts among divergent ends are to be settled. Ends, priorities, and values all lie outside the range of reason. They are no more than our value allegiances, the

---

[4] David Hume, *A Treatise of Human Nature* (London: A. Millar, 1738), bk. 2, pt. 3, sec. 3. For Hume, the only inappropriate desires are those that depend on cognitively irrational beliefs.

[5] For strict consistency, a rigorous Humean should, by analogy, hold that cognitive reason too is only hypothetical—that it tells us only that certain beliefs must be abandoned *if* we hold certain others, and that no beliefs are contrary to reason as such, so that "it is not contrary to reason to think one's finger larger than the entire earth."

[6] Herbert A. Simon, *Reason in Human Affairs* (Stanford: Stanford University Press, 1983), pp. 7–8.

product of a rationally blind attachment to some fundamentally extrarational commitment. (In this context, oddly enough, Hume and Nietzsche are birds of the same feather.) But in leaving the issue of our interests altogether out of it, this sort of approach plainly takes too narrow a view of what reason is all about by writing off the whole sphere of the evaluative use of reason.

To reemphasize: There is not only an informative rationality that relates to means but also an evaluative rationality that relates to ends. We can reason not only about matters of efficiency of goal attainment but about the appropriateness of our goals as well. One can reason not only about matters of fact but also about matters of value. It is surely a dictum of reason not only to accept that which (in the light of the available evidence) is acceptance worthy but also to prefer that which (in the light of available indications) is preference worthy. It *is* contrary to reason (albeit to evaluative rather than cognitive reason) to prefer the lesser good to the greater or the greater evil to the lesser or to subordinate real needs to feckless wants. Only by doing violence to the nature of reason—only by ignoring or dismissing the evaluative side of reason with its concern for what is worthy of preference—can Hume maintain the sort of position he does.

Even Hume himself stands committed (both in the *History of England* and *An Inquiry Concerning the Principles of Morals*) to the idea that passion as such is not really quite the end of the matter, because for him some passions (the "good" ones associated with the objects of the Glorious Revolution of 1688) are worthy, and others (especially those of "enthusiasm") are not. But what instrument have we for this crucial work of appraisal, except reason? The philosophical Hume thought that "rational sympathy" would do—but it too is in the end deeply problematic, given its apparent tendency to pull different people in different directions. Unevaluated "natural sympathy" of the sort envisioned by Hume will not in the end accomplish the job that needs to be done. For such uninstructed inclinations may *explain* how people act but cannot *justify* it. If rationality is what indeed concerns us, then evaluation, however difficult, is in the end the only way to go.

Hume's profound error lay in his taking a part of reason to be the whole of it. For, reason at large must care for ends as well as means. If our ends (our goals and values) are themselves inappropriate—if they run counter to our real and legitimate interests—then no matter how sagaciously we cultivate them, we are not being fully rational. (A voyage to a foolish destination, no matter how efficiently conducted, is a foolish enterprise.) Hume mistakenly effected a total divorce between reason and choice: "I have prov'd that reason is perfectly inert, and can never either prevent or produce any action or affection."[7] But while reason indeed cannot of itself "prevent or produce" action, the fact remains that it can justify and thereby motivate action through providing good reasons for it. When rational inquiry indicates to me that doing act A is beneficial, then—insofar as I am rational—it impels me toward this action. Alternatively, if it indicates that the action is detrimental, it impels me away from it. Reason's task in relation to action is to provide *grounds* for or against. Of course, the consideration that something is the rational thing for an agent to do in the circumstances will not move one to do so unless one also takes the stance "I shall heed the instructions of reason." But just this stance, of course, is routinely mandatory for all those of us who see ourselves as rational agents and set ourselves to act accordingly. And this means that any disconnection of reason from action is quite mistaken. To see reason as irrelevant to the validation of choice and action over and above matters of efficiency is to misrepresent it to the point of caricature.

Nor will it do to reduce the impetus of reason to the factual issue of needs and wants as interdistinguished from the normative source of best interests. People can clearly have desires (for harm to enemies) or needs (for drugs on which they have come to depend) that go clean against their real interests. The evaluative/normative aspect simply does not reduce without residue to the factual/descriptive.

An interesting and somewhat desperate move to transcend the gulf between wants and interests—between "what one wants" and "what is good for one"—is represented by Henry Sidgwick's influential proposal to equate the latter with *what one would want if*—if one were fully informed, undisturbed by passion, painstaking in visualizing consequences, and involved with other such strictly intellectual capabilities.[8] But such a stance is predicated on the highly questionable (albeit ancient) idea that an incapacity in the processing of information is the only impediment to appropriate evaluation—that "if we but knew," we would have to make our evaluations correctly. But this is eminently problematic. Clearly, it is not lack of information alone that prevents the monomaniac or the masochist from evaluating matters aright. Failures to assess means to ends are one thing; failures to think sensibly about values and priorities, another.

The crucial fact is that there is not only inferential ("logical") reason but also evaluative ("axiological") reason. Just as rational people believe only what is beliefworthy for someone in the circumstances, so they value only what is valueworthy, what is *deserving* of being valued. And the determi-

---

[7] *A Treatise of Human Nature*, ed. L. A. Selby Bigge (Oxford: Clarendon Press, 1964), p. 458.

[8] Henry Sidgwick, *A Method of Ethics*, 7th ed. (London: Macmillan, 1928), pp. 111–12.

nation of value worthiness requires the sensible application of appropriate standards—in short, reasoning. It is quintessentially the work of reasoning to determine what sorts of commitments are rational (i.e., conforming to reason) and what sorts are not. (And this is so whether the "commitments" at issue are beliefs or evaluations.)[9]

Concern for the rationality of ends is important precisely because cognitive rationality is not all, because information is not the only thing that counts in life. Knowledge of matters of descriptively nonevaluative fact is only one good among others; reason has other matters to attend to as well.[10] The instrumental rationality at issue in finding the effective means to chosen ends is only a part of rationality. For means may well be directed toward inappropriate ends. An embezzler, say, or a self-destructively neurotic person can be quite efficient in figuring out how to attain objectives. But this partial sort of rationality does not render such activities rational *tout court*. The Humean dogma that the nature of our ends is immaterial to rationality must accordingly be rejected. Being intelligent about *some* things does not make one unqualifiedly intelligent. Evaluative rationality is an indispensable component of rationality overall.

The Crucial Role of Interests: Wants and Preferences Are Not Enough

As this perspective indicates, rationality involves two sorts of issue: means and ends. The rationality of means is a matter of factual information alone—of what sorts of moves and measures lead efficiently to objectives. But the rationality of ends is a matter not of information but of legitimation. It is not settled just by factual inquiry but involves appraisal and evaluative judgment. In the larger scheme of things both aspects are needed: ends without requisite means are frustrating; means without suitable ends are unproductive and pointless. Accordingly, rationality has two sides: an *axiological* (evaluative) concern for the appropriateness of ends and an *instrumental* (cognitive) concern for effectiveness and efficiency in their cultivation. The conception of rationality fuses these two elements into one integral and unified whole.

Contentions like "Smith is selfish, inconsiderate, and boorish" do not lie outside the sphere of rational inquiry, nor for that matter do contentions like "Behavior that is selfish, inconsiderate, and boorish is against the best interest of people." The issue of *appropriate* action in the circumstances

---

[9] On the matter of rational vs. irrational ends, see Baier, *The Moral Point of View*, and Bernard Gert, *The Moral Rules* (New York: Harper & Row, 1973).

[10] On this theme, see the final chapter of the author's *Limits of Science* (Berkeley and Los Angeles: University of California Press, 1984).

in which we find ourselves is pivotal for rationality. Whether in matters of belief, action, or evaluation, we want—that is to say, often do and always *should* want—to do the best we can. For one cannot be rational without due care for the desirability of what one desires—the issue of its alignment with our real, as distinguished from our putative, or merely seeming interests.

The sensible attunement of means to ends that is characteristic of rationality calls for an appropriate balancing of costs and benefits in our choice among alternative ways of resolving our cognitive, practical, and evaluative problems. Reason accordingly demands determination of the true value of things. Even as cognitive reason requires that in determining what we are to accept we should assess the evidential grounds for theses at their true worth, so evaluative reason requires us to appraise the values of our practical options at their true worth in determining what we are to choose or prefer. And this calls for an appropriate cost-benefit analysis. Values must be managed as an overall "economy" in a rational way to achieve overall harmonization and optimization. (Economic rationality is not the only sort of rationality there is, but it is an important aspect of overall rationality.) Someone who rejects such economic considerations— who, in the absence of any envisioned compensating advantages, deliberately purchases benefits he or she deems to be worth a few pennies at the expense of millions—is simply not rational. It is just as irrational to let one's efforts in the pursuit of chosen objectives incur costs that outrun their true worth as it is to let one's beliefs run afoul of the evidence.

It is a grave mistake to think that one cannot reason about values—that values are simply a matter of taste and thus beyond the reach of reason, since "there's no reasoning about tastes." The fact that valid values implement and pivot upon our needs and our appropriate interests means that a rational critique of values is not only possible but necessary. For values that impede the realization of a person's best interests are clearly inappropriate. A priority scheme that sets mere wants above real needs or sets important objectives aside to avert trivial inconveniences is thereby deeply flawed. Even great values will have to yield to the yet greater. (Some things are rightly dearer to us than life itself.)

Economists, decision theorists, and utilitarian philosophers generally hold that rationality turns on the intelligent cultivation of one's preferences. But this is problematic in the extreme (as the preceding chapter argued). For the two formulas are equivalent only if one happens to have sufficiently enlightened preferences. And this of course is not necessarily so. What I want or merely may think to be good for me is one thing; what I need and what actually is good for me is another. To move from preferences and perceived interests to genuine benefits and real interests, I must be prepared to get involved in a rational critique of ends—to examine in the light of objective standards whether what I desire is desirable, whether my actual ends are rational ends, whether my putative interests are real interests. Genuinely rational persons are those who proceed in situations of choice by asking themselves not the introspective question "What do I prefer?" but the objective question "What is to be deemed preferable? What *ought* I to prefer on the basis of my best interests?"[11] Rational comportment does not just call for desire satisfaction; it demands desire management as well. The question of appropriateness is crucial. And this is an issue about which people can be, and often are, irrational; not just careless but even perverse, self-destructive, and crazy.

There is nothing automatically appropriate, let alone sacred, about our own ends, objectives, and preferences. For rationality, the crucial question is that of the true value of the item at issue. What counts is not preference but preferability—not what people do want, but what they ought to want; not what people actually want, but what sensible or right-thinking people would want under the circumstances. The normative aspect is ineliminable. There is an indissoluble connection between the true value of something (its being good or right or useful) and its being rational to choose or prefer this thing. And so, the crucial question for rationality is not that of what we prefer but that of what is in our best interests—not simply what we may happen to desire but what is good for us in the sense of contributing to the realization of our real interests. The pursuit of what we want is rational only insofar as we have sound reasons for deeming this to be deserving of being wanted. The question whether what we prefer is preferable, in the sense of *deserving* this preference, is always relevant. Ends can and (in the context of rationality) must be evaluated. It is not just beliefs that can be stupid, ill advised, and inappropriate—that is to say, *irrational*—but ends can be as well.

Evaluation thus lies at the very heart and core of rationality. For rationality is a matter of balancing costs and benefits—of best serving our overall interests. The question of worth is thus never far removed from the thoughts of a rational mind. The rationality of ends is an indispensable component of rationality at large. The rationality of our actions hinges critically both on the appropriateness of our ends and on the suitability of the means by which we pursue their cultivation. Both of these components—the cogently cognitive ("*intelligent* pursuit") and the normatively purposive ("*appropriate* ends")—are alike essential to full-fledged rationality.

But just what is it that is in a person's real or best interests? Partly, this is indeed a matter of meeting the needs that people universally have in

---

[11] A good exposition of the opposing position may be found in Frederick Schick, *Having Reasons: An Essay in Rationality and Sociality* (Princeton: Princeton University Press, 1984).

common—health, satisfactory functioning of body and mind, adequate resources, human companionship and affection, and so on.[12] Partly, it is a
matter of the particular role one plays: cooperative children are in the
interests of a parent, customer loyalty in those of a shopkeeper. Partly, it
is a matter of what one simply happens to want. (If John loves Mary, then
engaging Mary's attention and affections are in John's interests—some
things are in a person's interests simply because one takes an interest in
them.) But these want-related interests are valid only by virtue of their
relation to universal interests. Mary's approbation is in John's interest
only because "having the approbation of someone we love" is in anyone's
interest. Any valid *specific* interest must fall within the validating scope
of an appropriate *universal* covering principle of interest legitimation.
(The development of my stamp collection is in my interest only because
it is part of a hobby that constitutes an avocation for me, and "securing
adequate relaxation and diversion from the stress of one's daily cares" is
something that is in anyone's interests.) A specific (concrete, particular)
interest of a person is valid as such only if it can be subordinated to a
universal interest.

But what of "mere whims and fancies"? If I have a yen for eating grass,
is my doing so not a perfectly appropriate "interest" of mine? Yes it is. But
only because it is covered by perfectly cogent universal interest, namely
that of "doing what I feel like doing in circumstances where neither injury
to one nor harm to others or self is involved."

Some writers (J. P. Sartre, for example) see reason-providing considerations in the practical sphere as locked into a potentially infinite regress
that can be broken only by an ultimate appeal to unreasoned "reasons"
that lie in the domain of judgmental decisions and acts of will. But this is
just not how things go in the explanation and the validation of actions.
Here, the regress of reasons (A because B because C) will and must termi-
nate automatically and naturally with any normatively valid universal reason—an interest that it is only proper and appropriate for *anyone* to have
when other things are anything like equal. I want *this* sandwich because
I am hungry, and I want to stop feeling hungry (i.e., relieve those hunger
pangs) because it is painful not to. But there is just no point in going
further—and no need for it. When such a universal is reached, no further
elaboration is called for. (It is this circumstance that endows the matter of
the rational validation of ends with its importance.)

And so, in assessing the rationality of actions, we cannot just look to
personal motives but must invoke universally appropriate values as well.

---

[12] The issue goes back to the specification of the "basics" (*principia*) of the human good in
the Middle Academy (Carneades)—things like the soundness and maintenance of the parts
of the body, health, sound senses, freedom from pain, physical vigor, and physical attractiveness. Cf. Cicero, *De finibus* 5.7.19.

The fact that X wants A remains a mere motive for X's action in pursuing A (in contradistinction to a reason) until such time as it is rationalized through the fact that X recognizes A to have the desirable feature F, which is not just something that X wants but is something that any and every (reasonable) person would want in the circumstances at issue.[13] (Note, when X wants "to marry Mary," this remains unrationalized until such time as it is "covered" by the universal desideratum of "marrying a person one loves deeply.") Only such a legitimation *sub ratione boni*, as part of a universally cogent desideratum, can rationalize a valuation (or a choice or preference that flows from it). Strictly personal resolutions provide only motives, not reasons: only universal considerations can provide an adequate rationale for action. "X wants A." Why? "X wants B and sees A as leading to B." But why does X want B? With a *rational* want we can extend this regress until we reach something that is unrestrictedly (universally) desirable—something the wanting of which we, the questioners, see to make sense, in that we value it, think that everyone should do so, and think it pointless and needless to raise further questions. Only when X does that which we ourselves see as being "normal and natural" for people in general do we stop asking for further special explanations. At that point, the factor of rationality accomplishes its characteristic work.

Consider the contrast between:

professed wants: what I say or declare that I want or prefer;

felt wants: what I (actually) do want or prefer;

real (or appropriate) wants: what the reasonable (impartial, well-informed, well-intentioned, understanding) bystander would think that I ought to want on the basis of what is "in my best interests."

This last item is decisive for rationality—namely, what is in my "real" or "best" interests. Rationality is not just a matter of doing what we *want* (if this were so, it would be far simpler to attain); it is a matter of doing what we (rationally) *ought*, given the situation in which we find ourselves.

Relative value (utility, means-to-ends serviceability) is no doubt important. But without due heed to the categorically normative status of those ends themselves, relative evaluation is a futile exercise from the rational point of view. To proceed rationally we must care not just for the efficacy of means but for the worth of ends. Man is not only *Homo sapiens* but *Homo aestimans*. The most fundamental judgment we make regarding even merely hypothetical developments is whether they are or are not "a good thing." Being rational involves endeavoring to do well (intelligently) what we must by nature do, and evaluation is, emphatically, a part of this.

---

[13] We cannot appropriately define "the rational thing" as being "what every rational (reasonable) person would want," since this would be circular. But that, of course, does not preclude the contention at issue from specifying a necessary relationship.

Action in pursuit of what we ourselves desire is not automatically rendered rational by this fact. The crucial issue is one of evaluating that desire itself—of determining whether the desired object is actually desirable, something *worthy* of desire. (Desire may be enough to explain an action, but it is not thereby enough to qualify it as rational.) Other things being equal, it is rational to pursue one's wants. But generally other things are not equal. In the main, the point is not what we do want but what we ought to want, not what we desire but "what's good for us." And when these differ, rationality and desire part ways. (From the rational point of view it is counterproductive to pursue wants at the expense of needs and real interests.) Being desired does not automatically make something desirable, nor being valued valuable. The pivot is how matters *ought* to be.

In the nature of things, when something is classed as a value, it is placed within the category of putatively "good things," because its promotion and realization is viewed as inherently beneficial. This consideration points to one important way in which values can be criticized *abstractly* and on their own account. For here we can look to exactly what sorts of goods and benefits would accrue from the realization of the value.

People's ends and purposes are certainly not automatically valid. We can be every bit as irrational in the adoption of ends as in any other choice. Apparent interests are not automatically real; getting what one wants is not necessarily to one's benefit; goals are not rendered valid by their mere adoption. People's ends can be self-destructive, self-defeating impediments to the realization of their true needs. Rationality calls for objective judgment—for an assessment of preferability, rather than for a mere expression of preference. The rationality of ends, their rational appropriateness and legitimacy, is accordingly a crucial aspect of rationality. More is at issue with rationality than a matter of strict instrumentality, mere effectiveness in the pursuit of ends no matter how inappropriate they may be. When we impute to our ends a weight and value they do not in fact have, we pursue mere will-o'-the-wisps.

The rationality of ends is essential to rationality as such; there is no point in running—however swiftly—to a destination whose attainment conveys no benefit. Our true interests are not those we do have but those we would have if we conducted our investigative business and our evaluative business properly (sensibly, appropriately). Our welfare is often ill served by our wishes—which may be altogether irrational, perverse, or pathological.[14] This distinction of appropriateness of real, as opposed to merely seeming, wants and interests is crucial for rationality. The latter turns on what we merely happen to want at the time, the former on what

---

[14] See the author's *Welfare* (Pittsburgh: University of Pittsburgh Press, 1972). Cf. John Rawls, *A Theory of Justice* (Cambridge: Harvard University Press, 1971), p. 421. Rawls traces this line of thought back to Henry Sidgwick.

we should want, and thus on "what we would want if"—if we were all those things that "being intelligent" about the conduct of one's life requires: if our actions were prudent, sensible, conscientious, well considered, and the like.[15]

To be sure, a person's "appropriate interests" will have a substantial element of personal relativity. One person's self-ideal, shaped in the light of one's own value structure, will quite appropriately be different from that of another. Moreover, what sorts of interests one has will hinge in significant measure on the particular circumstances and conditions in which one finds oneself—including one's wishes and desires. (In the absence of any countervailing considerations, getting what I want is in my best interests.) All the same, there is also a large body of real interests that people share in common—for example, as regards standard of living (health and resources) and quality of life (opportunities and conditions)— and it is these factors of life sustainment and enrichment that are ultimately determinative of the validity of individualized interests. Both sorts of interests—the idiosyncratic and the general—play a determinative role in the operations of rationality.

The rationality of ends inheres in the simple fact that we humans have various valid needs—that we require not only nourishment and protection against the elements for the maintenance of health but also information ("cognitive orientation"), affection, freedom of action, and much else besides. Without such varied goods we cannot thrive as human beings—we cannot achieve the condition of human well-being that Aristotle called "flourishing." The person who does not give these manifold desiderata their due—who may even set out to frustrate their realization—is clearly not being rational.

These various "goods" are not simply instrumental means to other goods but aspects or components of what is in itself a quintessentially good end in its relation to us—human flourishing. What it involves and how it particularizes to the concrete situation of specific individuals is something complex and internally variegated. But it is this overarching desideratum that validates the rest. Flourishing as *humans*, as the sorts of creatures we are, patently is *for us* an intrinsic good (though not, to be sure, necessarily the supreme good). We are so situated that from our vantage point (and who else's can be decisive for us?) it is clearly something that must be seen as good. We need not deliberate about it, need not endeavor to excogitate it from other premises; for us, it comes direct, as an inevitable "given."

---

[15] The contrast goes back to Aristotle's distinction between *desire* as such and *rational preference*. Many aspects of Aristotle's ethical theory bear usefully on the present discussion.

No doubt Xenophanes of Colophon was right. Even as different creatures may well have different gods, so they might well have different goods. But no matter. *For us* the perfectly appropriate sort of good is *our* sort of good—the human good. In this regard, Aristotle did indeed get to the heart of the matter. For us, the human good is indeed an adequate foundation for substantive, practical rationality. Given that we are what we are, it is this that is decisive for us. We have to go on from where we are. It is in *this* sense alone that there is no deliberation about ends. The universally appropriate ends at issue in our human condition are not somehow freely chosen by us; they are fixed by the (for us) inescapable ontological circumstance that—like it or not—we find ourselves to exist as human beings and thus able to function as free rational agents. Their ultimate inherence in (generic) human needs determines the appropriateness of our particular, individual ends.

The springs of human agency are diverse. Our actions can be engendered in different ways. We act not for reasons alone but frequently from "mere motives"—out of anxiety, cupidity, habit, impulse. In such cases we also have ends and purposes in view, but often not appropriate ones. If rationality were merely a matter of unevaluated goals and purposes as such—if it were to consist simply in the "technical rationality" of goal-efficient action—then the established line between the rational and the irrational would have to be redrawn in a very different place, and its linkage with what is intelligent and well advised would be severed. But where there is no appropriate, and thus no meaningful end, rational agency ceases. (There will, of course, still be room for goal-directed action, but without *appropriate* goals it will be problematic from the rational point of view.)

Value Objectivity: The Prospect of Correct and Incorrect Evaluation

The question "Is there a tenable distinction between valuing that which is right or correct and valuing that which is wrong or incorrect?" has much concerned philosophers throughout the axiological tradition that stretches from clinical antiquity to Brentano and beyond. Its resolution is relatively uncontroversial and unproblematic in the case of means values, seeing that there is no fundamental problem about applying the concepts of correctness and incorrectness in the case of valuing things as means. Smith's valuing "dissolute living" as a means to "bad health" is correct if dissolute living produces bad health and incorrect otherwise. And again, there is no issue of principle in the case of valuing things according to a certain given standard. Whether or not, say, a certain measure would conduce to "the standard of living of the country" is, in the final analysis, a simply technical question that can in principle always be resolved by strictly factual considerations. The more difficult and problematic question is whether the issue of correctness versus incorrectness applies to valuing things intrinsically, as ultimate ends.

The issue was posed clearly and cogently by Aristotle:

> What affirmation and negation are in thinking, pursuit and avoidance are in desire; so that since moral virtue is a state of character concerned with choice, and choice is deliberate desire, therefore both the reasoning must be true and the desire right, if the choice is to be good, and the latter must pursue just what the former asserts. Now this kind of intellect and of truth is practical; of the intellect which is contemplative, not practical nor productive, the good and the bad state are truth and falsity respectively (for this is the work of everything intellectual); while of the part which is practical and intellectual, the good state is truth in agreement with right desire.[16]

To appreciate justly what is at issue, one must take seriously Aristotle's contention that "correct" and "incorrect" are just as applicable to desire and valuing as to belief or judgment. Consider the pairings:

belief	valuing or desire
correctness of belief	correctness of valuing or desire
believed to be true	valued or desired
actually true	valuable or desirable

An instructive analogy can be based on this correspondence: Take whatever one would regard as a plausible thesis with respect to the familiar left-hand column. (For example: "With respect to belief, we may characterize belief as correct if the item [i.e., proposition] believed is actually true.") Then use the correspondence to translate this thesis into the language of the right-hand column. The result will be a thesis that is also plausible—and indeed correct on the Aristotle-Brentano view. (In the example: "With respect to desire, we may characterize a desire as correct if the item [i.e., the thing desired] is actually of value.") On the basis of this analogy Brentano, following Aristotle, elaborated a complex theory of the correctness of desire and valuation.[17] And there is much to be said in favor of such an approach to the rationality of evaluation.

What makes evaluation a rational enterprise is the fact that values are objective in at least one of the various senses of that term, namely, in that evaluation is subject to *standards* of appropriateness and inappropriate-

---

[16] *Nicomachean Ethics* 1139a20–31 (Oxford trans.).

[17] For further details, see R. M. Chisholm, "Brentano's Theory of Correct and Incorrect Emotion," *Révue Internationale de Philosophie* 78 (1966): 395–415.

ness, or correctness and incorrectness. Only through standards can we reach that impersonality and generality of application that is crucial to objectivity. To get beyond the level of means evaluation (i.e., of assessment of efficiency in the realization of otherwise unevaluated ends), then we must also have criteria of inherent positivity that constitute standards for evaluation of ends. And in the case of us humans these must, in the final analysis, pivot on whether the items at issue somehow manage to serve a genuine interest of ours—that is, to function in some way conducive to enabling us to flourish as human beings. The objectivity of rational evaluation ultimately roots in the nature of our real interests. To be sure, this issue of real interests is itself in part normative. But this fact does not establish a vicious circularity; it simply reflects the fact that the value domain is probatively self-contained—that it lies in the very nature of things that in cogent reasoning about values we cannot reach evaluative conclusions without evaluative inputs.

The theory of value adopted here is thus at once *humane* (i.e., oriented to the constitution of rational beings of our type) and *objective*. It is worthwhile to dissipate the aura of paradox that looms here.

In rejecting subjectivity, the position denies that values lie in the eyes of the beholder—that people somehow "make them up as they go along." On the contrary: values are a matter of opinion-independent fact. However, their rooting in matters independent of human opinion—of our particular contingent beliefs—does not necessarily render such objective values independent of human thoughts (mental reactions). For the core of an objectifying value theory is that nature in general, and its sub-subdivision of humans in particular, are such that certain evaluations will in some part be people-correlative, realizable in and through a human medium alone. Even as certain electromagnetic waves need to be filtered through a human eye to depict objects as "red" or "green," so certain aspects of the real need to be filtered through a human mind to bring certain values to manifestation, and it is this circumstance that renders values objective. But of course being red is not subjective—it pivots on the perfectly objective fact of the sort of response that certain electromagnetic vibrations produce in interaction with a certain kind of monitor. Similarly the values at issue are matters of how certain circumstances evoke value responses in intention with a particular sort of mind. These evocations reflect perfectly real and objective cogents of the value structure of the real. The human mind does not "invent" them, but rather brings them to overt expression. We "discover" such evaluative conditions and relationships as (preexisting) aspects of nature, even as we discover preexisting aspects of nature when we observe natural laws. We humans *discern* them but they are not made up by us—their basis and grounding preexists in nature. After all, the laws of human medicine and human psychology—while representing integral parts of the objective law-structure of nature—are nowise invented (made up, subjectively devised) by humans; they can nevertheless only be manifested in and through them. And just this is the case with those humane values at issue here. Though perfectly objective, they are, nevertheless, only manifestable in and through humans.

It is in this sense and in this sort of way that the present approach to evaluation construes the idea that human values—values bound up with the modus operandi of rational beings of our type—should nevertheless be seen as objective.

The Idea of a "Value Economy" of a Life

The consideration of a person's *system* of values leads to the conception of an ideal. The life-history ideals and character ideals operative within our cultural tradition (the statesman, the inventive genius, the successful businessman, the champion athlete) are all suggestive of a certain plan of life—a curriculum vitae, or at least a part thereof—that unfolds over time in the guiding light of a governing commitment to certain values. These values serve to effect some degree of rational balance in the deployment of resources (in "budgets" of time and effort) toward the attainment of specifiable benefits for self and others.[18] And this means that one can criticize such ideals—among various other ways of criticizing—in the light of the constellation of values implicit within them. For these may involve what, in the particular operative setting, requires an exorbitant or inappropriate investment of resources for the attainment of the relevant complex of benefits. Values being inherently benefit oriented, the value holder may expend too much or too little on the pursuit of the benefits at issue. We thus arrive at the conception of imbalances in a value economy.

When we consider the constellation of value commitments of a person (or a society), the appropriateness of adopting a value can be assessed, not abstractly, but in context. One can test the value economy at issue against the background of the concept of a spectrum of well-ordered modes of life, each one of which is characterized by an appropriate and viable balance of value commitments, and each of which carries its characteristic pattern of rewards. In extreme instances, the entire value economy that is built into

---

[18] On an economic line of approach we can, for example, introduce the idea of the "marginal significance" of a value (i.e., the infinitesimal ratio of added benefit per increment of added cost), using this idea to depict the fact that, in the circumstances, the principal of some values will yield a larger return in overall satisfaction for a given investment of effort.

the framework of a life-history ideal can become obsolete by becoming infeasible under changed circumstances (i.e., the knight-errant, the master craftsman).

This brings out the contextual nature of this mode of value criticism, its dependence on the setting of a complex of the value commitments that one has under specific conditions and circumstances. It is clear that value criticism of this sort would never result in the verdict that a certain value (i.e., genuine value) is wrong or improper as such. Rather, its verdict would be contextual: it would maintain that a person, leading his or her life in a certain particular setting, oversubscribes or undersubscribes to a given value, given the nature of this setting. Such criticism, then, does not address itself to values directly and abstractly, but rather to the issue of adopting and implementing certain values under the concretely prevailing conditions.

This perspective highlights the idea of the relevance of values to the specific life environment that provides the operative setting within which a value is espoused. For with a change in this setting, a certain value may be greatly more or less deserving of emphasis, depending on the changes in the nature and extent of the corresponding benefits in the altered circumstances. Or again, the value may be greatly more or less demanding of emphasis, depending on changes in the cost of its realization in a given degree. In extreme cases, a value can become irrelevant when the life setting has become such that the historically associated benefits are no longer available (e.g., the current status of knight-errantry, chivalry, and, perhaps, noblesse oblige), or it can even become malign when action on it comes to produce more harm than good (as with certain forms of "charity"). The appropriateness of values and indeed the very status of some putative values as genuine values is vulnerable to changes in the social or technological (etc.) circumstances of life. Our values are instrumentalities that serve the human good—the realization of our real interests—and with changing conditions their appropriateness can change as well. These interests, taken as abstract units at the highest level of generality, are themselves stable, but the particular values that concretize their effective pursuit can come, with changing circumstances, to vary in their status of rational appraisal. For rationality as such is committed to the assessment of appropriateness, and the alteration of circumstances can— and almost always does—manage to undermine the appropriateness of concrete values.

The rationality of ends is an indispensable component of rationality at large for two reasons. First, rationally valued ends must be evaluatively appropriate ones: if we adopt inappropriate ends, we are not being rational, no matter how efficiently and effectively we pursue them. Second, we cannot proceed rationally without considering the ends-relative value of our means, inquiring whether the cost of those means (the resources we are expending through them) is consonant with the values supposedly being realized through the ends by asking: "If *those* costs are involved in *the means, then are the ends really worth it?*" Without rational evaluation, practical rationality becomes infeasible—with fatal consequences for rationality as a whole, given the systematic unity of reason.[19]

[19] Some aspects of the rationality of value and evaluations are also treated in the author's *Rationality* (Oxford: Clarendon Press, 1988).

Part II

SCIENCE AND HUMAN VALUES

Four

How Wide Is the Gap between Facts and Values?

The Problem

Can values be derived from facts? Is it possible to effect a valid inferential transition from factual premises to an evaluative conclusion?

This issue is well worth the considerable philosophical toil and struggle that has been expended on it over the years.[1] Large and substantial philosophical positions are at stake with this apparently small-scale and seemingly technical question. As Hume remarked, a person who makes mistakes in factual matters is at worst stupid or incompetent, but a person who is mistaken in evaluative matters—for example, who prizes what properly deserves to be disdained—would for this very reason be deemed perverse and wicked.[2] But if evaluations could be *derived* from facts, so that erroneous evaluations would be mere mistakes in inquiry and information processing, then this differentiation would be invalidated. Mistakes in evaluation would be more to be pitied than censured, and the ethical aspect of evaluation would become unraveled: evaluative errors would now betoken a cognitive inadequacy of some sort, an intellectual rather than a personal defect. Moreover, values would be rendered objective by subsumption within the factual domain, and the thesis "There's no disputing about values" would be demolished. Far-reaching consequences would ensue.

The issue of fact-to-values inference confronts us with a philosophical dialectic in which the following doctrines are in circulation:

    (1) *Value naturalism*: Value claims can (at least sometimes) be inferred from strictly factual contentions.

    (2) *Value reductionism*: Value claims can always be reduced to (or redefined in terms of) strictly factual contentions.

    (3) *Value subjectivism*: Evaluative questions are never objectively resolv-

---

[1] For the literature of the problem, see the extensive bibliography in the author's *Introduction to Value Theory* (Englewood Cliffs, N.J.; Prentice-Hall, 1969; reprint, Lanham, Md.: University Press of America, 1980) and in Geoffrey Sayre McCord, ed. *Essays on Moral Realism* (Ithaca, N.Y.: Cornell University Press, 1988). Among the informative discussions that postdate these bibliographies is Stephen W. Ball, "Facts, Values, and Normative Supervenience," *Philosophical Studies* 55 (1989): 143–72.

[2] *Treatise of Human Nature*, bk. 3, pt. 1, sec. 1.

able. The situation is in principle never such that a specific resolution of
a value issue can be rationally constrained by objectively establishable
considerations.

(4) *Fact objectivism*: Factual questions are always objectively resolvable—at
least in principle.

The logical interrelationships of these positions is such that:

Anyone who accepts	Must also accept
(2)	(1)
(1) and (4)	not-(3)
(2) and (4)	not-(3)

So much is straightforwardly inherent in the logical structure of the situation. And given the plausible fact-objectivism of (4), it becomes clear that
establishing (1), or a fortiori (2), could be a plausible route to not-(3)—the
denial of value subjectivism, which is the stalking-horse of these present
deliberations.

It will, however, be contended here that naturalism/reductionism is a
route that those of us who are value objectivists and therefore reject (3)
neither can nor need to travel. Specifically it will be argued that:

First, the value naturalism of thesis (1) is false, or at least highly implausible.

Second, the untenability of value naturalism carries that of value reductionism
in its wake, since not-(1) entails not-(2).

Third, the untenability of value naturalism therefore still leaves it open to the
fact objectivist (who subscribes to [4]) whether or not to be a value subjectivist—that is, whether or not also to accept (3). However,

Fourth, a plausible case can actually be developed for value objectivism—that
is, for not-(3), despite the failure of the value naturalism of thesis (1).

So much for describing the lay of the doctrinal land. Let us begin its explo-
ration.

Fact Statements and Value Statements Distinguished

A factual statement is, clearly, one that restricts itself to staking claims
about strictly "factual" matters—that is, to providing information about
the descriptive features and circumstances of things. It makes no attempt
to assess, judge, or evaluate. Most factual statements are indeed purely
so: they contain no evaluative terms at all, making no mention whatever
of any aspect of good or bad, worthy or unworthy, significant or insignificant. A value statement, by contrast, is one that asserts or implies something about the worth and value of things—whether overtly or implicitly,
explicitly or by implication, positively or negatively. A value statement,

accordingly, embraces claims regarding the inherent positivity or negativity of things—about what is to be prized (or devalued), approved (or disapproved), preferred (or spurned) or the like. What is at issue with value statements is not just a matter of factual or descriptive information but a contention or implication—explicit or implicit—that a pro or con attitude is in order, that people generally *should*, and right-thinking people actually *would*, manifest approval or disapproval toward something. Thus the statement "That is a Chinese vase" affords a model descriptive contention, "That is a pretty vase" a model evaluative one, the difference turning on the circumstance that "Chinese" is a straightforwardly descriptive term, and "pretty" a straightforwardly evaluative one.

However, while the distinction between the factual and the evaluative seems clear enough at the level of abstract theoretical principle, significant difficulties arise in concrete applicative practice. For example, various ordinary-language predicates are only context-dependently evaluative. Take "X is talented," for example. Here the question "At what?" becomes crucial. To say that X is talented at marksmanship (that X can shoot much more accurately than most marksmen) is to stake a straightforwardly factual claim. But to say that "X is talented at poetry" is to assert that X can write (not more but) better poems than most and thus stakes a claim that is ineliminably evaluative. For the most part, however, such second-order subtleties need not further concern us here.

In line with the preceding explanation, consider the following group of statements:

> Americans generally like dogs.
> Dogs are affectionate creatures; they normally form attachments to their masters.

These statements are factual. None of them asserts or implies, in and of themselves, that dogs have any particular evaluative status (whether positive or negative). By contrast, consider:

> Dogs are fine companions.
> Dogs are loyal friends to people.

These are evaluative statements that attribute virtues. Unlike that first pair—or for that matter, even "Dogs are no good at catching mice"—they do not just attribute certain descriptive characteristics to dogs but ascribe to them evaluatively positive features of some sort. Each has an implication for what right-thinking people would and should prize about dogs, in a way that the first pair of statements in and of themselves do not. In just this way, the claim that "social justice" is something that Jones prizes is a purely factual one, while the contention that "social justice" is beneficial—is to be prized on grounds of representing a desirable state of affairs—is distinctively evaluative.

Logical Difficulties

Under exactly what sorts of conditions are we going to class a statement as evaluative? Of course it has to contain value terms—somewhere along the line matters of value have to be mentioned. But that of itself will not do, seeing that a claim's involvement with value terms might occur in a wholly vacuous and noncommittal way. (If E is a bona-fide evaluative thesis, then the complex conjunction P & $(E \lor$ not-$E)$ will also contain value terms, but that of itself will not render this compound statement evaluative.)

In specifying what sorts of statements are evaluative, the best course is to proceed in stages, beginning with the unproblematic and expanding outward from there. Certain statements are patently evaluative. Like "Lions are noble creatures" or "Sensible people esteem virtue," they wear their evaluative status on their sleeves. But the evaluative status of other statements is not comparably immediate and emerges only indirectly because they can be seen to have patently evaluative consequences when merely factual confirmation is introduced. Thus consider the contention "Any trained mathematician will recognize the elegance of the classical demonstration of the irrationality of the square root of 2." If we suppose that X is a trained mathematician, then this thesis clearly has the evaluative consequence "X recognizes the elegance of the classical demonstration of the irrationality of 2's square root," which in turn has the consequence "The classical demonstration of the square root of 2's irrationality is elegant." Because of this implication, it seems plausible to take the line that the initial contention must also be classed as evaluative. But at this point difficulties arise.

A significant stumbling block for all theories of fact-value interrelation is the paradoxical circumstance that $F \lor V$ follows from a strictly factual premise F (and thus is itself presumably factual), while nevertheless $F \lor V$ in conjunction with a factual premise (namely, $\sim F$) yields the evaluative conclusion V (and thus is itself presumably evaluative).[3]

In fact, we face an aporetic situation, that of the inconsistent triad:

(CP) *The Consequence Principle.* Any statement that, even in the presence of some merely factual supplementation, has an evaluative statement as a

---

[3] This difficulty is mentioned in A. N. Prior's paper entitled "The Autonomy of Ethics," *Australian Journal of Philosophy* 38 (1960): 202ff., reprinted in his *Papers on Logic and Ethics* (Amherst: University of Massachusetts Press, 1976). Prior credits the argument to Dr. T. H. Mott in 1954. It is also discussed in George Mavrodes's essay "On Deriving the Normative from the Non-Normative," *Papers of the Michigan Academy of Arts and Sciences* 53 (1968): 353–65; as well as in Lars Bergström, "On the Logic of Imperatives and Deontic Logic," in *Mérites et limites des méthodes logiques en philosophie* (Paris: J. Vrin, 1885; reprint, Paris: Colloque de la Fondation Singer-Poliginac, 1984), pp. 211–33 (see p. 212).

logical consequence should itself be classed as evaluative (i.e., as belonging to the class E of evaluative statements):

If $(P \ \& \ F) \to V$, where F is factual and V evaluative $(V \in E)$, then $P \in E$.

(FFD) *The Factuality of Fact Denial.* If F is factual, then so is its negation, $\sim F$.

(D) *The Dichotomy Assumption.* Any statement P is either factual or evaluative but not both: P is factual iff not-$(P \in E)$.

The mutual inconsistency of these three theses can be shown by means of the following dilemma: Let us stipulate that V is evaluative $(V \in E)$ and that F is factual. And let us now inquire into the status of $F \lor V$.

Part 1. Suppose that $F \lor V$ is evaluative: $(F \lor V) \in E$.

1. $F \to (F \lor V)$, by standard logic
2. $(F \lor V) \in E$, by supposition
3. $F \in E$, from (1), (2) by the Consequence Principle
4. But (3) is contrary to the supposition that F is factual, in violation of the Dichotomy Assumption

Part 2. Suppose that $F \lor V$ is factual.

1. $[(F \lor V) \ \& \ \sim F] \to V$, by standard logic
2. $\sim F$ is factual, by the Factuality of Fact Denial
3. $(F \lor V) \in E$, from (1), (2) by the Consequence Principle
4. But (3) is contrary to the supposition that $F \lor V$ is factual, in violation of the Dichotomy Assumption.

The inconsistency of the triad (CP), (FFD), (D) means that one or another of these three theses must be denied. Given that (FFD) is pretty well inevitable, one seems to be left with only two alternatives:

either abandon (or revise) the Consequence Principle,

or abandon (or revise) the Dichotomy Assumption, and specifically to take the line that $F \lor V$ of a hybrid status that is neither (strictly) factual nor (strictly) evaluative.

To see more clearly which way to turn here, let us examine yet another inconsistent triad:

(FC) *Factuality Conservation.* If F is factual, and F entails P, then P is factual.

(FFD) as above.

(D) as above.

Now let it be that F is factual and V is evaluative, and consider the following course of reasoning:

1. $F \rightarrow (F \vee V)$, by standard logic
2. $F \vee V$ is factual, from (1) by Factuality Conservation
3. $\sim F$ is factual by the Factuality of Fact Denial
4. $\sim F \mathrel{\&} (F \vee V)$ is factual, by (2), (3)
5. $[\sim F \mathrel{\&} (F \vee V)] \rightarrow V$, by standard logic
6. V is factual, from (4), (5) by Factuality Conservation
7. But by the Dichotomy Assumption (6) is contradictory to the supposition that V is evaluative.

Since the Dichotomy Assumption is also central to this apory (in which the consequence principle is an innocent bystander), we had best make it our target for rejection.

On this basis, one would then shift from a two-sided fact-value dichotomy to a tripartite division of statements as factual, evaluative, and *hybrid*. And accordingly, one would assign to $F \vee V$ this third, hybrid status.[4] Fact and value are now seen as separated not by a sharp boundary line but by a broad corridor.

This shift has further consequences. For one thing, the decision to class $F \vee V$ as hybrid rather than factual constrains us to modify the principle of

> *Factuality Conservation* (FC): If P is logically derivable from factual statements, then P is itself factual.

For clearly $F \rightarrow (F \vee V)$, and we have nevertheless now decided *not* to class $F \vee V$ as factual. Accordingly the most we can do is to adopt the principle of

> *Modified Factuality Conservation* (FC*): If P is logically derivable from factual statements, then P is not strictly evaluative.

Given the rejection of the Dichotomy Assumption, these two formulations of the principle are not equivalent, as P could be hybrid.

Moreover, the decision not to class $F \vee V$ as evaluative also has severe implications for the Consequence Principle. For we obviously have the entailment:

$$[(F \vee V) \mathrel{\&} \sim F] \rightarrow V.$$

Since $F \vee V$ thus entails a value conclusion in the presence of mere fact, the Consequence Principle would have us class $F \vee V$ as evaluative, contrary to

---

[4] Lars Bergström proposes the analogous solution of seeing this statement as "a value judgment under some conditions, but not under others" ("On the Logic of Imperatives," p. 212). He instances the example: "I have Mozart's best symphonies among my records." If I in (descriptive) fact have *all* of them, the statement becomes a trivial truth; but if I in fact have only a third of them, it is clearly evaluative. The statement's evaluative status thus depends on its factual/empirical context rather than on its assertoric content alone.

the preceding approach. We must accordingly now also alter this principle, modifying it to:

(CP*) Any statement that, in the presence of mere facts, entails an evaluative conclusion is (for this very reason) not strictly factual.

But now, of course, with dichotomy abandoned, "not strictly factual" is now no longer tantamount to "evaluative."

The shift from a fact-value dichotomy to a triad of factual, evaluative, and hybrid enables us to thread our way through the logical complexities of the situation. And given these distinctions and modifications, we can continue to maintain the position that values cannot be derived from (mutually consistent) factual statements, despite the circumstance that the following two entailments both obtain:[5]

$$F \to (F \vee V)$$
$$[(F \vee V) \ \& \sim F] \to V.$$

The logical complexity of the issue of a cogent standard of evaluativeness makes it advisable to proceed without any attempt at a logically regimented criteriology, simply taking the line that we generally know an evaluative statement when we see one. However, we can keep something of a grip on the issue by retaining (CP*) and (FC*), not, to be sure, as criterial *standards* that define evaluativeness, but merely as partial—and negative—*guidelines*.

Values Not Derivable from Facts about Desires and Preferences

It is clear (and rather trivial) that strictly factual statements can be inferred from evaluative ones. From the evaluative thesis "It is a splendid thing that dogs chase cats" there clearly follows the strictly factual "Dogs chase cats." But what of the reverse situation, the inference of evaluations from facts?

At various junctures, philosophical theorists have proposed that judgments of value merely relate to the emotional reactions of people, thus reducing to theses regarding their likes and dislikes, approvals or disapprovals, preferences or dislikes. Value, on such an approach, is a matter of feeling. Just this is the position of *preferential value subjectivists*, people who hold that "to be of value" is (by definition) to be taken as tantamount to "to be preferred (liked, approved, desired, or the like) by some (particular) group or category of persons." Any such position will, of course,

---

[5] To be sure, the factual pair F, $\sim F$ yields V via the principle *ex contradictio quodlibet*. But this is clearly a degenerate case.

straightforwardly reduce evaluative claims to factual issues, since what people happen to prefer (like, etc.) is clearly a factual matter to be settled either directly, by asking them, or indirectly, by monitoring their behavior in choice situations.

This position faces decisive difficulties, however. One of the obstacles confronted by such a theory is the plain circumstance that there is no unproblematic way of crossing the inferential gap from "You (or I or most or all of us) like (prefer, approve of) such-and-such" to the conclusion that the item at issue is of value (is right or good or beneficial or the like). Thinking something to be good no more makes it so than thinking something to be true makes it so.[6] The gap from being desired to being desirable, from being preferred to being worthy of preference is one that cannot be crossed without paying the price of a commitment to some decidedly evaluative precommitment.

For example, consider the inference:

Smith likes dogs.
Smith is a generally knowledgeable person.

Therefore: Dogs are likable.

This argument does indeed move from factual premises to an evaluative conclusion (since "likable" here does not mean "*able* to be liked"). But not validly—with unproblematic cogency. For there is a missing (enthymematic) premise:

What generally knowledgeable people like, *deserves* to be liked.

This is clearly an evaluative premise (one that can provide for evaluative conclusions in the presence of strictly factual premises). And it is the tacit role of this evaluative premise that carries the burden of weight in the preceding argument.

Accordingly, any such view that reduces value attributions to claims about people's preferences (likings, etc.) shipwrecks on the circumstance that there is a substantial inferential gap between

People of group X prefer (like, etc.) items of sort S.

and

Items of sort S are of value (are preferable, merit liking, etc.).

There is no way of closing this gap short of introducing some additional evaluative premise to the effect that the preferences of X-members are

---

[6] There may, of course, be something of an *evidential* relationship going on, insofar as people qualify as reliable judges.

appropriate: that what they like indeed merits liking. To be sure, we can move inferentially from what *everyone should* (normatively) approve of, or from what (evaluatively) *right-thinking people do* approve of, to what has value. But here, of course, we infer value conclusions from premises that themselves are evaluative in nature rather than merely factual. After all, a claim about what somebody likes (whether an individual or a group) is a contention about this individual, while a claim that something has value is, first and foremost, a contention about that item. Facts about people's desires, preferences, or the like simply do not settle genuinely evaluative issues. Even after we know—however securely—that someone likes (prefers, etc.) something, the question always still remains open whether this liking is appropriate, reasonable, well advised (etc.). And until this question is resolved, the inference to an authentic evaluation is not really valid. The inferential step from what people *deem* valuable to what *has* value is no shorter than the step from what people *deem* true to what *is* true.[7]

To be sure, one can always make an explicit addition of an appropriateness stipulation to facts about people's evaluations, as in the following:

Smith likes dogs.
Smith's sentiments in this as in other instances are appropriate.

Therefore: Dogs are likable.

But of course any such facilitative premise is blatantly evaluative. Once it appears, we no longer have an inference to an evaluative conclusion from factual premises alone.

Nor does it help to shift the issue from individuals to groups. Consider the inference:

Most people dislike that painting.

Therefore: That painting is a poor one.

Or again:

People in general prefer sleeping to working.

Therefore: Sleeping is a superior activity to working.

---

[7] Note that, as this analogy rightly suggests, people's valuings or disvaluings can perfectly well provide prima facie *empirical evidence* for something's having or lacking value—"in normal circumstances most (sensible) people prefer preferable (i.e. preference-deserving) things." To move from "People prefer S" to "S is preferable," however, we must supply the clearly evaluative enthymematic premise: "What people generally prefer is indeed preferable."

These inferences are no more valid in and of themselves than are their individualistic analogues of the sort presented above. For here too we need an enthymeme that requires a supplemental value-premise to establish appropriateness, validity, or the like.

John Stuart Mill argued the desirability of happiness as follows: "The only proof capable of being given that an object is visible, is that people actually see it. The only proof that a sound is audible, is that people hear it: and so of the other sources of our experience. In like manner, I apprehend, the sole evidence it is possible to produce that anything is desirable, is that people do actually desire it. If the end which the utilitarian doctrine proposes to itself [namely, happiness] were not, in theory and in practice, acknowledged to be an end, nothing could ever convince any person that it was so."[8] It is commonly objected against this reasoning that *visible* = "capable of being seen" and *audible* = "capable of being heard," but *desirable* does not come to "capable of being desired" but rather "worthy of being desired." But Mill is not guilty of a confusion here. The linkage he (presumably) has in mind is not that being desired *constitutes* desirability through a meaning relationship of some sort but that it *evidentiates* desirability: that a good—and perhaps even the best—evidential ground we can secure to show that something is desirable is that people desire it. His reasoning is enthymematic:

> People universally seek happiness.
>
> People are sensible enough not to be systematically deluded. What all or most of them desire is something that (almost certainly) is worthy of being desired.

> *Therefore*: Happiness is worthy of being desired.

The reasoning here is indeed from fact to value, but only via an enthymematic premise that bridges the fact-value divide. For accordingly, any such inferential transition (along the lines endorsed by J. S. Mill) from what people factually desire to what qualifies as normatively desirable (i.e., *deserving* of being desired) hinges crucially on the availability of a premise to the general effect:

> Whatever people (commonly, generally, invariably) desire (prefer, prize) is worthy of being desired (preferred, prized).

But this enthymematic premise itself clearly has an evaluative status that prevents the value subjectivism at issue from achieving any *reductive* ends. To achieve cogency, the move from people's preferences or desires to something's being of value must always be mediated by some evaluative supplementation.

[8] *Utilitarianism*, chap. 4.

Another Failed Proposal: Value Consequentialism

Again, consider the position of certain *value consequentialists* who see value claims as reducible to fact because they hold that "to be of value" is (by definition) to be taken as tantamount to: "to produce consequences of type *T* for many (or most or all) people." In examining this position, we come to an immediate dilemma. Either type *T* is itself so characterized as to be evaluative (as embracing what is good or beneficial or the like), or, alternatively, type *T* may be specified as being something merely descriptive and strictly factual in character (say, as embracing what is pleasant). But in the former case, the value consequentialism at issue does not enable us to leap across the fact-value divide; it does no more than, in effect, to reduce the other types of value to the one at issue in type *T*. And in the second case there are two possibilities:

(i) What is at issue are people's subjective pro-reactions (welcomings, likings, satisfaction-yieldings, preferences, etc.).

(ii) What is at issue is some objective state of affairs (such as conducing to people's health or sense of well-being or social adjustment, etc.).

But in either event, the evaluative issue remains entirely open. For just why should the presence of those strictly descriptive consequences be seen as having an evaluative bearing? Without further ado regarding a particular issue, there is no reason to take *T* membership as having any relevance to the issue of value that is the object of the enterprise. In case (i) we are effectively carried back to the problems of value subjectivism considered above: a connection remains to be established between those pro-reactions and actually having value. And in case (ii) we are also driven back to the missing link of some underlying presupposition regarding the value of *T*-membership. In both cases, accordingly, the weight of the fact-value transitional argumentation is clearly borne not by the explicit factual premise but by an enthymematic evaluative premise regarding the value implications of *T*-membership.

Thus consider, for example, inferences that draw evaluative conclusions from facts about certain states of affairs from facts regarding their consequences to people, such as:

Undergoing experience *E* will (actually or probably) cause distress (to most people).

Therefore: It is wrong to subject people to undergoing experience *E*.

Despite its eminently plausible appearance, this inference simply does not work as it stands. For suppose that what is at issue to be some dental or medical procedure. The inference then presupposes an additional premise of the general type:

Doing E provides no benefits that outweigh the distress caused thereby.

And this needed premise is itself clearly of an evaluative nature.

Accordingly, the problematic status of value consequentialism is clear. This line of approach leaves the question of the value of the state of affairs at issue in a parlous state—either unresolved or begged.

Just this same sort of difficulty also defeats a naive utilitarianism that proposes to define the rightness of actions and the goodness of ends in terms of the pleasure, happiness, or satisfaction to which they gave rise. For consider the following:

Doing (or attaining) X gives pleasure (happiness, satisfaction, etc.) to many (most, all) people.

Therefore: Doing (or attaining X) is something that is good (desirable, valuable).

Clearly this inference is not a strictly valid one except when considered as an enthymeme in whose background lies the facilitative value-premise:

Whatever pleases (gives happiness or satisfaction to) many (most, all) people is ipso facto something good (desirable, valuable).

And the existence of malign pleasures (those, for example, occasioned by seeing a misfortune befall one's enemies) indicates that the premise is far from unproblematic.

Such deliberations serve to indicate that even if values are indeed determined by people, they are not determined by their mere approval as such, but by the circumstance that such approval betokens something normative on the order of promoting people's well-being or facilitating a realization of their real or true interests. Those value-validating inferences at issue accordingly involve further evaluative premises, though they are often kept enthymematically out of sight.

Failure Not Surprising

In looking back to first principles, one can see that it should not really occasion surprise that judgments of value cannot be derived from judgments of pure fact (let alone equated to them). Suppose, for the sake of argument, that a certain strictly factual statement F did indeed underwrite—even if only in the presence of other suitable facts F'—valid inference to a genuinely evaluative conclusion V: $(F \& F') \rightarrow V$. Then by virtue of the (revised) Consequence Principle, we have it that F is itself not factual, contrary to hypothesis. This consideration serves to cast a pretty dark shadow across the prospect of value-from-fact derivability. For in abandoning the Consequence Principle altogether—refusing to retain it even merely in the revised and weakened formulation—we would pretty much lose our conceptual grip on what the fact-value distinction is all about. The very idea of a statement's being evaluative would become effectively unworkable.

To be sure, we must, at this point face and resolve a case that is perhaps most difficult for our present analysis. As often happens in such situations, it is a case of surprising simplicity, namely that of the inference:

Dogs chase (all) cats.

Therefore: Dogs chase nice cats.

The premise of this patently valid inference is clearly factual and its conclusion plausibly qualifies as evaluative.[9] Does such an example not refute our thesis that factual premises do not yield evaluative conclusions?

Not really. For closer analysis shows that what is actually at issue in the preceding inference is the enthymematic syllogism:

All cats are chased by dogs.
[All nice cats are cats.]

Therefore: All nice cats are chased by dogs.

And here that enthymematic minor premise can (and should) be regarded as a nonfactual thesis, albeit one that states a trivial truth. The price of a consistent theory involves taking the not implausible line that certain truisms (such as "All nice cats are cats") should be classified as evaluatively hybrid.

The negative upshot of a quest for instances of "genuinely evaluative" conclusions entailed by "strictly factual" premises should occasion no surprise. The fact is that the only sensible and appropriate explication we have of what it is to be a "value statement" is such that the noninferability of such statements from strictly factual premises is a foregone conclusion. On any plausibly available view of what it is for statements to be "evaluative," it would unavoidably have to transpire that *any statement from*

---

[9] Observe that "Dogs always chase nice cats" combined with the obviously factual theses "Felix is a cat" and "No dog chases Felix" entails the clearly evaluative conclusion "Felix is not a nice cat."

which, in the presence of merely factual information, an authentically evaluative conclusion could be validly deduced would itself have to be considered as other than strictly factual. This consideration of itself defeats the idea that value claims can be derived from factual claims alone.

This argumentation effectively formalizes a line of reasoning whose informal course runs as follows:

> Factual statements do no more than state something to be descriptively the case; their acceptance has implications relating only to what is (or is not) to be accepted or believed.

> Evaluative statements always stake claims (explained or implicit) regarding what is to be valued or prized—or the contrary; their acceptance has implication for what (sensible) people ought to do in matters that transcend acceptance or belief.

> *Therefore*: Since evaluative statements always have a content that goes beyond what any merely factual statements can encompass, there is no valid way of deriving them from factual statements.

The general position at issue here is no more than a somewhat elaborated version of Hume's idea that "ought"-oriented conclusions cannot be derived from "is"-oriented premises. Given the proper construction of "value statement," it becomes a strictly conceptual truth that a logically cogent fact-to-value transition is infeasible. G. E. Moore's critique of the "naturalistic fallacy" stands secure.

The failure of value naturalism (the thesis that genuine value claims are at least sometimes derivable from strictly factual contentions) automatically carries in its wake the failure of value reductionism (that value claims can always be redefined in terms of factual contentions). In this regard, the tenor of our present position accords wholly with the logical positivists' doctrine that assertions of value are not reducible to factual claims.[10] (Though why the positivists thought that this fact would render them meaningless is anybody's guess. Their nonderivability from strictly factual statements surely does not invalidate evaluative statements but merely exhibits a definitive aspect of their nature.)

The crucial point is that the value realm is inferentially closed. One cannot enter it inferentially from without. To provide a discursive (inferential) validation of an evaluative conclusion, one must have recourse to at least some evaluative inputs as premises for the reasoning, even if only inherently trivial cases. Inferentially, values must root in values: where only "value-free" facts go in, values cannot come out.

[10] See A. J. Ayer, *Language, Truth, and Logic* (London: Macmillan, 1936; reprint, New York: Dover, 1952), chap. 6.

Implications

Does the collapse of the naturalistic project of deriving values from value-free facts not furnish a powerful argument in favor of value subjectivism? After all, if values are not to be derived from facts, then what sorts of considerations can possibly manage to validate them? If value claims cannot be extracted from strictly factual considerations, does this not relegate them to the parlous condition of mere matters of taste and potentially idiosyncratic individual feeling?

By no means! While it is indeed true that the fact-value divide cannot be crossed by valid deduction without using some evaluative premises (at least tacitly), it nevertheless can be crossed when these premises are trivial and truistic. For example, consider the inference:

Doing A would cause Smith needless (pointless) distress.

Therefore: It would be wrong for me (or anyone) to do A.

To be sure, this perfectly valid inference is only enthymematically so. To achieve the deductive stringency of formal validity it only requires recourse to the enthymematic premise:

It is wrong to do something that causes people needless (pointless, unnecessary) pain.

But this premise is unproblematically available. It is, in fact, close to trivial, since the mode of action at issue is a paradigm instance of moral transgression: given that pain is (clearly) something negative for us, its unnecessary infliction on some of us by others is a quintessential malfeasance.[11]

The salient consideration is that values *almost* emerge from facts. The gap between facts and values is often so small, though nevertheless crucially important, that it can be crossed by a step so short as to be effectively negligible, namely, by means of truisms.

The salient fact is that in innumerable situations, the transition from factual premises to evaluative conclusions is mediated by auxiliary (normally enthymematic) evaluative premises that are essentially trivial and truistic in that they turn merely on an adequate grasp of concepts and issues. The evaluative negativity of certain transactions and circumstances is immediate, perspicuous, and self-evident: it is simply a matter of evaluative resonance ("immediate appreciation") that some sorts of situations

---

[11] Cf. the discussion in the introduction of Judith Jarvis Thomson, *The Realm of Rights* (Cambridge: Harvard University Press, 1990).

are painful, unpleasant, incongruous, unacceptable. Certain evaluations are thus simply a matter of an experientially grounded grasp of fundamentals. The propositions that formulate such contentions are trivial, truistic, and able to dispense with any need for grounding in something further that supports ab extra. For example, the negativity of pain and with it the moral inappropriateness of its deliberate and needless propagation is an instance of such an evaluative truism.

What marks such an evaluative truism as enthymematically available is not its profound truth but its very triviality. If someone were to dissent from it, we would have no alternative but to take the view that this betrays the absence of any real grasp on the central concepts at issue (in the present case, what it is to be morally wrong). That is, we would have to take essentially the same reaction here that we would take toward someone who failed to acknowledge that "knives have blades." If someone were to deny "Knives have blades," we could not take the line that that person was overlooking some significant fact about the world, but simply that he or she did not have a firm grasp on what it is to be a knife. Similarly, if someone denied assent to "It is morally wrong to inflict needless pain on people," we would take the line that that person did not have a proper grasp on deep truths about morality, but merely that he or she simply did not know what morality is all about. And this same story holds not only for "injuring people needlessly" but also in an endless variety of other cases (such as "taking something that belongs to another simply because one wants to have it" on the negative side, and "helping someone in a way that involves no loss for other people" on the positive side).

This state of affairs takes the steam out of a negative resolution of the fact-derivability question in a debate about the subjectivity of values. For even though the inferential transition from fact to value must always make use of *some* evaluative theses, nevertheless such inferential mediators can be wholly unproblematic truisms that, as such, stand secure from the vagaries of potentially idiosyncratic value appraisals.

Thus subjectivism obtains no aid and comfort from our finding that values cannot be derived from facts alone, that explicitly or implicitly evaluative claims are always required to render such argumentation cogent. For this circumstance is stripped of any subjectivistic implications by the consideration that the requisite value-inputs can be altogether trivial and truistic. On this basis, the prospects of value objectivism are unaffected by a recognition that values cannot be derived from facts.

But does the existence of a fact-value gap not have dire consequences for the legitimacy of values? For on its basis it would transpire that if, by hypothesis or by thought experiment, we entered into a realm of thought from which all value commitments had been rigorously expunged, then we would never be able to work our way back from this strictly factual setting into the evaluative sphere. Yes indeed, this is the state of affairs. But of course the obvious inference from this is not "So much the worse for values" but rather "So much the worse for the acceptability of that initial value-abrogating hypothesis."

Just how wide *is* the fact-value gap? Well, on the one hand, facts and values are connected (rather than separated) by a band of hybrid statements at the fact-value interface. On the other hand, the inferential transition from strict facts to values cannot be crossed without bringing values into it. The situation regarding this central issue is clear: the fact-value gap is real and irremovable. Nevertheless, this inferential gap *is* also a very narrow one—so narrow that it can be crossed in many cases by employing something that is no more than a mere truism, albeit a truism that must be classified as nonfactual.

The Parallelism between Rational Inquiry and Evaluation

In the final analysis, the separation of the descriptive from the normatively evaluative that is expounded through a distinction between "facts" and "values" is very misleading. Factuality as such is something that is neutral as between strictly informative facts and additionally evaluative ones. Descriptive facts and normative ones are more closely interrelated than is generally recognized. In particular, they share a common epistemology. Rational cognition and rational evaluation run wholly parallel in point of validation because cognition too is an ultimately evaluative enterprise. Values and descriptive facts are both governed by objective, impersonal norms. Our knowledge of both sorts of facts—the descriptive/informative and the normative/evaluative—hinges on both sides upon the criteriological bearing of the question "What merits approbation?" To be sure, this overarching question bears a very different construction on each side of the issue, with *approbation – acceptance* on the side of descriptive information, and *approbation – endorsement* on the side of evaluative judgment. But the fact remains that acceptance too is an appraisal of sorts: an *epistemic* appraisal.

What sorts of considerations constitute a basis for positive epistemic appraisal? There are two sorts, the evidential and the probative. The evidential considerations are simply the available items of substantiating "data." The probative considerations include such factors as generality, order, simplicity—in short, the considerations that provide for a smooth and systematic coherence with our other overall commitments. Because inductive reasoning and cognitive systematization are two sides of the same coin, the parameters of systematic coherence are also part and parcel of our standards of epistemic approbation.

Rational appropriateness in the criteriology of cognition is determined as follows:

> Those descriptively informative theses (descriptive judgments) qualify as rationally acceptable (cognitively valid) that optimally systematize our cognitive data (where systematization proceeds under the aegis of normative standards of cogency).

In an entirely parallel way, we have the following situation on the side of the criteriology of evaluation:

> Those normatively evaluative theses (evaluative judgments) qualify as rationally acceptable (normatively valid) that optimally systematize our evaluative data (where systematization proceeds under the aegis of normative standards of cogency).

Both the descriptive and the normative deliberations require the "data of experience." In the alethic (descriptively truth-oriented) case, these are the data of *sensation* (sense perception) and their systemic extensions in factual theories. In the evaluative (normatively value-oriented) case, these are the data of *evaluation*—of pro or con appraisal—and their systemic extensions in normative rules. In both cases alike we proceed criteriologically in terms of the optimal systematization of experience— that is, by just the same device of seeking the best available extrapolation of the data, the interpretation that best coheres with the rest of our experience.

In the cognitive case, validity (here amounting to presumptive truth or factual correctness) calls for the optimal inductive systematization of our informative experiences under the aegis of principles of explanation. In the normative case, validity (here amounting to presumptive appropriateness or evaluative correctness) calls for the optimally cohesive systematization of our evaluative experiences under the aegis of principles of justification. The parallelism between the two cases is depicted in display 4.1, which portrays a value cognitivism that sees the processes of rational inquiry and of rational evaluation as proceeding in a strictly parallel way. On both sides, system building provides us with a screening process that includes the fitting and excludes the unassimilable, discriminating between what is tenable and what is not in the holistic context of our commitments overall. The fundamental idea is that of controlling validity through the optimal systematization of the relevant data that runs uniformly across both the cognitive and normative domains. In either case, this is a matter of systematization of experience:

> *cognition*: rational systematization of informative experience through principles of explanation;

Display 4.1 The Cognitive Parallelism of Inquiry and Evaluation

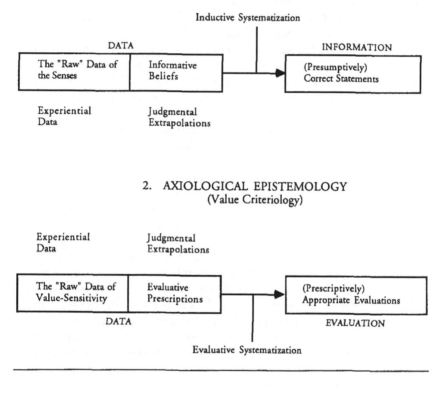

1. ALETHIC EPISTEMOLOGY
(Truth Criteriology)

Inductive Systematization

2. AXIOLOGICAL EPISTEMOLOGY
(Value Criteriology)

Evaluative Systematization

evaluation: rational systematization of affective experience through principles of justification.

Essentially the same standard applies throughout: a judgment is valid if it belongs to the most cogent systematization of the whole range of our relevant, alethically fact-oriented experience on the one side, and that of our relevant, axiologically value-oriented experience on the other. The coherence approach to value criteriology in terms of judgmental systematization accordingly runs wholly parallel to the coherence approach to acceptance criteriology.[12] The parallelism of the systemic process operative in both the cognitive and evaluative sectors engenders a symmetry of val-

---

[12] On coherence criteriology, see the author's *Coherence Theory of Truth* (Oxford: Clarendon Press, 1973) as well as chap. 2, "Truth as Ideal Coherence," of his *Forbidden Knowledge* (Dordrecht: D. Reidel, 1987), pp. 17–27.

idation on the sides of cognitive and evaluative reason that once again exhibits the fundamental unity of reason.

No wonder, then, that altogether analogous issues arise on both the cognitive and the evaluative sides. In the alethic case, we face the problem of bridging a (seemingly insuperable) gap between appearance and reality, between phenomenally subjective claims at the level of appearances and impressions, and ontologically objective claims at the level of being and actuality. The coherence criteriology of factual truth is of good avail here, for it authorizes the move from claims on the order of "There looks to be a cat on the mat" to claims on the order of "There actually is a cat on the mat" through optimal systematization. In making this move, we exploit the circumstance that this particular ruling regarding the nature of the real best systematizes our cognitive commitments overall. And an entirely parallel situation prevails on the evaluative, axiological side, where we face the problem of bridging a (seemingly insuperable) gap between subjective claims at the level of actual evaluation—between what strikes us as wicked (*seems* wicked) and what *is* wicked. The coherence criteriology of norms enables us in this case to leap across just exactly this gap. It puts us in a position to move inferentially from facts about how certain sorts of behavior affect people to evaluative generalizations on the order of "Taking the property of another without appropriate justification is wrong" through the mediation of the principle of best systematization.

On both sides of experience—both with the sensory "observation" and with the evaluative "assessment"—we thus leap across the gap separating subjective seeming ("appearance") from objective being ("reality") by one selfsame device: systematization of the data. In each case we enter into a realm of objective claims through rational triangulation from the data of experience. (Of course, the greater extent of the interpersonal uniformity of sensory as compared with evaluative experience makes the case of sensation simpler than that of evaluation. But the difference is one of degree rather than of kind.)

This fundamental parallelism means that value issues should also be seen in a "realistic" light. Matters of value, too, can and should be regarded as objectively validatable. The possibility of rational agreement or disagreement, of criticism, correction, and the like, arises on the evaluative side also. One must avoid the confusion of values and tastes. "There's no disputing about *tastes*" may be true, but "There's no disputing about *values*" is certainly not. Values too can be altogether objective. The status of value judgments as appropriate or inappropriate, correct or incorrect can be subject to person-indifferent standards, on whose basis value claims admit of rational support through impersonally cogent considerations.

To reemphasize: the rational validation of descriptively factual claims in empirical inquiry and of evaluative claims in normative evaluation proceed in ways that are, from the structural point of view, closely analogous. Both consist in the rational systematization of experience—informative and evaluative experience, respectively. The parallelism of alethic and axiological criteriology indicates that what is sauce for the informative/inductive goose is also sauce for the evaluative/normative gander. And this circumstance is highly important from the angle of our present concerns. For one thing, it illustrates from yet another direction of approach the holistic unity and integrity of reason. For another, it indicates that the very existence of an evaluative sector of reason hinges on the prospects of an objective rational inquiry into the nature and bearing of evaluative considerations. And this is all to the good. Given the systemic unity of reason, the whole of rationality would collapse into vacuity if rational deliberation about the evaluative considerations that validate our standards of cogency throughout were in principle impossible.[13]

A Postscript on Value Realism

A postscript on value realism is in order. Three distinctively different sorts of value realism can be envisioned:

> **1.** *Alethic realism.* Do evaluative contentions fall into the range of assertions characterizable as true or false?
>
> **2.** *Property realism.* Does the ascription of value to things of a certain sort (acts or artifacts, say) attribute objective (and thus evidentiable—perhaps even "observable") properties to those items?
>
> **3.** *Warrant realism.* Can evaluative contentions be supported by rationally cogent considerations that, when duly legitimated, can justify people in maintaining them?

Let us begin with the alethic case—the controversy over the question whether evaluative claims are to be categorized as having a truth status, as being true or false.[14] This mode of realism turns on the issue of whether evaluations can be assimilated to statements (assertions or propositions) in the specific regard that the particular appraisal categories true-false are applicable to them as well. This issue seemingly arises in the present context because it might seem that in describing certain evaluative claims as "trivial and truistic," our present discussion is predicated on an

---

[13] The insight of traditional skepticism is right in this regard—except that the skeptics perform *modus ponens*, where *modus tollens* is the appropriate tactic.

[14] The current state of this discussion as regards specifically *moral* values is depicted in Geoffrey Sayre-McCord, ed., *Essays in Moral Realism* (Ithaca, N.Y.: Cornell University Press, 1988).

affirmative, realism-endorsing stance on this issue. But this is not actually the case.

For present purposes, nothing substantial hinges on the specific appraisal categories true-false. All that matters for our present deliberations concerning the issue of objectivity is that some evaluative claims can be fitted out with a suitably straightforward legitimating rational warrant. Appraisal in the range of validatable-nonvalidable, warranted-unwarranted, correct-incorrect, appropriate-inappropriate, right-wrong is altogether sufficient, and the *truth* issue as such need not arise.[15] Where values are concerned, the issue of alethic realism is immaterial to that of objectivity.

To judge by the literature of the subject, many philosophers are under the impression that alethic value realism is the only way to avert a corrosive subjectivism of the it's-all-a-matter-of-taste variety. The idea seems to be abroad that evaluations must either lie in the catchment area of the true-false characterization, or else they are empty expressions of subjective inclinations. But this is surely nonsense. One can evaluate the rational credentials of questions, commands, hypotheses, and so forth, each in their own truth-noncommittal way, so why not evaluations? The appraisal categories for different sorts of utterances differ, as per the following examples:

> statements: true-false
> questions: sensible-absurd
> commands: appropriate-inappropriate
> evalutations: correct-incorrect

Why should evaluations be destroyed as rationally cogent objects if it were to turn out that the appropriate appraisal categories are not true-false but something like (say) well grounded or ill grounded?

In the end, the issues of alethic value realism is really not terribly interesting or significant, despite the great pool of ink that has been expended on it. Only those who labor under a mistaken impression that determination as true or false is the only conceivably appropriate pathway to rational legitimation can think that by addressing alethic realism they are getting at something crucial for the objective validity of evaluations. After all, even as regards statements there are many other sort of categories of rational appraisal other than true-false:

> appropriate-inappropriate
> foolish-shrewd

---

[15] In this light, our previous recourse to "truistic" statements has to be glossed not through a reference to truths as such but to statements whose acceptability validation is more or less immediate.

correct-incorrect
plausible-implausible
probable-improbable

There simply is no good reason to think that an alethic realism oriented to true-false with respect to values is the only way to prevent a value subjectivism that submerges the whole field of evaluation in a corrosive sea of subjective taste.

What thus matters for our present concern with objectivity is that evaluations can be validly supportable by rational considerations—that a sensible case can be made from endorsing them (as *justified*, not necessarily as *true*), that they can be supported by sensible considerations and convincing arguments. What counts is that we should be able to reason about evaluative issues by cogent reasoning that (fully) rational people are bound to accept as cogent and that all people in consequence should accept as such. The real issue—the area of conflict where the real philosophical action lies—is surely that of warrant realism.

And here the situation is not unpromising. As we have seen, the appropriateness of evaluations can be shown in many cases by validating considerations that are in fact trivial and truistic. But whether evaluative "truisms" are specifically true rather than simply being "self-evidently correct" or "obviously appropriate" is quite immaterial.

Yet how can one be a warrant realist if one abandons the idea that evaluations can be derived from facts? If the relevant facts of the matter do not sustain and substantiate our evaluations, then what can possibly do so?

The answer here is already implicit in the preceding deliberations. Evaluations do indeed supervene on facts, but they do so in view of "appropriate considerations" that are themselves evaluative, even though they may verge on triviality. The following argumentation is paradigmatic:

> In doing action A, Jones deliberately hurt Smith's feelings. [Fact]
>
> Neither in fact nor in Jones's thought on the matter was any constructive ulterior purpose served by Jones's doing A. [Fact]
>
> It is morally wrong to hurt people's feelings when doing so has no compensating possibilities in other respects. [Evaluative truism]

Therefore: Jones acted (morally) wrongly in deliberately hurting Smith's feelings.

The given facts of the case do indeed sustain that evaluative conclusion, but of course they do so only in the presence of the enthymematic evaluation. The value conclusion follows from the facts all right, but does so in view of (truistic) considerations that are themselves evaluative.

Finally, what of property realism? Do value ascriptions attribute actual properties to the items at issue? Well, properties perhaps (the term is surely a very broad one), but certainly not properties of the usual sort. For the "properties" at issue in value appraisals are:

dispositional;
mind-involvingly relational;
not perceptually observational but judgmentally evaluational.

Such properties are not instances of the familiar types; they are not "primary" properties (object descriptive), nor yet "secondary" ones (characterizing what sort of a perceptual reaction the object evokes on a normal observer under standard conditions of sensory observation), but something rather different.

If we are going to discuss whether or not their value features represent *properties* of objects, we first of all have to get clear about what sorts of properties there are. And here the philosophers' traditional conception of properties must undergo some broadening from the very outset. For the English empiricists have managed to focus the attention of philosophers on properties or qualities of two sorts:

Primary properties that represent *descriptive* features of the physical makeup of a thing. (The weight of an apple, for example, or its shape or size.)

Secondary properties that represent *sensorily perceptible* features. (The color of the apple, for example, or its taste.)

Primary properties characterize the physical makeup of the object in itself; secondary properties correspond to dispositions to produce certain sensory effects on normal observers. But what this listing patently ignores is that there are also:

Tertiary properties that represent *cognitively discernible* features—characteristics that (only) a suitably informed mind reflecting on the object and its context can come to recognize.

The "uniqueness" of an occurrence, for example, its being the only one of its kind, is certainly a property of it. But it is neither an integral aspect of its internal makeup nor a sense-discernible feature of it. Again, a man's "(physical) similarity to Napoleon" is undoubtedly a property of his but represents neither a primary quality nor a sensory disposition. Or again, consider the ink configuration "&." Its property of representing the conjunctive "and" is certainly not something discernible by observation alone, apparent as such to a perceptive Chinese, for example. Secondary qualities are supposed to be something that any physiologically normal person can observe. Tertiary properties, by contrast, are features that only a suitably informed and intelligent *thinker* can recognize. There is nothing mysterious about them, they are just something conceptually different from and more complex than secondary properties. An object's secondary properties pivot on its dispositions to evoke characteristic *affective* responses in the suitably responsive senses. Its tertiary properties pivot on dispositions to evoke characteristic *reflective* responses in the suitably informed mind. When a Greek vase is (truly) said to be "a typical second-century B.C. Cretan amphora," it is undoubtedly the case that an empirical property of some sort is ascribed to it. But that property is clearly neither primary nor yet secondary in the classical sense of that distinction, which was nowise designed to capture issues relating to features whose nature is dispositional, relational, context bound, and attributively inferential.

Now if we are going to see the value features as properties of things, then it is clearly at the level of tertiary properties that we shall want to proceed. And there is no good reason to expect any undue difficulties here. The "beauty" of a vase is something that, unlike its shape, is not going to be detectable by bare straightforward observation. Like its being "a typical product of its era," the validation of its attribution is going to require a great deal of peripheral information and principled reflection. For the ascription of a value to something involves an implicit claim about how this thing or situation at issue would figure in the reflective thought of an intelligent, unbiased mind that adequately reflected on its nature and ramifications.

While value contentions bring persons and their reactions onto the stage of consideration, evaluations are clearly not themselves secondary properties that turn on sensory responses. For tertiary properties carry us into a new, mind-correlative realism. We ascribe secondary properties on essentially causal grounds, but tertiary properties on essentially judgmental ones. Here thought is pivotal, and reasons come into it. And while secondary properties are specifically linked to the makeup of our human sensibility (our sense organs), nothing inherently species bound is involved in the reflectivity at issue with tertiary properties.

The dispositional status of secondary properties loosens their connection with the actual responses of actual observers: the issue is merely that if there were observers and if their observations were properly constituted, then what sort of response would the item evoke? And similarly with tertiary properties, where the issue is if these observers were duly apprised and if their evaluative endorsements were properly constituted, then what sort of response would the item evoke? The dispositional properties at issue thus relate to the item's response-evoking capacities and do not simply "lie in the eye of the beholder." Value thus lies in the object, not just in the response to it; it is an inherent feature *of an object* that it manifests in certain transactions in which it is "evoked" in appropriately endowed intelligent beings.

These tertiary properties are "supervenient" on an item's factual situation and context, encompassing its descriptive makeup and its descriptive embedding in the wider setting in which it figures. No doubt, if an item's primary and secondary qualities were different, its tertiary qualities might differ as well. But this supervenience proceeds in a way in which evaluative considerations are also involved. Our concrete evaluations are—when appropriate—indeed rationally constrained by the underlying facts, but constrained in ways that involve the operation of value principles.

The concept of *supervenience* has been invoked by R. M. Hare with respect to the relation between values and natural facts. "Let us take that characteristic of 'good' which has been called its supervenience. Suppose that we say 'St. Francis was a good man.' It is *logically impossible* to say this and to maintain at the time that there might have been another man placed exactly in the same circumstances as St. Francis, and who behaved in exactly the same way but who differed from St. Francis in this respect only, that he was not a good man."[16] But of course the "logical impossibility" at issue is not a matter of pure logic but rather a matter of those evaluative principles built into the use of evaluative terms like the ethical epithet "good man." The crucial role of such meaning-expository principles governing the use of value terms means that the "supervenient" dependency of evaluating on the "natural facts" is totally compatible with a rejection of a value naturalism that sees evaluative as derivable from matters of pure fact alone.

G. E. Moore did not serve the interests of philosophical clarity at all well in adopting the contrast terms "natural-nonnatural" to characterize a distinction for which, on his own principles, the less question-begging contrasts sensory-nonsensory or perceptual-nonperceptual would have been far more suitable.[17] For, in the final analysis, all that Moore means by calling the value characteristics of things "nonnatural" is that they do not represent observationally discernible features of their putative bearers, that they are, in their nature, not sensible. (However, to call them "supersensible" would introduce the wrong connotations here—what has "higher" or "lower" to do with it?) But to characterize the evaluative fea-

---

[16] R. M. Hare, *The Language of Morals* (Oxford: Clarendon Press, 1952), p. 145, cf. also John M. Mackie, *Ethics* (Hammondsworth: Penguin Books, 1977), p. 41.

[17] G. E. Moore, *Principia Ethica* (Cambridge: Cambridge University Press, 1903), chap. 1.

tures of things as nonnatural, as Moore unfortunately did, strongly suggests that something rather strange and mysterious is going on, that the purported condition of things is somehow extra- or super-natural. And invoking this mystery invites the misguided response that just as we have inner and outer senses to observe the natural properties of things, occurrences, or situations (the taste of an apple or the painfulness of a wound), so there must be some special sense-analogous faculty to determine their value status, a mysterious value insight or "intuition" to perceive their evaluative aspects. Forgetting the good Kantian point that evaluation is a matter of judgment on the basis of principles, much of Anglo-American moral theory thus followed Moorean inspirations down the primrose path of a value-insight empiricism that looked to some sort of perceptual or quasi-perceptual access to value, thereby stumbling once more into the blind alley of the older British theorists of moral sense or sensibility. This approach launched philosophers on the vain quest for a value sensibility—with all of its inherent insolubilia, including the prospect of evaluative color blindness and the intractable problem of how value perception (of any sort) can *justify* rather than merely *explain* evaluations.

The fundamental contrast, of course, should simply be that between what can be observed or inferred from observational data and that which cannot. The value of an item is no more accessible to perception than is the ownership of a piece of property. But that of course does not make it something mysterious and "nonnatural"—the special object of a peculiar detection-faculty, a value intuition. The crucial fact is that value is not sense perceptible but mind judgmental: something to be determined not simply by observation of some sort but by reflective thought duly sustained by background information and suitably equipped with an awareness of principles.

In ending this postscript, a brief summary is in order. We have distinguished three main versions of value realism: alethic realism, property realism, and warrant realism.

As regards alethic realism, our discussion has taken no definite position, having found no pressing need to do so, because the significance of this issue for the problem of objectivity that is at stake here has been greatly exaggerated.

As regards property realism, we have dismissed *primary* properties from our range of concern (since their evaluative features are clearly not inherent, nondispositional characteristics of things). And we have also dismissed *secondary* properties from our range of concern (since value is not a matter of disposition to affect a normal observer's sensory repertoire in a certain way). Instead, we have adopted a realism of *tertiary* properties, since the issue of appropriate evaluation is indeed one of an item's disposition to figure in a certain sort of way in the thought processes of duly informed and enlightened reflective appraisers.

Finally, as regards the justificational realism of rational warrant, our position has been that it is just this issue that lies at the heart of the value-realism controversy. As the preceding discussion has tried to show, there is good reason for believing that evaluations can indeed be rationally substantiated, notwithstanding the circumstance that values cannot be derived from facts.[18]

[18] This chapter is a revised version of an essay of the same title initially published in the supplement to *Philosophy and Phenomenological Research* 50 (1990): 297–319.

Five

Values in the Face of Natural Science

Reconciling Darwinism and Purpose: The Hermeneutical versus the Causal Perspective

Philosophers and scientists sometimes maintain that a Darwinian evolutionary account of the origin of mind and its operations is bound to be deficient because it leaves no room for intentionality, with the result that meaning and purpose are banished not just from the sphere of inanimate nature but from the human domain as well. The theory of evolution provides for the emergence of new organic types through the competitive elimination of those organisms that are comparatively less efficient in the struggle for reproductive survival within the niche at issue. Such a purely "mechanical" account of organic development, so opponents of the theory sometimes argue, is fundamentally inadequate because all characteristically mental operations involve meaning, value, and purpose—normative factors that natural selection simply omits from nature's scheme of things. An evolutionary account is accordingly seen as inherently flawed in its reductive elimination of the entire characteristically human dimension of ideation with its correlatives of meaning, value, and purpose. The evolutionary origin of our thought mechanisms—so it is said—is somehow at odds with an intentional (or purposive or teleological or "spiritual") dimension to our substantive thinking.

Now if it were indeed the case that, as a matter of general principle, evolution could not provide for the entire gamut of characteristically mental operations—or, even worse, stood in conflict therewith—then of course evolution would thereby prove itself to be an inherently defective instrumentality of explanation in this domain. Such a view is, however, gravely mistaken, and an understanding of the misimpressions it embodies is necessary to secure a just appreciation of the place of values in the scheme of things.

All that is required to operate the process of evolution (along the lines of a Darwinian natural selection) with respect to the resources of mind is that there be an inheritable, physically transmissible *basis* for the operations of mind by way of the brain and its operations as the agency for the neurophysiological processes associated with thinking in its various forms. An evolutionary account of the emergence of mental capabilities requires no more than the physical replication over time of creatures whose capacity for mental processes inheres in and results from the operations of their physical endowment. This does indeed mean that our mental faculties and functions must be regarded as the causal product of our physical equipment and its physical operations. But of course such a supposition as to their *causal basis and developmental origins* is totally devoid of any implications for their *substantive nature* as ideational processes that involve purpose and meaning. The causal operations of thought processes is one thing; their experienced substance and import is quite another.

Evolution often brings to the fore new activities and processes that radically transcend their developmental origins in the scale and scope of their operation. DNA molecules are an assemblage of physical atoms, but they encompass the key to organic life—human life included. Birds doubtless initially developed song for signaling warnings of danger, but that did not preclude the evolutionary transmutation of such song behaviors into means for establishing territoriality against potential competition. The physical rooting of an activity or process does not confine or circumscribe its functional character.

The emergence of new modes and levels of operation, function, and comportment that transcend the capabilities of their causal origination is, in fact, characteristic of evolutionary processes, whether biological or physical. For the first microseconds of cosmic history after the big bang there was no chemistry. The early stages of the universe had no place for biology. There was no foothold in nature for laws of sociology or market economics before the origin of humans. The emergence of new phenomena at different levels of scale and organizational complexity in nature means the emergence of new processes and laws at these levels. The transition from protophysical to physical and then to chemical and onward to biological law reflects a succession of new strata of operational complexity. And this holds good for purposive intelligence as well—it is a new phenomenon that emerges at a new level of operational complexity. New products and processes constantly develop from earlier modes of organization, bringing new orders of structure into being. The emergence of the psychological processes of ideation that open up realms of meaning and purpose is just another step in this course of development of new levels of functional complexity in nature.

It is important to bear in mind, moreover, that while causal explanation proceeds from a mind-external point of view and in mind-detached terms of reference, such cognitive functions as meaning, valuing, intending, and the like can be comprehended as such only from within, through hermeneutical understanding based on actual experience. The *physical* processes that lie at the causal basis of thought are, as such, fully open to second-party ("external") examination, description, explanation, and modeling. But the *ideational* aspect of thinking is formulated in terms of reference that must be interpreted in the light of one's own firsthand experience (though of course it can be described to others who have similar experiences at their disposal). The causal order of occurrence relationships and physical-process explanations is something very different from the hermeneutical order of meaning relationships and ideational explications. There is, accordingly, a crucial difference between having a causal account of the physical-process concomitants of human mental operations (of the sort that biological evolution provides) and having experiential access to its products "from within." Meaning, intending, and their hermeneutical cousins all involve intellectual resources that are at the disposal only of someone who also has the requisite sort of foothold within the realm of mind. Only by experiencing them—by actually carrying out the sorts of activities at issue—can one comprehend them. Understanding their nature requires performing them, and performing them requires having a mind that engages in those particular mental processes. (*Explaining* their occurrence, however, can in principle be managed "externally," so to speak, in terms of reference that call for no such actual experiential involvements.)

Proper heed of this distinction between the productive causal basis and the descriptive functional nature of mental operations leads to the recognition that one must not ask an evolutionary account of mind to do the impossible in this regard. Such an account can perfectly well explain the developmental origination of mental operations in terms of their causal basis. But it cannot make their inner experiential character intelligible. The *existence* of mental functions like meaning and purpose can be accounted for on evolutionary principles. But their *qualitative nature* is nevertheless something that can be adequately comprehended only "from within," from a performer's rather than an observer's perspective.

One can fully understand a *physical* process like the spider's web-weaving without being a spider—without ourselves being in a position to engage in this process and so without knowing what it feels like to perform the activity. But one cannot fully understand a *cognitive* process like seeing colors or interpreting symbols or having intentions without experiencing this sort of thing. It is one thing to explain how operations originate causally, and something very different to know what it is like to perform them. The cause-and-effect physiology of inebriation can be learned by everyone. But only the person who drinks can comprehend it in the "inner" experiential mode of cognitive access. The mental performances that reflect meaning and purpose can be understood only from within the orbit of experience (though their occurrence can doubtless be detected and accounted for through external scientific-causal examination). The hermeneutical comprehension of meaning, intending, purposing, valu-

ing, and the like is bound to experience—to a performer's perspective—
and thus differs from the neurophysiology of brain processes that is in
principle accessible to external observers. The former items reflect issues
that evolutionary explanations simply do not address, owing to their altogether different orientation to the causal dimension of the matter.

Evolutionary Origins

Evolutionary biology precludes thoughtful planning as an available explanatory mechanism in accounting for the developmental emergence of
creatures. But it clearly does not preclude the evolutionary development
of creatures capable of thoughtful planning.

An evolutionary account of the physical mechanisms involved in mental
operations is thus by no means reductive, let alone eliminative, of the
inner hemeneutical dimension of intentionality and meaning. In addressing (however successfully) the issue of the physical conditions and processes that engender (i.e., causally produce) those mental operations at
issue with intending, purposing, meaning, and so forth, it is by its very
nature silent regarding their phenomenological character, which can be
grasped only "from within." An evolutionary productive/causal account
is developed from the angle of the *observer's* perspective, whereas the
substantive content of these processes has of necessity to be understood
as proceeding within the hermeneutical vantage point of a *performer's*
perspective. The former, scientific, evolutionary, neurophysiological account of the causality of thought processes does nothing to eliminate or
diminish the contentual aspect of meaning and purpose, which can be
appreciated only from an "internal," experiential standpoint. But incom-
pleteness is one thing, and defectiveness quite another. The former (evolutionary) account is nowise deficient or defective for failing to provide
for the latter (phenomenological/hermeneutical) one, which is in principle impossible because of the different levels of consideration that are
at issue.

Intentionality and its accompaniment of aims, purposes, and the like
form part of the thought machinery of thinkers, even as mathematical
operations like addition and subtraction do. How minds evolve in nature
and come to acquire such talents and capacities is one thing, but what they
accomplish by carrying them on is another. Biological evolution has to do
with the first; intentionality with the second. Evolution operates with respect to the workings of mind, with its processes; intentionality is a matter
of its products. There is, and can be, no incompatibility between them,
seeing that altogether different issues are involved: biological evolution in
the one case, cultural evolution in the other.

All that we can reasonably ask of a biologically evolutionary account of mental operations is that it should explain the developmental emergence of the capacities and processes of thought. The inner phenomenology of thinking lies beyond evolutionary biology's range—not because of its deficiencies, but simply because it addresses altogether different issues. We cannot fault an evolutionary account of mind for failing to provide that which no causal account of mind's origination could possibly deliver on its own—cognitive access to the inner, phenomenological nature of mental experience. The nature of the *apparatus* of thought and its physical modus operandi does not descriptively characterize the *substance* of our thinking. A Darwinian account of the development of our capacities for mental operation accordingly leaves open scope for purpose and meaning because it does not—and cannot by its very nature—shut the door on issues that it simply does not address. And it clearly cannot be faulted for failing to deal with an issue (namely, *the nature of understanding and intentionality*) that lies entirely outside the range of its causal concerns.

An evolutionary account of intelligence is indeed predicated on a position that is "mechanical" and "materialistic" in viewing the mind as having a causal basis for its operations in the processes of the body (and the brain in particular).[1] But this sort of causal-origin materialism is nowise at odds with a hermeneutical perspective that maintains that we understand various of the world's processes in terms of concepts and categories drawn from the "inner" experience of the mind's self-observation. Evolution's "mechanical," causal accounting for our experiences of purposiveness and intentionality is not in any way at odds with the inner experienced aspect of these phenomena. The former issue belongs to the domain of the causal explanation of experiencing as events in the physical world, the latter to the phenomenology of our experiences as phenomena in the world of thought.

Evolutionary theory can explain our capacity for purposive mental activities and can account for our frequent exercise of this capacity. But what it cannot do is to explain away the "inner" nature of such exercises as thought processes in whose conceptual makeup the ideas of meaning and purpose play a key role.

The crucial fact is that there are two entirely different levels of deliberation: the physical order of causal processes and the ideational order of ideas, meanings, reasons, and the like. And these two orders are wholly removed from one another—there is no way to get from one to the other by traveling within it. Perhaps, presumably—nay, even probably—the physical order of causes is productively responsible for the existence of

---

[1] For a good overview of the philosophical issues involved, see Paul Churchland, *Matter and Consciousness* (Cambridge: MIT Press, 1984).

the conceptual order (via the neurophysiology of brain processes). But this does not bear upon the qualitative interior of the ideational order, which, so far as its nature is concerned, is simply something dimensionally distinct from and conceptually incommensable with the causal order. Each order is self-enclosed and autonomous, hermetically sealed in its own domain. Whatever causal connections there may be do not and cannot constitute a conceptual connection.[2]

How those "mental" processes are generated—whatever causal machinations may underlie their occurrence—is simply irrelevant to the *experienced* nature. On that experiential plane we operate on another level of consideration and deal with an entirely different order. Where there were brushmarks on paper or gruntlike noises from human mouths, there are now concepts, meanings, and ideas. Where there were air vibrations, there is music. The characteristic—and fascinating—thing about the symbolic synapse is that it manages to fasten together somehow the physical order of process with the mental order of concepts, that the workings of the mind manage to transmute that physical brain electronics into intellectual objects, ideas of meaning.

The Darwinian dimension of the "explanation" of the causal origin of the mind's resources belongs to the causal order. The aspect of purpose, meaning, and intentionality appertains to the ideational order of our thought processes. And the twain can meet only in the causal and not in the conceptual order. Biological Darwinism can touch upon the physical and physiological side of the operations of this *brain* but does not bear upon the ideational side of the conceptual processes of the *mind*. The reason that evolution does not and cannot eradicate purpose is simply that evolution deals with a category of processes that are disjoint from—and dimensionally different from—those processes at issue when intentionality and purpose come upon the stage of consideration.

The eminent English biologist J. B. S. Haldane once protested, "If my opinions are the result of chemical processes going on in my brain, they are determined by the laws of chemistry, not those of logic."[3] But this argument is surely problematic. It is like saying, "If my chess moves are the result of muscular motion, they are determined by the laws of physiology, not those of problem solving." If the brain processes involved in opinion formation become (to some extend) aligned, via evolution, to the laws of logic, then clearly it becomes possible to have it both ways. Contrary to this author's dogmatic either-or, there is no conflict here. While chemis-

---

[2] Some of these issues are dealt with in greater detail in the author's *Conceptual Idealism* (Oxford: Basil Blackwell, 1973).

[3] Quoted in K. R. Popper, *The Open Universe: An Argument for Indeterminism* (Totowa, N.J.: Rowman & Littlefield, 1982), p. 89.

try (or neurophysiology) may explain how the brain works, "logic" as operative through intentionality and purpose can explain what it does with these capabilities.

A Darwinian account of the origin of mind accordingly does not—and by its very nature cannot—conflict with intentionality and purpose because different things are at issue. It would simply be foolish, however, to deny the originative power of evolutionary processes. To say that a purposive being cannot arise by evolution in a theretofore purpose-lacking world is much like saying that a seeing being cannot arise by evolution in a theretofore vision-lacking world or that an intelligent being cannot arise by evolution in a theretofore intelligence-lacking world. A commitment to the spirit of Darwinism may well impede an acceptance of the purposiveness *of* nature, but it clearly does not and cannot impede an acceptance of purposiveness *in* nature through the evolutionary emergence within nature of beings who themselves have purposes, intentions, goals, and so forth. No doubt, Darwinian natural selection ill accords with an anthropomorphism of nature, but it certainly does not preclude an anthropomorphism of human beings.

Homo sapiens is an amphibious being, a creature of two realms, the material and the mental. The former encompasses our physical and biological dimension, the latter our intellectual and spiritual dimension—our involvement with matters of thought, feeling, and valuation. Which dimension is paramount? Is it not clearly the former? Is the mental perhaps wholly encompassed in physical nature via the workings of biological evolution?

The answer is negative. Our mental *activities* are doubtless materially engendered, but our mental *performances* are not, seeing that what we achieve by these activities is something else again. The intellectual/spiritual side of ourselves is not a product of material nature; it is *a product of our own doing*. Something has intervened between physical process and mental product, namely the actions and performances of *Homo sapiens* as such. (In this regard we humans are self-made.) The mental (spiritual/intellectual) roots *causally* in the material realm, but not *hermeneutically*. The dimension of meaning—of concepts and ideas—is self-contained. The mental performances of humans are, no doubt, causally based in our material resources (in our brains), but on their ideational, hermeneutical side they are self-contained and rooted in our thoughts. Our physical endowment explains our capacity for thought, but only thought itself explains the substantive nature of our thinking.

The long and short of it is that acceptance of an evolutionary account of the origination and operation of human intelligence leaves ample scope for meaning, value, and purpose in the domain of our human doings and dealings. Did it not do so, its own adequacy would thereby come into question. But it would surely be both naive and mistaken to think that the normative sphere of human assessment is somehow undermined or negated by an account that sees our performance in this domain as rooted in capacities that humankind has acquired through its development in the natural course of evolutionary events. The causality of process is irrelevant to the experiential significance of products. After all, neither our logic nor our mathematics is somehow diminished by the fact that the capacity to develop and operate these disciplines is something that has come our way in the evolutionary course of things. The evolutionary basis of the human capacity for valuing, purposing, and meaning destroys the realm of value, purpose, and meaning no more than does the evolutionary basis of the capacity for understanding undermine the importance and validity of the things we come to know.[4]

Knowledge Itself as a Value

Knowledge brings benefits. We humans have evolved within nature into the ecological niche of an intelligent being. In consequence, the need for understanding, for "knowing one's way about," is one of the most fundamental demands of the human condition. We are not so much *Homo sapiens*, the knowing people, as *Homo quaerens*, the inquiring people.

The basic demand for information and understanding presses in upon us, and we are impelled toward (and are pragmatically justified in) bestirring ourselves toward getting it satisfied. The great Norwegian polar explorer F. Nansen put it well. What drives people to explore the uninviting polar regions, he said, is

> the power of the unknown over the human spirit. As ideas have cleared with the ages, so has this power extended its might, and driven Man willy-nilly onwards along the path of progress. It drives us in to Nature's hidden powers and secrets, down to the immeasurably little world of the microscopic, and out into the unprobed expanses of the Universe. . . . it gives us no peace until we know this planet on which we live, from the greatest depth of the ocean to the highest layers of the atmosphere. This Power runs like a strand through the whole history of polar exploration. In spite of all declarations of possible profit in one way or another, it was that which, in our hearts, has always driven us back there again, despite all setbacks and suffering.[5]

----

[4] These themes are explored further in chap. 7 of the author's *A Useful Inheritance* (Savage, Md.: Rowman & Littlefield, 1989).

[5] Quoted in Roland Huntford, *The Last Place on Earth* (New York: Atheneum, 1985), p. 200.

The need for knowledge is part and parcel of our nature. A deep-rooted demand for information and understanding presses in upon us, and we have little choice but to satisfy it. And once the ball of information seeking is set rolling, it keeps going under its own momentum, far beyond the limits of strictly practical necessity.

It is a situational imperative for us humans to acquire information about the world. We are rational animals and must feed our minds, even as we must feed our bodies. *Homo sapiens* is a creature that must, by its very nature, feel cognitively at home in the world. Relief from ignorance, puzzlement, and cognitive dissonance is one of cognition's most important benefits. These benefits are both positive (realizing the pleasures of understanding) and negative (reducing intellectual discomfort through the removal of unknowing and ignorance and the diminution of cognitive dissonance). The basic human urge to make sense of things is a characteristic aspect of our makeup—we cannot live a satisfactory life in an environment we do not understand. For us, an adequate cognitive orientation in the world is itself a practical need: cognitive disorientation is actually stressful and distressing. The discomfort of unknowing is a natural component of human sensibility. To be ignorant of what goes on about us is almost physically painful for us—no doubt due to nature's programming because it is so dangerous from an evolutionary point of view. As William James observed: "The utility of this emotional effect of [security of] expectation is perfectly obvious; 'natural selection', in fact, was bound to bring it about sooner or later. It is of the utmost practical importance to an animal that he should have prevision of the qualities of the objects that surround him."[6]

The benefits of knowledge are twofold: the internally theoretical (or purely cognitive) and the externally practical (or applied). The theoretical/cognitive benefits of knowledge relate to its satisfactions in and for itself, for understanding is an end unto itself and is, as such, the bearer of important and substantial benefits, albeit ones that are purely cognitive, relating to the informativeness of knowledge as such. The practical/pragmatic benefits of knowledge, in contrast, relate to its role in guiding the processes by which we satisfy our (noncognitive) needs and wants. With us humans, the satisfaction of our needs for food, shelter, protection against the elements, and security against natural and human hazards all require information. And the satisfaction of mere wants comes into it as well, seeing that for us humans the satisfaction of some wants is itself a need. We can, do, and must put knowledge to work to facilitate the attainment of our goals, guiding our actions and activities in this world into productive and

[6] William James, "The Sentiment of Rationality," in *The Will to Believe and Other Essays in Popular Philosophy* (New York: Longmans, Green, 1897), pp. 78–79.

rewarding lines. And this is where the practical importance of knowledge comes into play.

Bafflement and ignorance—to give suspensions of judgment the somewhat harsher names that are their due—themselves exact a substantial price from us. The need for information, for cognitive orientation in our environment, is as pressing a human need as that for food itself, and more insatiable. We humans want and need our cognitive commitments to compose an intelligible story, to give a comprehensive and coherent account of things. Cognitive vacuity, dissonance, or disorientation can be as distressing to us as physical pain.

The impetus to inquiry—to investigation, research, and acquisition of information—can thus be validated in strictly economic terms with a view to potential benefits of both theoretical and practical sorts. We humans need to achieve both an intellectual and a physical accommodation to our environs. For us, knowledge is a requisite essential to our being the sorts of creatures we are: the value of knowledge is something deep rooted in our human needs.

Knowledge as One Good among Others

But important though knowledge is, it is only one good among others. Even in its most developed form (i.e., in science), knowledge is not a be-all and end-all. It too is subject to the humane deliberations of valuation and value. For science, like other human enterprises, is itself a domain where values play a decisive role, in particular one that relates to the value of information both for itself and for facilitating control over the course of nature's events—to cognitive and practical goods. Moreover, the pursuit of knowledge is itself governed by norms, with the conception of "making good a claim" figuring as a mediating link between the cognitive and the normative.[7] Our factual contentions and commitments themselves must, where appropriate, rest on a right or entitlement of a certain sort—a right to maintain something under the aegis of epistemic ground-rules. The pivotal consideration here is that of its being right, fitting, and proper for someone in certain epistemic circumstances to endorse a certain thesis. Rational acceptance is a cognitive act governed by appropriate normative standards, so that inquiry itself can, and should, be viewed as a mode of practical activity, as a cognitive praxis governed by evaluative norms and criteria.

---

[7] Hilary Putnam's *Reason, Truth, and History* (Cambridge: Cambridge University Press, 1981) provides interesting discussions of this issue.

This said, however, it must be recognized that man does not live by knowledge alone. Other legitimate and important human enterprises exist and delimit the significance of science within the sphere of our concerns. While knowledge represents an important aspect of the good, it is only one star in the firmament of human desiderata—one valuable project among others, whose cultivation is only one component of the wider framework of human purposes and interests. The quality of our lives turns on a broad spectrum of personal and communal desiderata such as physical well-being, human companionship, environmental attractiveness, social congeniality, cultural development, and so on—values toward whose attainment the insights afforded by science can often help us, but which themselves nevertheless fall outside its domain.

While the cultivation of knowledge is indeed only one worthy human project among many, it is, however, a particularly important one. Its pursuit as a good in no way hinders the cultivation of other legitimate goods; on the contrary, it aids and facilitates their pursuit, thereby acquiring an instrumental value in addition to its value as an absolute good in its own right. Whatever other projects we may have in view—justice, health, environmental attractiveness, the cultivation of human relations, and so on—it is pretty much inevitable that their realization will be facilitated by the knowledge of relevant facts. Thus, even though the pursuit of knowledge is certainly not our only appropriate task, it is nevertheless an enterprise whose normative standing is high because knowledge serves to facilitate the realization of any other legitimate good: any and every such good is cultivated the more effectively by someone who pursues its realization knowledgeably.

Scientific Knowledge as One Mode of Knowledge

Moreover, even in the strictly cognitive domain, scientific knowledge is only one sort of knowledge: there are other valid cognitive projects apart from the scientific. The epistemic authority of science is great, but not all-inclusive. For natural science is a mission-oriented endeavor, with its goal structure formed in terms of the traditional quartet of description, explanation, prediction, and control of nature. It inquires into what sorts of things there are in the world and how they work at the level of law-governed generality, focusing primarily on the lawful modus operandi of the natural processes that characterize the furnishings of nature. Given this mission, the concern of science is, and must be, with the public face of things—with their objective facets. It strives for reproducible results, and its focus is on those objective features of things that anybody can discern (in suitable circumstances), regardless of one's particular makeup or experiential background. Science deliberately sets aside the observer-relative dimension of experience. As the English philosopher F.C.S. Schiller put it:

> Large tracts of actual experience are submerged and excluded as "subjective," in order to focus scientific attention upon the selected and preferred sections of experience which are judged fit to reveal objective reality. . . . Thus the differences between experienced particulars, even when not denied outright, are simply assumed to be irrelevant for scientific purposes, and are ignored as such. It is by this assumption alone that science is enabled to construct the common world of intersubjective intercourse, or "objective reality," which different observers can contrive to explore.[8]

The "facts" to which science addresses itself are accordingly those that arise from intersubjectively available observation rather than personal and potentially idiosyncratic sensibility. Its data are those universals accessible to man qua man, rather than those that are in some degree subjective and personal, accessible only to individuals of a particular background or experiential conditioning. Thus, science rejects the individualized, affective, and person-linked dimensions of human cognition—sympathy, empathy, feeling, insight, and "personal reaction"—as a source of data (though not, of course, as objects of study). The phenomena it takes as data for its theory projection and theory testing are publicly accessible. Affective sensibility—how things strike people within the context of their personal (and perhaps idiosyncratic) experiences and their particular sociocultural setting—is something science leaves aside by concentrating on the impersonally measurable features of things. This quantitative orientation of our natural science means that the qualitative, affective, evaluative dimension of human cognition is bypassed.

And so, no matter how far we manage to push science forward along the physical, chemical, biological, and psychological fronts, there are issues of human concern that will remain intractable by scientific means—not because science is impotent within its range but because they lie outside it. We shall aways have questions about people and their place in this world's scheme that lie outside the problem mandate of science.

In natural science we investigate what is and what can be, relative to the laws of nature. The more remote regions of possibility—the more imaginative realms of what might be and what might have been—lie outside our purview in natural science, which, after all, does not deal with purely imaginative constructions and conjectured possibilities. Virtually by definition, natural science is oriented in its concern for laws and pro-

---

[8] F.C.S. Schiller, *Must Philosophers Disagree?* (London: Macmillan, 1934), pp. 5–7.

cesses toward what detectably exists in nature and does not deal with the speculative domain of what is not but yet might be. Its concern is with the modus operandi of the real; the realm of the imaginatively hypothetical is outside its sphere. The artistic, imaginative aspect of human creativity—the projection of abstract form in art or music—thus lies outside its range of concern. Poetry, drama, religion, proverbial human wisdom, and so on all carry messages distinct from those conveyed within the medium of scientific discourse. The limits of science inhere in the limits of its cognitive mission and mandate: the "disinterested" depiction and rationalization of objective fact.

The "knowledge" of science is descriptive rather than normative, with the issue of evaluatively responsive appreciation—of what sorts of things are worthwhile—simply left aside. However value laden the *pursuit* of scientific knowledge may be on the side of process, on that of its products—the *content* of its findings—science remains value neutral. Throughout its substantive concerns, science is "value-free": its approach to the characterization of phenomena is simply devoid of the element of personal evaluation. The affective, appreciative, emotively evocative side of human knowledge, the intuitive and unreasoned ways of knowing, the mechanisms through which we standardly understand other people and their productions, all lie outside science's range of concern. Although science can study them from an externalized point of view, it cannot internalize them and accept them at face value. Natural science aims at mastery over nature—at controlling it both intellectually and physically. It prescinds from the enterprise of appreciating nature in an evaluative mode.

Our knowledge of the value dimension of experience—our acknowledgment of these features of things in virtue of which we deem them beautiful or delightful or tragic—remains outside the range of science, where it is not experiential sensibility but explanatory understanding that is the crux. Issues of evaluation and appreciation are not matters to be settled by scientific inquiry into nature's ways, which teaches us the why and wherefore of things but does not instruct us about their worth. It is not that the deliverances of science have no value implications for us but rather that when we draw these, we leave the realm of science behind.

Many people sense a shudder of dismay when science turns its cold, objective gaze upon man and his works—as though our deepest human values were somehow being put at risk. But nothing could be more foolish. To fear science as antithetical (rather than simply indifferent) to human values and interests is not only discomforting, it is irrational and inappropriate, because it is based on a profound misunderstanding of what science is all about. The fact that a human being is an agglomeration of chemicals, a complex of flesh and bone evolved by natural selection from creatures of the primeval slime, is no reason why he or she cannot also be a friend. Objectively, the playing of a violin is no more than a scraping on catgut, the glow of a sunset no more than a shower of radiation. Does that prevent them from reaching heights of transcendent beauty? To speak of conflict here is to confound diverse perspectives of consideration, to confuse different levels of thought and inquiry.[9] The scientific mode of understanding takes the externalized route of causal explanation, not the internalized route of affective interpretation. The cognitive approach of science to man's understanding of man deliberately puts aside the recognition of others as fellow humans that is characteristic of all genuinely human relationships among people. Science is not opposed to these concerns, it is irrelevant to them; it simply ignores them, having other fish to fry.

Accordingly, as the "idealist" tradition of German philosophy from Hegel to Heidegger has always right-mindedly insisted,[10] the quest for scientific knowledge is simply one human project among others. Reacting also against the Greek view that *epistēmē* is supreme, this tradition replaced the old theological doctrine that faith transcends knowledge with the latter-day variant that valuation transcends knowledge. Such a position has much to recommend it.

But perhaps science should change our values. Perhaps scientific understanding should alter our valuing habits, even as it does, quite properly, recommend certain changes in our habits of eating and exercising. But this is a careless way of thinking. Science is able to recommend lifestyle changes precisely because certain values—health, well-being, vigor, and life itself—are presupposed as fixed givens. Similarly science would rationally recommend value changes only in the interest of predetermined values. It simply cannot abolish, abrogate, or alter that which it must presuppose as given in order to offer any recommendations at all.

Science, then, has its limitations. It is no be-all and end-all: it cannot answer all the questions that matter to us. But of course we are dealing here with the limitation of a range of concerns as such, and not with limitations of capacity within this range. The "limitations" at issue are simply mission-inherent. Science has a definitive and determinate mission of its own in rationalizing the objective empirical facts, and here, as elsewhere, determination is negation: because science is a certain definite kind of enterprise, there are also things that science is not. These other cognitive

---

[9] To be sure, the pursuit of scientific work in some areas entails not only price but also risks. But only science itself can provide us with the information needed to assess these in an intelligent way. Nothing said here conflicts with the idea that the pursuit of science has its costs, which must be weighed on the scale along with others.

[10] See Martin Heidegger, *Being and Time*, trans. and ed. J. Macquarrie and E. Robinson (London: Routledge & Kegan Paul, 1962), sec. 32.

ventures are not alternatives to science, because the orientation of their concern inclines toward other directions. They are not different ways of doing the same job but look to doing altogether different sorts of jobs. And so, these other cognitive projects are not in a position to compete with science in its own domain; in fact, there is not a question of competition, because diverse objectives are at issue. Those who play different games are not in competition with each other.

Thus, it must be stressed that we are not dealing here with something that is a defect or a shortcoming. It is a limitation imposed by the aims of the enterprise, the objectives that characterize the very nature of science as the thing it is. The characteristic cognitive task of science is the description and explanation of natural phenomena—the answering of our how and why questions about the workings of the world. Normative questions regarding the inherent value of things—their significance, legitimacy, and the like—are simply "beside the point" of this project. The fact that there are issues outside its domain is not a defect of natural science but an essential aspect of its nature as a particular enterprise with a mission of its own. It is no more a defect of science that it does not deal with belles lettres than it is a defect of dentistry that it does not deal with furniture repair. It is no deficiency of a screwdriver that it does not do the work of a hammer.

Theorists who maintain that scientific knowledge is the be-all and end-all, that what is not in science textbooks is not worth knowing (or, worse yet, false), are ideologists with a peculiar and distorted doctrine of their own. For them, science is no longer a particular sector of the cognitive enterprise but an all-inclusive worldview. This is the doctrine not of science but of scientism. To take this stance is not to celebrate science but to distort it by casting the mantle of its authority over issues it was never meant to address.

Ludwig Wittgenstein wrote: "We feel that even if all *possible* scientific questions be answered, the problems of life have still not been touched at all. Of course there is then no question left, and just this is the answer."[11] This austere perspective pivots on the view that scientific issues are the only ones there are—that where no scientific question is at issue, nothing remains to be said, and that factual information is the end of the cognitive line. If this position is adopted, then questions relating to normative and evaluative issues of significance, meaning, and validity—questions relative to beauty or duty or justice, for example—can all be set at naught. Such a response does indeed resolve the "problems of life," but only by casting them away into the outer darkness. This scientific positivism is indeed antipathetic to human values. As one acute writer has observed:

[11] Ludwig Wittgenstein, *Tractatus Logico-Philosophicus* (London: Routledge & Kegan Paul, 1933), sec. 6.52.

[Such a doctrine] is an attempt to consolidate science as a self-sufficient activity which exhausts all possible ways of appropriating the world intellectually. In this radical positivist view the realities of the world—which can, of course, be interpreted by natural science, but which are in addition an object of man's extreme curiosity, a source of fear or disgust, an occasion for commitment or rejection—if they are to be encompassed by reflection and expressed in words, can be reduced to their empirical properties. Suffering, death, ideological conflict, social classes, antithetical values of any kind—all are declared out of bounds, matters we can only be silent about, in obedience to the principle of verifiability. Positivism so understood is an act of escape from commitments, an escape masked as a definition of knowledge.[12]

But of course nothing within or about science demands such a dehumanization of our sensibilities. To take this stance is not to celebrate science but to distort it into a doctrinaire scientism.

Man is a member not just of the *natural* but of the specifically *human* order of things. There is more to reality than science contemplates; in the harsh but stimulating school of life, we humans are set examinations involving problems for whose resolution our science courses by themselves do not equip us. Our problems—and our opportunities—transcend the scientific domain.

The Autonomy of Science

While the terrain of science is far from all-inclusive, the fact nevertheless remains that in its own province, science stands supreme. All the properties and states of physical things, any and all of nature's occurrences and events, the behavior and doings of people—in short, every facet of "what goes on in the world"—can be regarded as appropriate objects of scientific scrutiny and explanation. No matter of natural fact lies in principle outside the domain.

Paul Feyerabend maintains in *Against Method* that science is itself no more than one form of ideology and that we would be well advised to replace it with an anarchistic potpourri of speculation according to which "anything goes." The claims of science to provide objective and useful information about the world are, he argues, no better than those of myth or idle speculation.[13] But this sort of thing is easier said than substantiated. Where are those informative disciplines, rival to standard science,

---

[12] Lasek Kolakowski, *The Alienation of Reason*, trans. N. Guterman (Garden City, N.Y.: Doubleday, 1968), p. 204.

[13] Paul Feyerabend, *Against Method* (London: Verso, 1978). See also his "How to Defend Society against Science," *Radical Philosophy* 11 (1975): 1–22.

that embrace alternative modes of medicine, engineering, and so on capable of matching the standard science in applicative effectiveness? Where are the rival theory-systems that can approach science in predictive power? The point, of course, is not that alternative belief structures about the world are theoretically impossible or evaluatively unappealing; it is simply that, in comparison with orthodox science, they are hopelessly ineffectual. As a basis for governing our interactions with nature successfully, they are utter failures.

The situation is simple and straightforward. If we want to know about the constituents of this world and their laws of operation, we have to turn to science—and in fact to the science of the day. Whatever its shortcomings or limitations, science is "the only game in town" with respect to successfully implementable information regarding the operations of nature. There is no place else to turn for information worthy of our trust. (Tea-leaf reading, numerology, the Delphic oracle, and the like are not serious alternatives.) If we want to be informed about the furnishings of the world and their modes of comportment, there is simply nowhere else worth going to.

On its home ground, science has no effective challenge, no serious competition. Whatever its limitations and lack of completeness, natural science is wholly self-sufficient within its proper domain of the explanation and prediction of natural phenomena. And this is how the matter must stand, given the crucial fact that science is autonomous. Corrections to science must come from science. Science is inexorably "complete" in regard to its self-sufficiency. The key point was made long ago in Hegel's *Phenomenology of Spirit*: we cannot set limits to our (scientific) knowledge of reality, because any relating of knowledge to reality has to come from within that knowledge itself.[14] Inquiring thought cannot get outside itself to compare its deliverance with "the real truth." There is no viable external standard by which the deliverances of science can be appraised. We have no choice but to follow science where it leads us. There is no other, science-external cognitive resource to monitor its operations. Shortcomings in scientific work can emerge only from further scientific work. The defects of science can be removed only by the further results of science.

The acceptability of scientific claims is a matter to be settled wholly within science through considerations internal to the scientific enterprise. A "science" viewed as subject to external standards of validity and correctness is simply not deserving of the name. Scientific claims must—whenever corrected at all—be corrected by further scientific claims. This fun-

---

[14] G.W.F. Hegel, *Phänomenologie des Geistes*, trans. A. V. Miller (Oxford: Oxford University Press, 1977), secs. 73–76.

damental fact is the rock bottom that provides the only basis on which the doctrine of the *self*-sufficiency of science can find its foothold.

Thus, while there are also other sectors of the cognitive sphere, and natural science is only one cognitive discipline among others, nevertheless within its own sphere it is sovereign. Within the region of its appropriate jurisdiction, so to speak, science is supreme because it stands unrivaled and alone. Whatever be its limitations, science is our only resource for dealing adequately with the issues that constitute its proper domain. And so, while science does indeed have various sorts of limitations, none of them affords grounds for complaint or reproach about the work of scientists as such—let alone for abandoning their project.

Moreover, the values at issue in the pursuit of scientific work as such are crucially important components of our value economy as a whole, seeing that understanding, discovery, truthfulness, honesty, candor, cooperation, dedication, and the like all are parts of the value structure of scientific inquiry at its idealized best. The norms of good scientific practice are not simply that but also salient examples of important human values at large.

In the final analysis, then, there is no inherent antagonism between science and human values. On the one hand, knowledge is itself an important human value; on the other, science must itself be seen as a praxis governed by values, since it is only by means of standards of adequacy and accuracy that an appropriate body of scientific knowledge can be constructed. Properly understood, the cognitive enterprise of science and the evaluative enterprise of rational assessment are not conflicting but complementary. Seen in its proper perspective, science offers no threat to human values but should be seen as supporting them in various crucial respects.

Part III

VALUES AND HUMAN NATURE

Six

What Is a Person?

Personhood

Perhaps the most significant and far-reaching single fact about us is that we are *persons*. For it is this, above all, that determines our self-image and our self-understanding—our view of the sort of beings that we ourselves are. Being persons (i.e., duly self-appreciative rational agents) is even more important for us, more crucial to our status in the world's scheme of things, than our being *people* (members of the species *Homo sapiens*). Human beings are merely members of a biological species; persons are members of a functionally constituted category that transcends merely biological limits.

But what is it to be a person? Seven conditions are essential.

1. *Intelligence.* One must be an intelligent being, able to acquire and process information—to acquire, maintain, and modify consciously held beliefs about the world and one's place within it.

2. *Affectivity.* One must be able to evaluate, to react to developments in the affective range of positive-negative, seeing the world's developments as good or bad, fortunate or unfortunate. A being who lacks preferences, who views everything with indifference (threats to its own very existence included), would not be a person.

3. *Agency.* One must be capable of goal-oriented action, seeing oneself as a free agent who is able not only to pursue goals but to initiate them, to set them for oneself. As philosophers have insisted since Aristotle's day, persons are not only agents but *autonomous* agents whose goals proceed from within their own thought processes and who are accordingly responsible for their acts.[1]

4. *Rationality.* One's actions (including mental actions like beliefs and evaluations) must proceed under the aegis of intelligence. They must by and large proceed from reasons that are grounded in aims and values to which one is committed.

5. *Self-understanding.* One must understand oneself in these terms, that is, conceive of oneself as an intelligent free agent, operating in the dimension of belief, action, and evaluation.

---

[1] Note that *agency* itself has various further ramifications. For example, agents' deliberations must have a time dimension—a future with reference to which they plan, and a past for whose actions they can be responsible.

6. *Self-esteem.* One must value oneself on this basis, and see this aspect of oneself as an important and valuable feature. That is, one must have a self-respect rooted in one's appreciation of oneself as an intelligent free agent.

7. *Mutual recognizance.* One must also acknowledge other duly qualified agents as persons and be prepared to value them as such. To see oneself as a person is coordinate with seeing others as such: persons must function in a context of community. Sociopaths and psychopaths who do not acknowledge other agents as persons thereby do not qualify as such themselves, though this of course does not prevent them being people (i.e., humans).

These conditions are severally necessary and jointly sufficient conditions for qualifying as being "a person" in the standard sense of that term. A person is thus a being who can function in certain particular ways and goes about doing certain characteristic sorts of things—in particular, one who operates in the sphere of ideation, evaluation, and action in a way that duly coordinates each of these functions with the others. The concept of a "person" is certainly a complex one that involves many constituent components, both descriptive and normative. However, one cannot be more or less of a person. Being a person turns simply on whether or not certain specific requirements are met. (One can, of course, meet fewer or more of these requirements, but that is not the issue.) Personhood is a matter of yes or no, and not one of degrees: a given creature either is or is not a person (though, to be sure, our information may be insufficient to effect a determination in this regard).

Interestingly, it does not lie in the concept of a person that such a being must necessarily have a body. To be sure, one must be able to act, but this agency could in theory be purely mental—involving solely, say, the direct communication between minds through a sympathetic resonance of some sort. Only contingently—only in worlds (such, presumably, as ours) where the transmission of information requires sending physical signals and where its recording requires a physical depository—will persons have to be embodied.

Note that conditions (1)–(4) relate to capacities, to what a person *can* do (namely, think, evaluate, act, reason), while conditions (5)–(7) relate to what a person *does* do, to the sort of use that is made of these abilities. To be a person one must use one's capacities in a certain sort of way (in point of self-understanding, self-esteem, and mutual recognizance). And this means that those who deem themselves to be persons—who "stake a claim" to be such—must in consequence assume from sheer self-consistency a commitment to endeavor to comport themselves in this way. Accordingly, the idea of a person has an indelibly moral dimension.

To be a person it is emphatically not enough to be an intelligent agent (otherwise the higher primates would be persons). To be a person, one must not only be conscious, but self-conscious: one must not only be a knower of facts and performer of action, but must be aware of oneself as such. Persons, as such, must regard themselves as persons. A person must not only possess knowledge, but knowledge of a very special sort, namely, reflexive self-knowledge. In view of this fact, even the possession of reason does not suffice to make a person. (Boethius's definition of a person as a rational being, *persona est naturae rationalis individua substantia* [*De duabus naturis*, chap. 3], simply will not do.) A merely rational being can be less than a person; the reflexive issue of how it is that one thinks of oneself plays a crucial role.

Still, rationality—the feature of having most of what one does proceed from the motivation of reasons—is a salient characteristic of personhood. And this rationality appertains to belief, evaluation, and action alike. Accordingly, persons are not just affective but rather evaluative creatures. Their reactions pro and con do not proceed on the basis of feelings alone—of pleasures and pains, likes and dislikes. Rather they involve approval and disapproval, evaluations that are based on reasons. The preferences of sensible persons in matters of thought, action, and evaluation generally can be and frequently are assessments—evaluations based on reasons. As rational beings, persons must be able to "give an account of themselves"—to render what they do in matters of belief, action, and evaluation intelligible (to themselves, of course, but thereby also potentially to others).

Persons are free and responsible agents. They are free and responsible in that when they act, they generally "*could* have acted otherwise" in the specific sense that they *would* have acted otherwise if some difference in the circumstances would have motivated them to do so. (The explanatory unraveling of this "if" clause is a very long story, for whose telling the present occasion is not the most suitable.) Accordingly, personhood involves autonomy and self-direction. It means that a full and adequate explanation of what an agent *does* (in contrast to "what happens to" him or her) requires reference to what this agent is and wants, values, prefers, and the like. Free agents are beings for whom conscious wants and preferences—rather than mere instincts and urges alone—provide the determinants of action.

But what about those who think of themselves as free but really lack freedom—people who are hypnotized, say, or whose minds are controlled by an evil scientist's machine? Such people are puppets, as it were, and operate under the control of another. This sort of thing can presumably happen, but given our understanding of the world's realities, rarely does so. Our understanding of the real world exiles this sort of thing to the outer regions of remote possibility. Here, as elsewhere, our concept of a person is geared to our substantive understanding of the world's ways. As it stands, the idea of freedom is built into our very concept of agency. It makes no more sense to hypothesize an agent whose acts are systematically unfree than it does to hypothesize an English speaker whose understanding of words is systematically mistaken. Even as such an individual just is not an English speaker, so one of the former sort just is not an agent.

In contrast, what about people who actually are free agents but simply fail to see themselves as such—say, because they are scientific or theological determinists who deem themselves to be acting out a role preprogrammed for them by some external agency? The situation here is a complicated one. For on the one hand, the fact remains that such individuals simply do not qualify as persons, strictly speaking. On the other hand, they doubtless have the potential of becoming so, and for that very reason deserve to be acknowledged as such by the rest of us.

Accepting people as rational free agents who bear the moral responsibility for their actions is an integral and ineliminable part of seeing them as persons. It is not that we have somehow learned this about others; rather, it reflects an indefeasible presumption (analogous to the presumption that a minor is incapable of rape or murder). The generalization that "persons are rational free agents" is a tautology. The particularization "X is a person" is the product not of an inference but of a decision—"I shall treat X as a person"—though, to be sure, a decision that is not arbitrary but grounded in evidence that supports but never completely constrains it. In recognizing someone as a person—as an autonomous, free, responsible, rational agent—we do not passively reflect observed facts about them but are actively engaged in treating them in a certain sort of way, failing which we would fall not so much into epistemic as into moral error.

Personhood stands at one end of a complex spectrum. Every human being forms the center of a many-circled social world. Around us there proliferate innumerable social units and groups to which we belong, whether by choice or by the hand of fate: families, clans, fellow employees, team- or club-mates, fellow citizens or countrymen, coreligionists, members of our cultural group in our civilization, the human race, and, last but not least, the wider, potentially cosmic confraternity of rational beings at large. By our nature as the social beings we are, we are emplaced within a large, variegated series of overlapping and complexly intersecting groupings. Each carries certain commitments, obligations, and duties, from the smallest unit or member of a particular family to the very largest, the community of persons, of rational agents at large.

Becoming a Person

To be a person one must think of oneself in a certain sort of way. One must view oneself as an individual self, an intelligent free agent with a unified identity over time whose present decisions reflect a responsibility for past action and whose present commitments are to be taken as binding for the future.

Homo sapiens is a creature of reflexivity of self-orientation and even a self-centeredness of sorts. For it is in being self-consciously aware of ourselves as ourselves—as beings of the sort we are—that our personhood comes into being. (Its next, no less crucial phase is, to be sure, other oriented—it lies in the transition from I to us, that is in accepting others as being of the same sort of ourselves.) For us, the world has a certain egocentric immediacy, being based on the here (i.e., with where we ourselves are) and now (i.e., with these present actions of ours).

Persons accordingly are constituted reflexively, by self-definition. In this context, it is how we see ourselves, both as individuals and in relation to others, that makes us into what we are. Being a person calls for thinking of oneself in a certain sort of way—as an intelligent free agent who, by virtue of this circumstance, is a possessor of worth and a bearer of rights in relation to others. In this regard, then, to see oneself in a certain sort of way (namely, as a person) is through this very act to make a certain sort of thing of oneself (namely, a person). In this regard, persons are "self-made": being a person is a matter of having a certain sort of self-image. It requires conceiving of oneself as a person—as an intelligent free agent who is capable of acting in line with his or her own choices and interacting with others on a basis of reciprocity. Accordingly, to be a person one must have the conception of a person, or a pretty close approximation thereto.

Persons are evaluative beings. Not only must they be able to believe and to act in the light of their beliefs, but their actions must be geared to values: to preferences and priorities on whose basis a rational being can see the objects of its desires as being desirable. Evaluation is crucial to personhood. And this matter of evaluation is something pervasive. In particular, persons can evaluate their values—can endeavor to assess the extent to which they are rationally defensible.

Miguel de Unamuno asked, "If we are in this world *for* some purpose, whence could this 'for' be taken but from the very depths of our will?"[2] But this oversimplifies the matter. Our purpose, our "mission in life" is not elective—it lies not in our will but in our nature. Its roots lie not in what we want but in what we are—or in what we find ourselves to be in the course of our efforts at self-understanding. To be a person is to be a creature that thinks of itself as having aims and ends—ideally including a commitment to realize in and for itself those values that are at issue in being a person.

To be a person one must be capable of seeing oneself as such, and accordingly must have the concept of a person. This at bottom is why

---

[2] "Si estamos en el mundo *para* algo, de dónde puede sacarse ese *para* sino del fondo mismo de nuestra voluntad?" (Miguel de Unamuno, *Del sentimiento trágico de la vida*, ed. Felix Garcia [Madrid: Espasa-Calpa, 1976], p. 226).

most higher primates—or, for that matter, our ancestors before the evolution of *Homo sapiens*—do not qualify as persons. Such creatures can
all think and choose and act. But presumably their conceptual repertoire is too impoverished to enable them to think of themselves as
such, that is, as beings who can think and choose and act in the light
of those choices. To be a person requires having a certain sort of self-
image, and early on in the history of our race the conception of a self was
presumably missing or underdeveloped. Until people developed the
rather sophisticated conception of "personal selves" as "intelligent free
agents," they were not persons. To be a person one must deem oneself
as such, and this involves thinking of oneself as a certain kind of being,
an agent who acts and (at least potentially) interacts with others of its
own kind, a being who takes causal and moral responsibility for its own
actions.

A person is thus a very complex sort of being. In consequence of
this circumstance, very different conceptions of personhood are in circulation. On the one side lies the Hegelian conception, which approaches
personhood in terms of one's position in relation to others within the
framework of a social order. The crux of personhood lies in the mutual
recognizance and reciprocal acceptance that characterizes one's acceptance by others. On the other side lies the Nietzschean conception of
persons as entirely self-made. For Nietzsche, a personal self is something
one becomes through asserting one's independence of all else and insisting on the privacy of one's own inwardness. One forms oneself as an
authentic person by asserting a scale of self-oriented values as guides
for fashioning a life of one's own—even as an artist creates his or her work
by imposing inner personal demands on the materials at hand. But the fact
is that both of these approaches are one-sided and imbalanced. Personhood is a holistic complex that enhances both elements together. A person
without idiosyncrasies—without the evaluative basis for an inwardly constituted stance toward the outer world—is a mere empty shell. But those
who, though otherwise qualifying as persons, exist permanently unto
themselves alone, without the potential for relationships of community
and interaction with others, are enmeshed in an impoverishing isolation
that makes them freaks rather than genuine persons. The self-assertion
and self-understanding of personhood are both modes of relating oneself
to others, and the reciprocal recognizance of persons in a matter of appreciating and valuing the fact that each individual has the right and the duty
to an inner life of his or her own, providing for the assertion of a variety
of personal aims and values. Personhood combines two sides: the one
directed inward, the other outward. To assert the predominance of one
to the exclusion of the other is to diminish and distort the conception
at issue.

The Value Dimension

Personhood is something inherently normative. To be a person in the full sense of the term is to see oneself as capable of acting in the light of values appropriately deemed valid. Specifically this means that one must value personhood itself, seeing that reason demands respect: it is a requirement imposed by one's own reason that rationality should be valued. As long as personhood is not valued for what it is, the conception of it still remains unachieved. Accordingly, the evaluative dimension is crucial to the full-fledged conception of a person. To have this conception of oneself is not only to consider oneself as a being of a certain kind but to *value* oneself for it—that is, to deem oneself a bearer of value for this very reason.

To be a person is thus to see oneself as a unit of worth and bearer of rights. And this is something that generalizes to others as well. A full-fledged conception of personhood can develop only in a social context. To regard oneself as a possessor of worth and a bearer of rights *in virtue of being a person* is thereby to accord a certain status to persons in general. It is to see persons in general as occupying a special place in the scheme of things, as constituting a special category of beings with whom one has a particular kinship and toward whom one consequently bears particular responsibilities.

If I am to see myself as rationally entitled to consideration because I have a certain status or condition S (because I am a person), then I must see S as a feature that underwrites consideration generally: if it entitles *me* to consideration, it correspondingly entitles *anybody*. Thus if I expect consideration—let alone respect—from others because I have S, then I must myself be prepared to respect S in others. The principles of rational cogency are impersonal; they do not respect the peculiarity of individuals. One's self-perception as a person must be such as to lead one to require certain claims and entitlements to consideration, to having one's own claims and needs taken into account. (From early childhood on, the idea of getting and giving one's due—of "playing fair"—comes into it.) One cannot sensibly value personhood in oneself except by valuing personhood as such, and consequently valuing it also in others. (For example, a being entirely unmoved by the suffering of others of its own kind would not qualify as a person.)

The fact is that evaluation—and, in particular, a prizing of those capacities involved in personhood—is essential to being a person. It is interesting to note the extent to which people do in fact respond evaluatively to the world's developments. Something that newspaper readers soon come to recognize about themselves is that few and far between are the developments in human affairs to which we are altogether indifferent—which, when we look in our heart of hearts, we see with total detachment and neither welcome nor deplore to some extent. And the same holds true even of remote historical events. Once we understand the issue involved, we find it hard not to take sides. Even when the issues are remote from us and our own forefathers, we nevertheless generally have the sense of positive or negative response, of a personal stance, of a definite evaluation pro or con, one way or the other toward the ways in which people interact with one another.

The Communal Aspect

We are born *people* (members of the species *Homo sapiens*) but become *persons*. Only as we progress through childhood and learn to think of ourselves as responsible agents—intelligent free individuals interacting with others as such—do we become full-fleged persons. (No doubt this communal development reflects a tendency that evolutionary processes have programmed into our developmental history, so that personhood is de facto more closely affixed to humanity than abstract theory alone suggests.) Personhood does not represent a biological mode of existence within organic nature, but a social mode of existence within an environing culture. Personhood thus has an inextricably social dimension. The conception of a (full-fledged) person is subject to a principle of reciprocity expectation. To qualify as a person oneself involves acknowledging and accepting as such the other creatures who seem plausibily qualified as being persons. And it involves the expectation that they will reciprocate. In deeming others to be persons, and thereby as entitled to being valued as such—qualified to have me treat *their* interests, their rights and concerns, as deserving *my* respect—I also expect them to see me in exactly this same light. Consequently, if others whom I recognize as persons treat me as a mere thing and not as a person, it injures my own personhood; it undermines my ability to see myself as a person.

William James says somewhere that we will be moral beings only if we believe that we are free agents, because only then will we deliberate about our actions with a view to reasons and thereby become morally responsible for them. But the real point here is a more fundamental one. It is precisely because persons as such form part of a mutually recognizant community of rational agents that persons are ipso facto beings who fall within the domain of morality. (Morality does not inherently root in a social compact. If extraneous persons were to come upon the scene, perhaps from outer space, we would at once have certain moral obligations to one another—to respect one another's "rights" as persons, and the like—which would certainly not need to be products of a prior "agreement," real or tacit.)

To be a person is to have a certain sort of self-image. But what of small children, the mentally handicapped, the merely heedless or thoughtless, and so on? What are we to say of someone who, for one reason or another, never forms any real self-image at all? Should we say that they thereby disqualify themselves as persons?

Well . . . yes and no. Strictly and literally, they do not satisfy the standards of personhood and are thus seemingly disqualified. But this does not quite settle the matter. For to be a person is not only to make certain claims for oneself but also to make corresponding concessions to others. In particular, it involves giving others the benefit of doubt when it comes to acknowledging them as congeners, as fellow persons. Accepting them as qualified persons is implicit in our own claims to personhood. Recognizing others as persons is not solely a matter of observation and information but always involves some element of evaluative generosity. The class of authentic persons—of people who see themselves and others as such—constitutes a family united by a bond of respect that is generally mutual but sometimes unilateral. Part and parcel of what defines one as a person is the "professional courtesy" (as it were) of acknowledging others as such— the preparedness to accept them as fellow members of "one larger family" that also includes oneself and ones more immediate associates.

Moreover, the limits of this family do not even stop at the boundaries of the human community. Should there be other, nonhuman rational agents in the universe whom we have good reason to see as possessed of a sufficiently developed self-image to value themselves as such, then we would have strong reason to accept them as persons also. It is thus (just barely) conceivable that "thinking machines" could come to qualify as persons.

But what is one to say about those who dilate the boundaries of personhood, who propose to exclude women, say, or children, or foreigners from this domain? Simply that they thereby put their own personhood in doubt. For being a person requires having the concept of a person, and someone whose conception is flawed in so substantial a way thereby compromises his or her claims to having an adequate grasp of the concept. It is part and parcel of the value dimension of personhood to acknowledge and esteem as a fellow person those who (like the very young) have the prospect of a future exercise of the capacities of personhood (intelligent agency, etc.) and also those who (like the incapacitated old) have the dignity of a previously manifested exercise of these capacities. Those who do not recognize and value other plausible person-candidates as such—who see personhood potential in others as insignificant—thereby cast their own personhood into doubt.

There is, of course, an enterprise of artificial intelligence that is nowadays much in the news. But is there also a comparable domain of artificial personhood? When (or rather if) we are led to acknowledge that computers can "think," must we then not also acknowledge them as persons? Clearly not!

As we saw at the outset, personhood involves (among other things) four essential requirements: (1) intelligence, (2) rational agency, (3) self-assertion, and (4) social reciprocity. Now in the case of computers, (1) seems possible and perhaps even plausible. But (2) is problematic, and (3)–(4) are out of reach. Or that at least is how the matter looks at present. But were the situation ever to change so radically that good reason came to exist for granting that "thinking machines" can achieve capacities (2)–(4) as well, then there would be no choice but to acknowledge them as persons. That would be simply part and parcel of the "benefit of doubt" aspect of being persons ourselves. But for the present, at any rate, the realization of this prospect seems not merely remote but unrealistic.

Personal Identity

What is it that individuates a particular person as such? What is the characteristic factor that makes a person into him- or her-*self*?

The self or ego has always been a stumbling block for Western philosophy because of its recalcitrance to finding accommodation within the orthodox framework of substance ontology. The idea that "the self" is a thing (substance), and that whatever occurs in relation to "my mind" and "my thoughts" is accordingly a matter of the activity of a homunclulus-like agency of a certain sort (a "mind"-substance) is no more than a rather blatant sort of fiction—a somewhat desperate effort to apply the substance-attribute paradigm to a range of phenomena that it just does not fit.

It is, after all, rather repugnant to conceptualize persons as things (substances)—oneself above all. Aristotle already bears witness to this difficulty of accommodating within a substance metaphysic the idea of a self or soul. It is, he tells us, the "substantial form," the *entelechy*, of the body. But this strategem raises more problems than it solves, because the self or soul is so profoundly unlike the other sorts of entelechy examples that Aristotle is able to provide.

People instinctively resist being described in thing-classificatory terms. As Sartre remarks, a wrongdoer may well concede "I did this or that act" but will resist saying "I am a thief," "I am a murderer."[3] Such characterizations indicate a fixed nature that we naturally see as repugnant to ourselves. People standardly incline to see themselves and their doings in processual terms as sources of purposive activities geared to the satisfac-

---

[3] J. P. Sartre, "Bad Faith," in his *Being and Nothingness*, trans. H. E. Barnes (New York: Pocket Books, 1953), pp. 107–9.

tion of needs and wants. In application to ourselves, at any rate, static thing-classifiers are naturally distasteful to us.

If one is intent upon conceiving of a person within the framework of a classical thing-metaphysic, then one is going to be impelled inexorably toward the materialist view that the definitive facet of a person is his or her body and its doings. For of everything that appertains to us, it is clearly one's physical body that is most readily assimilated to the substance paradigm. Think here of David Hume's ventures into self-apprehension.

> From what [experiential] impression could this idea [of *self*] be derived? This question is impossible to answer without a manifest contradiction and absurdity; and yet it is a question which must necessarily be answered, if we would have the idea of self pass for clear and intelligible. . . . For my part, when I enter most intimately into what I call *myself*, I always stumble on some particular perception or other, of heat or cold, light or shade, love or hatred, pain or pleasure. I never can catch *myself* at any time without a perception, and never can observe anything but the perception.[4]

Here Hume is perfectly right. Any such quest for observational confrontation with a personal core substance, a self or ego that constitutes the particular person that one is, is destined to end in failure. If one insists on narrowing experience to observation, then Hume's analysis holds. The only "thing" about ourselves we can get hold of observationally is the body and its activities.

However, while we may have difficulties apprehending what we *are*, we have no difficulty experiencing what we *do*. Our bodily and mental activities lie open to experiential apprehension. There is no problem with experiential access to the processes and patterns of process that characterize us personally—our doings and undergoings, either individually or patterned into talents, skills, capabilities, traits, dispositions, habits, inclinations, and tendencies to action and inaction are, after all, what characteristically defined a person as the individual he or she is. What makes my experience mine is not some peculiar qualitative character that it exhibits but simply its forming part of the overall ongoing process that defines and constitutes my life. Personal identity is a matter of processual integration.

Once we conceptualize the core "self" of a person as a bundle of actual and potential processes—of actions and capacities, tendencies, and dispositions to action (both physical and psychic)—then we have a concept of personhood that renders the self or ego experientially accessible, seeing

---

[4] Hume, *A Treatise of Human Nature*, bk. 2, pt. 4, sec. 6, "Of Personal Identity." In the appendix, Hume further elaborates: "When I turn my reflection on *myself*, I never can perceive this *self* without some one or more perceptions; nor can I ever perceive anything but the perceptions. It is the composition of these, therefore, which forms the SELF."

that experiencing itself simply consists of such processes. On a process-oriented approach, the self or ego (the constituting core of a person as such, that is, as the particular person he or she is) is simply a mega-process—a *structured system of processes*. The unity of person is a unity of experience—the coalescence of all of one's diverse microexperiences as parts of one unified macroprocess. (It is the same sort of unity of process that links each minute's travel into a single overall journey.) The crux of this approach is the shift in orientation from substance to process—from a unity of hardware, of physical machinery, to a unity of software, of programming or mode of functioning.

The fundamentality of psychic process for the constitution of a self was put on the agenda of modern philosophy by Descartes and most acutely so. Miguel de Unamuno says that Descartes got it backward, that instead of *cogito, ergo sum res cogitans* one should say: *sum res cogitans, ergo cogito*.[5] But this is simply not so. Descartes's reversal of Scholasticism's traditional substantialist perspective is perfectly in order, proceeding from the sound idea that activity comes first (*Im Anfang war die Tat*)—that what we do defines what we are.

The salient advantage of this process-geared view of the self as the unfolding of a complex process of "leading a life (of a certain sort)"—with its natural division into varied and manifold subprocesses—is that it does away with the need for a mysterious and experientially inaccessible unifying subtantial object (on the lines of Kant's "transcendental ego") to constitute a self out of the welter of its experiences. The unity of self comes to be seen as a unity of process—of one large megaprocess that encompasses many smaller ones in its makeup. We arrive at a view of mind that dispenses with the Cartesian homunculus, the "ghost in the machine," and looks to the unity of mind as a unity of functioning—of operation rather than operator. Such an approach wholly rejects the thing-ontologists' view of a person as an entity existing separately from its actions, activities, and experiences. A "self" is viewed not as constituted in terms of a thing with its physical components but as the product of a processual identity.[6]

On this basis, the Humean complaint—"One experiences feeling this and doing that, but one never experiences *oneself*"—is much like the complaint of the person who says, "I see him picking up that brick, and mixing that batch of mortar, and troweling that brick into place, but I never see

---

[5] Unamuno, *Del sentimiento trágico de la vida*, p. 52.

[6] There remains, of course, the philosophically interesting question of the extent to which the particular processes of a person's actual life can be hypothetically altered without abolishing the individual at issue. Presumably if I had not breakfasted this morning, I would still be the person I am, while if I had been raised by a Chinese family in Canton, I might not be. Cf. the author's discussion in chap. 6 of his book *The Primacy of Practice* (Oxford: Basil Blackwell, 1973).

him building a wall." Even as "building the wall" just exactly is the complex process that is composed of those various particular activities of putting on now this brick, now that one, so—from the process point of view—one's self just is the complex process composed of those various particular physical and psychic experiences and actions in their systemic interrelationship. A person is as a person does. What individuates someone as a person, then, is something processual—namely, the way in which he or she carries on those salient processes (intelligence, rational agency, self-assertion, and social reciprocity) that constitute the defining core of personhood.

The Inherent Obligations of Personhood

Though man is—as Pascal said—but a reed, he is a *thinking* reed. Though a mere pawn on the world's immense chessboard, people are—or can be—knowledgeable pawns. We are weak and mortal creatures at the mercy of nature and of chance, but the exercise of intelligence affords us a glimpse into the realm of the infinite and the timeless. Reason is the prime source of human power—and of human nobility. Many of the great things we can achieve in this world we can accomplish only through its means. Such greatness as we have, we owe in large measure to the possession of reason. It is thought, intelligence—the exercise of rationality in the interests of knowledge, valuation, and right action—that sets humans apart from other creatures and renders us (mere animals that we are!) akin to the gods.

As a rational being, *Homo sapiens* is endowed with some measure of self-determination—enough to be capable of making its idealized vision of what it should be determine at least in part what it actually is. Our claim to rationality means that our nature is not wholly given, that we have the ability to contribute in at least some small degree to making ourselves into the sorts of creatures we are.

What mechanisms can ensure the coordination of human behavior for the general good? There is of course the path of force, constraint, and coercion, but that is hardly an attractive option. Again, there is the path of rhetorical appeal, propaganda, subliminal suggestion, and the advertising arts. But this way of eliciting agreement is ultimately unworthy of man in violating his dignity as a thinking being. Only through rational persuasion—through appeal to one's reason—can we do justice to another's rational humanity. Kant put the matter well: "Nothing is so sacred that it may be exempted from this searching examination [of reason] which knows no respect for persons. Reason depends on this freedom for its very existence. For reason has no dictatorial authority; its verdict is always simply the agreement of free citizens, of whom each one must be permitted to express, without let or hindrance, his objections or even his veto."[7] Only an appeal to persuasive grounds in *convincing* people, only a recourse to their intelligence, is a truly worthy means of obtaining their compliance. It alone acknowledges the dignity of man and assures the treatment of others as we ourselves would wish to be treated—as people who can come to responsible decisions when presented with the relevant information.

The possession of rationality—our capacity to act on the basis of good reasons whose normative force we ourselves recognize as such, rather than acting wholly under the constraint of "external" compulsions and influences—is exactly what makes us free agents. Free will is the capacity to choose and "do as we want"—whether to heed the call of reason or to ignore it. But when somebody is convinced or persuaded *rationally*, it must be on grounds that they themselves acknowledge as appropriate. It is thus only in heeding reason's call that we are fully free by proceeding on the basis of reasons whose cogency we ourselves recognize and acknowledge. Internal compulsion—the peremptory dictate of temperament or will—is as contrary to true freedom as external compulsion. Only in heeding reason's call do we exercise our freedom, and thereby at the same time we realize our most positive human potential.

One recent writer sees rational argument as coercive, complaining that "a successful . . . argument, a strong argument, *forces* someone to a belief."[8] But this gets it completely wrong. Probatively cogent rational argumentation does not—cannot—take us beyond acknowledged premises. It is wholly noncoercive and can succeed only in leading people to where their *own* beliefs and their *own* convictions naturally take them. Rational "compulsion" is compulsion in name only—it is a "compulsion" that proceeds from within the orbit of our own thought processes and our commitments and thus is no actual compulsion at all. Reason is inherently noncoercive because it can take us only where the ruling part of ourselves, the rational part, is prepared to go.

As Spinoza rightly emphasized, reason provides for the essential basis of man's freedom—his autonomy as an agent. The fact that we can choose in the light of what we ourselves judge to be acceptable or desirable—that we can think and act as we deem fit by the standards that we ourselves acknowledge as rationally appropriate—frees us from the burden of deeming ourselves altogether subject to the impetus of external constraints. It is in exercising our *reason* (not our *will*, whose moving impetus is gener-

---

[7] Immanuel Kant, *Critique of Pure Reason*, A739/B767.

[8] Robert Nozick, *Philosophical Explanations* (Cambridge: Harvard University Press, 1981), p. 4.

ally some "external" drive or influence) that we realize ourselves as self-determined beings for whom the only ultimately decisive authority lies in the internal forum of our own thought processes.

The glory of reason is that it liberates its possessors from the control of "external" forces, endowing them with a claim to at least partial self-determination. In viewing ourselves as rational beings, we lay claim to an (at least partial) freedom from the impetus of external forces outside the range of such authority as we ourselves endorse. And in seeing others as proceeding rationally, we credit them with a similar status, manifesting a respect for their status as persons that we would in turn expect and welcome from them. Viewing our fellows as rational beings is a matter of hoped-for reciprocity—of "treating others as we would have them treat us." It is their potential for rational agency that makes humans into persons.

The characteristic thing about a person is being an intelligent free agent endowed with self-understanding and self-esteem. It is their potential for rational agency that makes people into the sorts of beings they are. But why should we humans strive to realize this potential? Why should we comport ourselves as rational agents who align and coordinate their beliefs, actions, and evaluations under the guidance of reason?

The answer is straightforward. We ought to comport ourselves rationally because rationality is an essential part of our self-conception as human persons. Rationality thereby represents a crucial aspect of our deepest self-interest—our being able to maintain a proper sense of legitimacy and self-worth by being able to see ourselves as the sorts of creatures we claim to be. The issue is one of the reflexive self-coherence and self-consistency of a creature that sees itself as partially self-made in view of its free rational agency.

It is through this fundamental *ontological* imperative that mere counsels of reason are transmuted into commands issued by one side of our nature (the rational) to ourselves at large. We have to do here with an injunction issued by an authoritative part of ourselves to the whole. Our claim to be rational free agents of itself establishes our position in the world's scheme of things, with the result that rationality becomes a matter of duty for us, of ontological obligation.

In his *System of Moral Philosophy*, Francis Hutcheson characterized morality as a matter of so acting that we can reflectively approve of our own character, of so acting that one need make no excuses for oneself toward oneself. But in much the same way, the fundamental ontological impetus to self-development is a matter of acting in the light of what sort of person one ought to be—of so comporting oneself that one can unhesitantly approve of oneself as being that which one has, through one's own actions, made of oneself. The ontological imperative toward self-realization—and the rational and moral imperatives it carries in its wake—are simply part and parcel of this fundamental impetus and commandment. Our deepest nature calls on us to be on good terms with ourselves and thus, in turn, requires due heed of our rationality. What is at stake is our very identity as beings of the sort we do and should see ourselves as being.

The crux of the imperative to personhood is thus the fundamental duty to make good use of the opportunitites that come our way to realize ourselves as fully as possible—the fundamental duty of self-realization. To be sure, rational agency is not programmed into us like an animal's instinct. We are free creatures. And as such we do well to walk in the paths of reason not because considerations of necessity dictate that we must but because considerations of desirability indicate that this affords the greatest real advantage for us as the sort of creatures we are. At this point there is a coalescence of what we are and what we ought to be. We can, of course, act contrary to reason. But we cannot do so reasonably, that is, with any plausible expectation that any good will come of it, that our interests will somehow be productively served thereby.

The value aspect is crucial here. Our ontological obligation to personhood roots in the reflexivity involved in being a person: the fact that persons are self-comprehending, self-developed, and self-responsible. The complex and sophisticated nature of their mental operations—the fact that persons are self-comprehending—makes them special and especially worthy. The fact that one can appreciate oneself as a being capable of appreciation is basic to our capacity to appreciate fully anything else whatsoever. To be a person one must not only be able to do evaluation, but one must actually exercise this capacity—in particular, exercise it with respect to oneself. A being for whom being a person is something of no value would, for that very reason, be precluded from qualifying as one.[9]

---

[9] Some of the issues of this chapter are further developed in the author's *Human Interests* (Stanford: Stanford University Press, 1990).

Seven _____

The Power of Ideals

The Role of Ideals

Ideals are values of a rather special sort. They pivot about the question "If I could shape the world in my own way, how would I have it be?" *Every* voluntary action of ours is in some manner a remaking of the world—or at any rate, of a very small corner of it—by projecting into reality a situation that otherwise would not be. To act intelligently is to act with due reference to the direction in which our own actions shift the course of things. And this is exactly where ideals come into play. Our ideals guide and consolidate our commitment to human virtues in general and moral excellences in particular. Courage and unselfishness provide examples. Acts of courage or of selflessness often go beyond "the call of duty," exhibiting a dimension of morality that transcends the boundaries of obligation in a way that is typical of ideals.

In an influential 1958 paper, the English philosopher J. O. Urmson stressed the ethical importance of the Christian conception of works of supererogation (*opera supererogationis*),[1] reemphasizing the traditional contrast between the *basic* morality of duties and the *higher* morality of preeminently creditable action that reaches "above and beyond the call of duty." Such supererogation is accordingly best conceived of not in terms of duty but in terms of dedication to an ideal. The values at issue are often symbolized in such role models as heroes and saints—people who perform in the pursuit of the good to an extent that goes well beyond anything that "could reasonably be asked of them."

A knowledge of their ideals gives us much insight into what people are like. "By their ideals shall ye know them." We do know a great deal about someone when we know about his or her ideals—about that person's dreams, heroes, and utopias. The question of what gods somebody worships—power or fame or Mammon or Jehovah—speaks volumes about the sort of person we are dealing with. (To be sure, there yet remains the question of how dedicated this person to those ideals, how energetically and assiduously he or she puts them to work.)

[1] J. O. Urmson, "Saints and Heroes," in *Essays in Moral Philosophy*, ed. A. I. Melden (Seattle: University of Washington Press, 1958). On this theme, see also David Heyd, *Supererogation: Its Status in Ethical Theory* (Cambridge: Cambridge University Press, 1984).

An ethic of ideals can accommodate what is at issue in the moral dimension in ways in which a mere ethic of duty cannot. We have no duty to our fellows to become a saint or hero; this just is not something we owe to people, whether singly or collectively—and not even to ourselves. Here we are dealing with something that is not a matter of obligation but one of ideality—of dedication to an inner impetus to do one's utmost to make the world into a better place that is rather different from what it actually is.

Human aspiration is not restricted by the realities—neither by the realities of the present moment (from which our sense of future possibilities can free us), nor even by our view of realistic future prospects (from which our sense of the ideal possibilities can free us). Our judgment is not bounded by what *is*, nor by what *will* be, nor even by what *can* be. For there is always also our view of what *should* be—what might ideally to be. The vision of our mind's eye extends to circumstances beyond the limits of the possible. A proper appreciation of ideals calls for a recognition of man's unique dual citizenship in the worlds of the real and the ideal—a realm of facts and a realm of values.

It is remarkable that nature has managed to evolve a creature who aspires to more than nature can offer, who never feels totally at home in its province, but lives, to some extent, as an alien in a foreign land. All those who feel dissatisfied with the existing scheme of things, who both yearn *and strive* for something better and finer than this world affords, have a touch of moral grandeur in their makeup that deservedly evokes admiration—unless, like Maximilien Robespierre, they propose to sacrifice others to the pursuit of their own vision.

Skeptically inclined "realists" have always questioned the significance of ideals on the grounds that, since they cannot ever actually be realized as such, they are presumably pointless. But this fails to reckon properly with the facts of the situation. For while ideals put before us situations that, in a way, are mere fictions, these fictions nevertheless direct and canalize our thought and action. Like "peace on earth," they may be unachievable, but they can nevertheless strongly influence how we manage our affairs. To be sure, an ideal is not a goal we can expect to attain. But it serves to set a direction in which we can strive. Ideals are irrealities, but they are irrealities that condition the nature of the real through their influence on human thought and action. Stalin's cynical question "But how many divisions has the pope?" betokens the Soviet realpolitiker rather than the Marxist ideologue. (How many soldiers did Karl Marx command?) It is folly to underestimate the strength of an attachment to ideals. Though in itself impracticable, an ideal can nevertheless importantly influence our practice and serve to shape the sort of home we endeavor to make for ourselves in a difficult world.

Ideals take us beyond experience into the realm of imagination—outside of what we do find, or expect to find, here in this real world, into the region of wishful thinking, of utopian aspiration, of what we would fain have if only (alas!) we could. Admittedly this envisions a perfection or completion that outreaches not only what we actually have attained but even what we can possibly attain in this sublunary dispensation. However, to give this up, to abandon casting those periodic wistful glances in the "transcendental" direction, is to cease to be fully, genuinely, and authentically human. In following empiricists and positivists by fencing off the ideal level of deliberation behind "No Entry" signs, we diminish the horizons of human thought to its grave impoverishment. (As is readily illustrated by examples from Galileo and Einstein, there is a valid place for thought experiments that involve idealization even in the domain of the natural sciences themselves.)

The idealized level of contemplation provides a most valuable conceptual instrument. For it affords us a most useful contrast conception that serves to shape and condition our thought. Like the functionary in imperial Rome who stood at the emperor's side to whisper intimations of mortality into his ear, so idealizations serve to remind us of the fragmentary, incomplete, and parochial nature of what we actually manage to accomplish. If the ideal level of consideration were not there for purposes of contrast, we would constantly be in danger of ascribing to the parochially proximate a degree of completeness or adequacy to which it has no just claims.

Prohibiting our thought from operating at the idealized level of a global inclusiveness that transcends the reach of actual experience would create a profound impoverishment of our intellectual resources. To block off our entry into the sphere of perfection represented by the ideal level of consideration is to cut us off from a domain of thought that characterizes us as intellectually amphibious creatures who are able to operate both in the realm of realities and in that of ideals.

Expelled from the Garden of Eden, we are exited from the whole sphere of completeness, perfection, comprehensiveness, and totality. We are constrained to make do with the flawed realities of a mundane and imperfect world. But it lies in the depths of our nature to aspire to more. Beset by a "divine discontent," we cannot but yearn for the unfettered completeness and perfection that (as empiricists rightly emphasize) the limited resources of our cognitive situation cannot actually afford us. Not satisfied with graspable satisfactions, we seek far more and press outward "beyond the limits of the possible." It is a characteristic *and worthy* feature of man to let his thought reach out toward a greater and more harmonious comprehensiveness than anything actually available within the mundane sphere of secured experience. *Homo sapiens* alone among earthly creatures is a being able and (occasionally) willing to work toward the realization of a condition of things that does not and perhaps even cannot exist—a state of affairs where values are fully and comprehensively embodied. We are agents who can change and transform the world, striving to produce something that does not exist except in the mind's eye, and indeed cannot actually exist at all because its realization calls for a greater perfection and completeness than the recalcitrant conditions of this world allow. Our commitment to this visionary level of deliberation makes us into a creature that is something more than a rational animal—a creature that moves in the sphere of not only ideas but ideals as well.

The Utility of Ideals

What do ideals do for us? What useful role do they play in the human scheme of things? The answer runs something like this. Humans are rational beings. People can act and must choose among alternative courses of action. This crucial element of choice means that our actions will be guided in the first instance by considerations of "necessity" relating to survival and the requisites of physical well-being. But to some extent they can, and in an advanced condition of human development must, go far beyond this point. Eventually they come to be guided by necessity-transcending considerations, by wants rather than needs, by our "higher" aspirations—our yearning for a life that is not only secure and pleasant but also meaningful in having some element of excellence or nobility about it. Ideals are the guideposts toward these higher, excellence-oriented aspirations. As such, they motivate rather than constrain, urge rather than demand.

The validation of an ideal is thus ultimately derivative. It does not lie in the (inherently unrealizable) state of affairs that it contemplates—in the unachievable perfection that it envisions. Rather, it lies in the influence that it exerts on the lives of its human exponents through the mediation of thought and action. To be sure, one ideal can be evaluated in terms of another. But to deploy our ideological commitments for appraising ideals is ultimately question begging—a matter of appraising values in terms of those same values. To appraise ideals in a way that avoids such circularity we must leave the domain of idealization altogether and enter into that of the realistically practical. The superiority of one ideal over another must be tested by its practical consequences for human well-being. "By their fruits shall ye know them." In appraising ideals, we must look not to the nature of these ideals alone but also to their work—their actual effects in applicative operation. For the key role of an ideal is to serve as an instrument of decision making, a sort of navigation instrument for use in the pursuit of the good. And here the homely practical goods—survival, health, well-being, human solidarity, happiness, and the like—come into their own once more. Those higher values ultimately validate their legitimacy through their bearing on the quotidian ones. To be sure, we cannot validate ideals by abstract demonstration. We live in a world without guarantees. All we can say is: "Try it, you'll like it—as you move in this direction, you'll find with the wisdom of hindsight that you have achieved useful results that justify the risks."

By urging us to look beyond the limits of the practicable, ideals help us to optimize the efficacy of our praxis. Their significance turns on what we do with them in the world, on their utility in guiding our thought and action into fruitful and rewarding directions, wholly notwithstanding their unrealistic and visionary character. Their crucial role lies in their capacity to help us to make the world a better place. There is no conflict between the demands of (valid) practice and the cultivation of (appropriate) ideals. The bearing of the practical and the ideal stand in mutually supportive cooperation.

The impracticability of its realization is thus no insuperable obstacle to the validation of an ideal. This issue of its feasibility or infeasibility is simply beside the point, because what counts with an ideal is not the question of its attainment but the question of the overall benefits that accrue from its pursuit. Having and pursuing an ideal, regardless of its impracticability, can yield benefits such as a better life for ourselves and a better world for our posterity. The validation of an ideal thus lies in the pragmatic value of its pursuit. As Max Weber observed with characteristic perspicuity, even in the domain of politics, that art of the possible, "the possible has frequently been attained only through striving for something impossible that lies beyond one's reach."[2]

Conflicting Ideals

Ideals do not speak with one voice. There are, of course, competing ideals. Aldous Huxley once wrote: "About the ideal goal of human effort there exists in our civilization and, for nearly thirty centuries, there has existed a very general agreement. From Isaiah to Karl Marx the prophets have spoken with one voice. In the Golden Age to which they look forward there will be liberty, peace, justice, and brotherly love. 'Nation shall no

---

[2] "Nicht minder richtig aber ist, dass das Mögliche sehr oft nur dadurch erreicht wurde, dass man nach dem jenseits seiner Kraft liegenden Unmöglichen griff" ("Der Sinn der 'Wertfreiheit' in den soziologischen und ökonomischen Wissenschaften," *Logos* 7 [1917]: 63; reprinted in *Gesammelte Aufsätze zur Wissenschaftslehre* [Tübingen: Mohr, 1922], p. 476).

more lift sword against nation'; 'the free development of each will lead to
the free development of all'; 'the world shall be full of the knowledge of
the Lord, as the waters cover the sea.'"[3] Susan Stebbing took Huxley
sharply to task here:

> In this judgment Mr. Huxley appears to me to be mistaken. There is not now,
> and there was not in 1937 when Mr. Huxley made this statement, "general
> agreement" with regard to "the ideal goal of human effort," even in Western
> Europe, not to mention Eastern Asia. The Fascist ideal has been conceived in
> sharpest opposition to the values which Mr. Huxley believes to be so generally
> acceptable, and which may be said to be characteristic of the democratic idea.
> The opposition is an opposition with regard to modes of social organization; it
> . . . necessitates fundamental differences in the methods employed to achieve
> aims that are totally opposed. The ideal of Fascism is power and the glorification
> of the State; the ideal of democracy is the development of free and happy human
> beings; consequently, their most fundamental difference lies in their different
> conception of the worth of human beings as individuals worthy of respect.[4]

And Stebbing is quite right. Conflicting ideals are a fact of life. Different
priorities can be assigned to different values, and to prize A over B, is
incompatible with prizing B over A. But of course, the prospect of goal
alternatives no more invalidates one's ideals than the prospect of spouse
alternatives invalidates one's marriage. The justification and power of an
ideal inhere in its capacity to energize and motivate human effort toward
productive results—in short, in its practical efficacy. Ideals may involve
unrealism, but this nowise annihilates their impetus or value precisely
because of the practical consequences that ensue upon our adoption of
them.

But what are we to make of the fact that competing and conflicting ideals are possible—that not only can different people have different ideals,
but one person can hold several ideals that unkind fate can force into situations of conflict and competition ("the devoted spouse" and "the successful politician," for example)? Clearly, we have to make a good deal of this.
Many things follow, including at least the following points: that life is complex and difficult; that perfection is not realizable; that lost causes may
claim our allegiance and conflicts of commitment arise; that realism calls
on us to harmonize our ideals even as it requires us to harmonize our other
obligations in working and overall economy of values. It follows, in sum,
that we must make various reciprocal adjustments, harmonizations, and

---

[3] Aldous Huxley, "Inquiry into the Nature of Ideals and the Methods Employed for Their
Realization," in his *Ends and Means* (London: Macmillan, 1937), p. 1.

[4] L. Susan Stebbing, *Ideals and Illusions* (London: Routledge & Kegan Paul, 1948), pp.
132–33.

compromises. But one thing that does not follow is that ideals are some-how illegitimate and inappropriate.

The general principle of having ideals can be defended along the follow-ing lines:

> Q: Why should people have ideals at all?
> A: Because this is something that is efficient and effective in implementing their pursuit of values.
> Q: But why should they care for the pursuit of values?
> A: That is simply a part of being human, and thus subject to the fundamental imperative of realizing one's potential of flourishing as the kind of creature one is.

The validity of having ideals inheres in the condition of man as an amphib-ian who dwells in a world of both facts and values.

Admittedly, ideals cannot be brought to actualization as such. Their very "idealized" nature prevents the arrangements they envision from constituting part of the actual furnishings of the world. But in the sphere of human endeavor we cannot properly explain and understand the reality about us without reference to motivating ideals. The contemplation of what should ideally be is inevitably bound to play an important role in the rational guidance of our actions.

In life, as in effective sharpshooting, we must often aim too high. To attain the achievable limits of the possibilities inherent in our powers and potentialities, we must in fact seek to go beyond them. And just here lies the great importance of the ideal realm. Human action cannot in general be properly understood or adequately managed without a just apprecia-tion of the guiding ideals that lie in the background. For man's interven-tion in the real world sometimes is—and often should be—conditioned by his views of the ideal order in whose direction he finds it appropriate to steer the course of events.

This situation has its paradoxical aspect. Ideals may seem to be other-worldly, or remote from our practical concerns. But in a wider perspec-tive, they are eminently practical, so that their legitimation is ultimately pragmatic. The imperative to ideals has that most practical of all justifica-tions in that it facilitates the prospects of a more satisfying life. Paradoxical though it may seem, this pragmatic line is the most natural and sensible approach to the validation of ideals.

The validation and legitimation of ideals accordingly lie not in their (infeasible) applicability but in their utility for directing our efforts—their productive power in providing direction and structure to our evaluative thought and pragmatic action. It is in their power to move the minds that move mountains that the validation and legitimation of appropriate ideals must ultimately reside.

The "Unrealism" of Ideals

Ideals are visionary, unrealistic, and utopian. But by viewing the world in
the light of their powerful illumination, we see it all the more vividly—
and critically. We understand the true nature of the real better by considering it in the light reflected from ideals, and we use this light to find our
way about more satisfactorily in the real world. The power of ideals lies in
the circumstance that the efficacy of our praxis can be enlarged and en-
hanced by looking beyond the limits of the practicable. Ideals can render
us important service when we "bring them down to earth."

To be sure, our ideals ask too much of us. We cannot attain perfection
in the life of this world—not in the moral life, the life of inquiry, or the
religious life. Authentic faith, comprehensive knowledge, and genuine
morality are all idealizations, or destinations that we cannot actually
reach. They are hyperboles that beckon us ever onward, whose value lies
in their practical utility as a motivating impetus in positive directions.

On this account, ideals, despite their superior and splendid appearance, are actually of a subordinate status in point of justification. They are
not ultimate ends but instrumental means, subservient to the ulterior values whose realization they facilitate. They are indeed important and valuable, but their worth and validity ultimately reside not in their intrinsic
desirability ("wouldn't it be nice if . . .") but in their eminent utility—in
their capacity to guide and to facilitate the cultivation of the values that
they embody.

Such an approach to the issue of legitimating ideals has a curious aspect
in its invocation of practical utility for the validation of our ideals. It maintains that the rational appropriateness of our commitment to an ideal lies
in its practical utility for our dealings with the real through its capacity to
encourage and facilitate our productive efforts. Such an approach does not
adopt a "Platonic" view of ideals that sees them as valuable strictly in their
own right. Rather, their value is seen as instrumental or pragmatic: ideals
arc of value not for their own sake but for ours, because of the good effects
to be achieved by using them as a compass for orienting our thought and
action amid the shoals and narrows of a difficult world, providing guidelines for acting so as to make one's corner of the world a more satisfying
habitat for ourselves and our fellows.

The Grandeur of Ideals

To say that the ultimate legitimation of ideals is pragmatic is not to say that
they are merely practical—that they are somehow crass, mundane, and
bereft of nobilty. By no means! The pragmatic justification of ideals has
effectively no bearing on their nature at all. Their validation may be utili-

tarian, but their inherent character can be transcendent. And so there need be nothing crass or mundane about our ideals as such.

With societies and nations, as with individuals, a balanced vision of the good calls for a proportionate recognition of *the domestic impetus* concerned with the well-being of people, home and hearth, stomach and pocketbook, good fellowship, rewarding work, and so forth. But it also calls for recognition of *the heroic impetus* concerned with acknowledging ideals, making creative achievements, playing a significant role on the world-historical stage, and doing those splendid things upon which posterity looks with admiration. Above all, this latter impetus involves the winning of battles not of the battlefield but of the human mind and spirit. A lack of ideals is bound to impoverish a person or a society. Toward people or nations that have the constituents of material welfare, we may well feel envy, but our admiration and respect could never be won on this ground alone. Excellence must come into it. And in this excellence-connected domain we leave issues of utility behind and enter another sphere—that of human ideals relating to humankind's higher and nobler aspirations.

Homo sapiens is a rational animal. The fact that we are animals squarely emplaces us within the order of nature. But the fact that we are rational delivers us from an absolute rule by external forces. It means that our nature is not wholly given, that we are able to contribute in at least some degree toward making ourselves into the sort of creatures we are. A rational creature is inevitably one that has some capacity to let its idealized vision of what it should be determine what it actually is. It is in this sense that an involvement with ideals is an essential aspect of the human condition.

Conclusion

Their fictional nature accordingly does not destroy the usefulness of ideals. To be sure, we do not—and should not—expect to bring our ideals to actual realization. Yet an ideal is like the Holy Grail of medieval romance: it impels us onward in the journey and gives meaning and direction to our efforts. Rewards of dignity and worth lie in these efforts themselves, irrespective of the question of actual attainment. When appraising people's lives, the question "What did they endeavor?" is no less relevant than the question "What did they achieve?"

The objects at issue in our ideals are not parts of the world's furniture. Like utopias and mythic heroes (or the real-world heroes we redesign in their image by remaking these people into something that never was), ideals are "larger than life." The states of affairs at issue with ideals do not and cannot exist as such. Look about us where we will, we shall not find them actualized. The directive impetus that they give us generally goes under the name of "inspiration." They call to us to bend our efforts toward certain unattainable goals. Yet, though fictions, they are eminently practical fictions. They find their utility not in application to the things of this world but in their bearing upon the thoughts that govern our actions within it. They are not things as such but thought instrumentalities that orient and direct our praxis in the direction of realizing a greater good.

Ideals, though instruments of thought, are not mere myths. For there is nothing false or fictional about ideals as such—only about the idea of their actual embodiment in concrete reality. Their pursuit is something that can be perfectly real and eminently productive. (It is at this pragmatic level that the legitimation of an ideal must ultimately be sought.) Indeed ideals are, if not essential, then eminently useful. For they are major formative components of the value commitments that provide us with guidance for the management of our lives and with yardsticks for the assessment of their meaningfulness.

Still, given the inherent unrealizability of what is at issue, are ideals not indelibly irrational? Here, as elsewhere, we must reckon with the standard gap between aspiration and attainment. In the practical sphere—for example, in craftsmanship or the cultivation of our health—we may strive for perfection, but we cannot ever claim to attain it. Moreover, the situation in inquiry is exactly parallel, as is that in morality or in statesmanship. The cognitive ideal of perfected science stands on the same level as the moral ideal of a perfect agent or the political ideal of a perfect state. The value of such unrealizable ideals lies not in the (unavailable) benefits of attainment but in the benefits that accrue from pursuit. The view that it is rational to pursue an aim only if we are in a position to achieve its attainment or approximation is simply mistaken. As we have seen, an unattainable end can be perfectly valid (and entirely rational) if the indirect benefits of its pursuit are sufficient—if in striving after it, we realize relevant advantages to a substantial degree. An unattainable ideal can be enormously productive. Optimal results are often attainable only by trying for too much—by attempting to reach beyond the limits of the possible.

It seems particularly incongruous to condemn the pursuit of ideals as contrary to rationality. For one thing, rationality is a matter of the intelligent pursuit of appropriate ends, and ideals form part of the framework with reference to which our determinations of appropriateness proceed. No less relevant, however, is the fact that a good case can be made for holding that complete rationality is itself something unrealizable, given the enormously comprehensive nature of what is demanded (e.g., by recourse to the principle of total evidence for rationally constituted belief and action). Neither in matters of thought nor in matters of action can we ever succeed in being totally and completely rational; we have to recognize that perfect rationality is itself an unattainable ideal. And we must be realistic about the extent to which we can implement this ideal amid the harsh realities of a difficult world. Yet even though total rationality is unattainable, its pursuit is nevertheless perfectly rational because of the great benefits that it palpably engenders. It is thus ironic that the thoroughgoing rationality in whose name the adoption of unattainable ends is sometimes condemned itself represents an unattainable ideal whose pursuit is rationally defensible only by pragmatically oriented arguments of the general sort considered here.

To be sure, such a pragmatic validation of ideals leaves untouched the issue of *which* particular values are to prevail. The approach is a general one and thus does not address the justification of particular ideals. It indicates the importance of having some ideals or other, leaving the issue of specific commitments aside. Addressing this issue requires more than an abstract analysis of the nature and function of ideals; it calls for articulating and defending a concrete philosophy of life. Such an issue is beyond the range of our present deliberations.

The fact remains that it is important—and crucially so—for a person to have guiding ideals. A life without ideals need not be a life without purpose, but it will be a life without purposes of a sort in which one can appropriately take reflective satisfaction. The person for whom values matter so little that he or she has no ideals is thereby deprived of guiding beacons to furnish that sense of direction which gives meaning and point to the whole enterprise.

Homo sapiens is an amphibious being who inhabits the realms both of reality and of possibility. And while we must dwell and labor in the one, we always do so with a view toward the other. The person whose wagon is not hitched to some star or other is not a full-formed human being but is less than he or she can and should be. Someone who lacks ideals suffers an impoverishment of spirit for which no other resources can adequately compensate.

Ideals, more than any other single factor, designate us as dual citizens of the world of the "is" and of the "ought"—of the domains of physical existence and that of value. And exactly this *potential* for operating in this second domain makes us humans into that which we *actually* are. Our involvement with ideals accordingly constitutes one of the mainstays for any doctrine of philosophical idealism that stresses the role of values in the shaping of the real.[5]

[5] Some of the ideas of this chapter are developed more fully in the author's *Ethical Idealism* (Berkeley and Los Angeles: University of California Press, 1987).

Eight _____

The Meaning of Life

Insignificance

In the opening passage of an essay on the meaning of life, the contemporary English philosopher David Wiggins assigns this issue to "the class of questions not in good order, or best not answered just as they stand."[1] But however awkward and inconvenient a philosopher may find it to grapple with such questions posed by ordinary people, they cannot in good conscience be avoided.

To be sure, a philosopher must unravel complications. For the question of the meaning of life does have a misleading air of directness about it. The closer one looks at it, the more complicated and many-sided it becomes. In particular, it straightaway admits of four distinctly different interpretations in line with the variant determinations of the schema: "Does ⟨human life at large/a particular individual life⟩ have a ⟨purpose/value⟩?" Its inherent fissures have the consequence that different people approach the issue of life's "meaning" very differently.

Various writers approach the issue from the angle of the question "Does ⟨the existence of⟩ humanity at large have a *purpose*?" and then see the question as resolved through the distinction between life-inherent and life-transcendent purposes. As one recent writer insists, "Claims of [purposive] justification come to an end within life [itself]. . . . No further justification is needed to take aspirin for a headache, [or] attend an exhibition of the work of a painter one admires. . . . No larger context of further purpose is needed to prevent these acts from being fruitless."[2] And this being so with transactions *within* life, it is then held to be true all the more as regards living one's life *as a whole*. In this way, the question of the meaningfulness of life is first viewed in essentially purposive terms and then dismissed as a real difficulty with the observation that living the good life is simply a purpose within itself.

---

[1] David Wiggins, "Truth, Invention, and the Meaning of Life," *Proceedings of the British Academy* 62 (1976), reprinted as essay 3 of his collection *Needs, Values, Truth* (Oxford: Clarendon Press, 1987).

[2] Thomas Nagel, "Absurdity," in *Mortal Questions* (Cambridge: Cambridge University Press, 1979), p. 12.

Again, other theorists, proceeding via the idea that a purpose must be *somebody's* purpose, consider the issue in a theological light. Should we conceive of the existence of humankind to serve some sort of purposive intention on the part of a creator-God? In this way, one recent writer on the subject treats the issue in such a way that "Is life meaningful?" is construed as being tantamount to asking: "Is there room for a personal relationship between human beings and a supernatural perfect being ruling and guiding men?"[3] But this approach of course begs a very large question. Why should it be a relationship with *God* that is needed to make life meaningful?[4] Why should a relationship to "the world at large" or "other people" or perhaps even simply to our own selves not be sufficient?

In deliberating about the meaning of life, one must also be careful to distinguish the question "Does life have *value?*" from the question "Does life have a *purpose?*" For purpose is end oriented; it is generally a matter of the realization of extrinsic aims or objectives—ones that lie outside and beyond the particular factor that is at issue. But value is frequently intrinsic and internal to its bearer rather than being geared to the realization of some ulterior end. Valuing is something different from—and larger than—purposing. No doubt our purposes involve something we value, but our values themselves need not be inherently purposive. One can quite appropriately prize a sunset or a poem or a baby as being something good, something of value in itself, without raising the instrumentalistic issue of purposes, of what beyond and outside of itself it is good for. And this holds true for life as well. A life can be meaningful for its bearer without serving a further purpose of some sort.

In the light of this distinction, it is clear that the issue that is on the minds of ordinary people when they wonder or speculate about the meaning of life seems generally to be best represented by the question "Does human life have a value?"[5] And a widely held point of view—particularly

[3] Kurt E. Baier, *The Meaning of Life* (Canberra: University of Canberra Press, 1957; Inaugural Lecture, Canberra University College), introductory section, *ad fin.*

[4] In Dostoevsky's novel *The Possessed*, Kirlov commits suicide because he thinks that when one no longer has faith in the existence of God, one's life loses all point and should be ended. But while this is thinking, it is clearly quite foolish thinking. Again, in the article cited above, Wiggins cites Wolfgang Amadeus Mozart's rather elitist claim that "we live in this world to compel ourselves industriously to enlighten one another . . . and to apply ourselves always to carrying forward the sciences and the arts." According to Wiggins, this claim is based on "the now (I think) almost unattainable conviction that there exists a God whose purpose ordains certain specific duties for all men." But Mozart does not say word one about God. And it is surely problematic to say that a claim that *might* have a certain basis *must* have this basis.

[5] Among recent writers, Robert Nozick sees this point most clearly. He writes: "Meaning involves transcending limits so as to connect with something valuable; meaning is a transcending of the limits of your own value, a transcending of your own limited value. Meaning is a connection with an external value" (*Philosophical Explanations*, p. 610).

popular among philosophers of a naturalistic orientation—accordingly focuses on the insignificance of people. "The life of a man," David Hume
wrote, "is of no greater importance to the universe than that of an oyster."[6]
Bertrand Russell suggested that, amour propre apart, there is no good
reason for seeing us humans as superior to the amoeba.[7] And clearly there
is some justice to such a perspective. In nature's vast cosmic scheme of
things we humans are to all appearances cast in the distinctly minor role
of an insignificant member of an insignificant species. On the astronomical
scale, we are no more than obscure inhabitants of an obscure planet.
Nothing we are or do on our tiny sphere of action within the world's vast
reaches of space and time makes any substantial difference in the world's
large and long run. The glories that were Greece and the grandeur that
was Rome have pretty much melted away with the snows of yesteryear.
Perhaps the proverb exaggerates in claiming that, regardless of what we
ourselves do, "It will all be the same one hundred years hence." But eventually, the last trace of our feeble human efforts will certainly vanish under
the all-consuming ravages of time.

There is in fact much justification for letting a sense of futility and
worthlessness pervade our thinking about our own personal place in the
world. It is not implausible to say that we just don't count—that nothing
we do really matters in the world's grand scheme. Space is frighteningly
large, time awesomely long, causality the interplay of impersonal forces.
The world as modern science portrays it is not a very friendly place. Even
here on earth, nature is red in tooth and claw all about us. And people
themselves are all too often a frightening mixture of phobias and neuroses,
with *Homo sapiens* as their own worst enemy, ever ready to destroy the
good things that somehow manage to emerge.

Still, this is hardly the end of the matter.

Making a Difference

The issue that people generally have in mind in posing the question of
"the meaning of life" is, in this light, best construed as an *evaluative* question: Given the imperfection of man and the impermanence of his achievements, and given our insignificance in the larger cosmic scheme of things,

---

[6] "Of Suicide," in *Essays Moral, Political, and Literary*, ed. E. F. Miller (Indianapolis:
Liberty Fund, 1985). One wonders how the universe informed Hume of this conclusion.

[7] Bertrand Russell, "Current Tendencies," in *Our Knowledge of the External World* (London: Allen & Unwyn, 1923): "A process which led from the amoeba to man appeared to the
philosophers to be obviously a progress—though whether the amoeba would agree with this
opinion is not known." But surely a not insignificant consideration here is that the amoeba is
not in a position to agree or disagree with anything!

just exactly what is the point of our existence? *Does it really make any difference what we do with our lives?* That, in general terms, is the core question: Does what we do really matter?

But matter to whom? A spectrum of ever-widening possibilities opens up here: ourselves, our near and dear ones, our environing group (co-workers, countrymen), our nation or civilization, our species, intelligent beings in general (those on other planets potentially included), reality at large (the universe), the world spirit (or God). Right from the start, one must resist the temptation to think that what we do only *really* matters if it matters at the bottom end of this series. One must reject the terrible and profound delusion that making a *real* difference requires making a *big* difference. Size and scale are surely not the only appropriate measures of significance. When something matters even only locally—merely for ourselves—that too endows it with a perfectly appropriate value and importance of its own. What is central to the issue of the meaning of life is whether what we do can and does really matter—not necessarily to God or to the universe but to ourselves. It is clearly just this—namely, mattering for us—that counts *for us*, since that is who we are.

The crucial point for meaningfulness, then, is not making a *big* difference but making a *real* difference. And the crux here is setting high standards for oneself and effecting one's emotions in terms of the impersonal criteria provided by those standards. For then the worth of what we do in our sphere of agency and action is something that, however "parochial," is there objectively for all to see. The reason for looking to objective standards to indicate the meaningfulness of life is not that one's existence needs the approval of others—and not even of God—but to ascertain that approval (valuing) by anybody, onself included, is in order (i.e., is appropriate). And the standard by which we must surely judge the value of life is not somebody's subjectively grounded idiosyncratic opinions but the objective question of whether living affects a prospect for realizing the good things acknowledged as such by all sensible people.[8] A life that is satisfying for oneself and constructive vis-à-vis others is of value by virtue of these very facts. And this circumstance, which doubtless does matter to its bearer, should also matter to the rest of us who stand by as observers. It has a meaning that is there for anyone to read. Clearly a life's value for its bearer and its value in its wider context are simply components of its value at large, and it is exactly this that is at issue in assessing the overall meaningfulness of a life. In considering the meaning of life, the pivot point is the matter of its value—that is, its value in general, which includes, but also is of larger scope than, the satisfactions it affords its particular bearer.

---

[8] What sort of good things? There are clearly many of them: happiness, creativity, morality, and so on.

Man a Machine?

But does this sort of evaluative appreciation really suffice to render life meaningful? Is the worth of human life not decisively undermined by the unfolding progress of science—by the ongoing process of discovering that *Homo sapiens* is merely a machine, a mere mechanism, albeit one of nature rather than artifice?

In 1748, Julien Offray de la Mettrie published in Leiden his startling treatise *L'Homme machine* (*Man a Machine*), giving vivid expression to the stark naturalism that culminated the intellectual ethos of this iconoclastic era. De la Mettrie's view may have looked foolish at a time when the most complicated machines were clockworks and windmills, but it certainly seems far less so in the present era of electronic "thinking machines" programmed to display "artificial intelligence." Perhaps, then, man is no more than a machine?

The shock effect of the idea of man's being a machine lies in the very fallacious impression that this circumstance would somehow *change* what man in fact is. For we incline to think that this would mean that man would thereby be devalued, that human life would then cease to be significant. But how does this follow? If one accepts that someone's body consists of chemical elements—mainly water—whose market value is but a few dollars, does that have any implications for his value as a *person*? Why should it? The closer one looks, the less apparent is the reason.

People sometimes feel themselves threatened by a line of argumentation along the lines of the following reasoning:

Man is a machine.
Machines cannot do X (have feelings, have free will, etc.).

Therefore: Man does not do X (have feelings, have free will, etc.).

But to maintain the second premise is in effect to beg the question once the first is asserted. All we can say is that *typical* machines do not behave in this way. But a human being, indeed if a machine, is certainly not a typical machine. The shock value of claiming that people are machines comes from the circumstance that it is all too easy to make the fallacious leap from the contention "man is a machine" to the conclusion "man is a *typical* machine." But of course this no more follows than there follows from the prosaic "man is an animal" the far-fetched conclusion "man is a *typical* animal."

Dictionaries generally define "machine" in such terms as "a mechical or electronically operated device designed for performing a predesignated task." Given this sort of specification, human beings and animals are obviously not machines. But this finding is not particularly interesting for the discussion because it rests the issue on a prejudicial formulation that rules out from the very start any prospect of considering the idea that one might be a machine. Such verbal force majeure apart, the question remains: *is* man a machine, albeit an organic, biological one, rather than a mechanical, artifactual one?

To pursue this question intelligently would in the first instance require a pretty exact specification of just exactly what "a machine" is. And this is certainly not easy to come by. The breathtaking modern development in the capacities and complexities of "thinking machines" that makes it possible to contemplate man's being a machine without ludicrous incongruity have also cost us any secure intellectual grasp on just what it is to be a machine. Nobody has yet provided a clear and cogent explanation of just exactly what is to count as "a machine" in the current scheme of things. In the absence of such an explanation, the question "Is man a machine?" poses an imponderable issue.

But even if it were to turn out in the end to be appropriate to categorize man as a machine, this eventuation would flatly fail to dehumanize us. If man indeed is a machine, then it is certainly a very peculiar one—one that is organic, intelligent, capable of feeling, suffering, loving, and so forth. If man is a machine, then machines can do some pretty non-machine-like things. The result would be to revolutionize not just our ordinary idea of man but our ordinary idea of machine as well.

Yet if man were a machine, would that not mean that man has no soul? Well . . . would it? What is "a soul" anyway? Clearly it is not some sort of physical component of one's body—like a kidney or liver. Soul is not a thing but a process cluster, a mode of action. Presumably a human soul *is* what it *does*—its being resides in the human capacity to think, feel, aspire, love, and the like. Thus even if man were a machine, this would not mean that people lack souls. On the contrary, the consequence would simply be that machines can have souls. If the being of a soul lies in what an ensouled creature can do, then should machines be able to do what people can, they too will have souls. If man indeed were a machine, the net effect would not be to dehumanize man but to produce a drastic change in our understanding of the nature of machines by effectively humanizing at least some of them.

Sometimes theorists try to bend the issue into other shapes; for example, might human beings be made artificially, somehow be synthesized in a laboratory? Even if this could be done, it would not show we are machines. It would simply go to show that the range of things that one can make in a laboratory includes not only chemicals and machines but also (perhaps more surprisingly) people.

To summarize: There is no particularly good reason to think that we humans indeed are simply machines. But even if we were, we would be machines of an unusual sort (things that are, in principle, by no means theoretically impossible), namely, machines endowed with free will, machines not designed and programmed by other agents but actually evolved in a way that puts them themselves in charge of what they do. Man's being a machine would not downgrade the value of human life but could be bound to revolutionize our view of machines.

Free Will

But can we really qualify as responsible agents who are indeed in charge of our actions? For what of the dread prospect that we are mere automata in that our will is not free and everything we do is merely the result of the play of natural forces beyond our control?

People who deny free will generally proceed on the basis of contemplating a physical order of natural process that determines all the world's events, human actions included, through the operation of impersonal causes. On this basis, they launch upon the following plausible argumentation:

Whatever people do falls within the scope of laws of nature.

Actions falling within the scope of laws of nature are for this very reason necessitated in nature's impersonal order and are accordingly not free.

Therefore: Everything people do is determined by a causal necessitation operating independently of the wishes and choices of human agents.

On this view, our actions are every bit of as much necessitated by the impersonal forces of nature as is the downhill flow of water or the motion of a billiard ball. They only seem to be governed by our choices and decisions; in fact they are the product of an impersonal necessity that works in and through our bodies.

This familiar line of reasoning is seriously flawed, however. To have free will is in the first instance to be in a position to act from motives, goals, and values that one has—to have one's actions proceed from the "motivational" sectors of one's thinking via one's own decisions and choices. It is a matter of the "inner," thought-embedded determination of what one does, and not a matter of the severance of one's actions from any and all determinations whatsoever. A free act is not one that is free of all determination but one free of determination of a certain particular sort, namely, from determiners that operate "externally" in total detachment from one's own wants, preferences, wishes, and the like. Its agent "could have done otherwise" all right, but only if the agent's choices and decisions had been different—which itself could have happened only if his or her values, goals, and decisions had been different. Where our "free acts are concerned," no explanation in the order of causal determination can be at once adequate and factor the agent out of it. That second premise is accordingly false.

But is the capacity to implement one's own agenda—to act on the basis of one's own feelings, wishes, desires, preferences, and the like—really enough to render one a free agent? For what if one's agenda of choice and decision is itself set by factors beyond one's control? Then everything hinges on the *nature* of that "external" determination, on the sort of mechanism at issue. In particular, if this is a matter of manipulation by an external controller, by rendering one's own putative decisions subject to the will of another, then the matter stands very ill for freedom.

Freedom of action consists in being in operative control of one's doings. It is a matter of autonomy, of independence of other wills—of hinging on one's own choices, preferences, wishes, and so forth and being able to function independently of the choices, wishes, and so on of other agents. Freedom pivots on an agent's independence of other *agents* and their machinations—not on an independence of operative *causes*. After all, all of us—free agents included—are part of the world's fabric of lawful operation, and everything we do is to this extent conditioned and conceivably even "determined" by factors of nature and nurture over which we have no control. But this sort of impersonal "determination" has nothing to do with freedom of the will. For what is crucial here is simply the matter of a determination by other wills or by constraints upon the agent's will that operates wholly from without, without reference to that will itself. What freedom precludes is a causality that bypasses the will of the agent— either because it involves no wills at all (i.e., no decisions, preferences, choices, etc. of anybody's, oneself included) or because it involves only those of other agents. Freedom, in sum, is not at odds with determination as such, but only with agent-bypassing determination.

We return at this point to deliberations in chapter 6 about the nature of persons. To be a person, one must be able to act freely—one must have "free will." And this certainly does not mean that there would cease to be any persons if it turned out that the world is altogether a theater of materialistic/deterministic causal processes. For it is no determination as such that precludes freedom, but the determination of factors other than those internal to the agent's desires, wishes, preferences, and so forth. If there were an "inner determinism"—if an agent's actions were the causal product of the operation of its own materialistic brain—then the causal condition of effective control over one's own actions would still be satisfied. The freedom at issue is not freedom from any and all determination but freedom from *external* control—which is compatible with an internally rooted determinism via an agent's own motives and "states of mind." The crux of the moral autonomy at issue in personhood is that an adequate understanding and explanation of the agent's actions requires making a refer-

ence to the thought processes that reflect their motivational orientation.
And the crucial fact for present purposes is that our standard normality-
geared approach to the world we live in enables us to put aside the para-
noia of worriment about "us-bypassing" external manipulative agents (deceiving demons, wicked all-powerful scientists, and the like). We are free
rational agents because we see ourselves in this light, accept one another
as such, and have no earthly reason to think that the world's realities are
at odds with these policies of ours.

We thus arrive at a version of the sensible doctrine of "compati-
bilism"—that freedom of the will is compatible with a softened determinism in the order of natural processes, because "freedom" is not a matter of
exemption from causal determinism but itself involves a determination
of sorts, namely, one in which those "events" represented by decisions, choices, and so forth and those "dispositions" involved in wishes,
preferences, and so on are crucial for the adequate explanation of human
actions. A freedom of acting and a determinism of acts are simply not
mutually exclusive contraries. In principle, an action can be at once determined *and* free, as long as the pattern of determination maintains its linkage to the wishes and choices of the agent.

Does Science Destroy Value?

All the same, if the world is more or less as physical science nowadays
depicts it, does this not deprive life of meaning and value? Does the world
picture of science not abolish any room for value in the world's scheme
of things?

But how could it possibly do so? Physical science tells us a *causal* story;
it describes the mechanics of how things work in the world—their physical
makeup and the processes that make them tick. But this does not undermine the value of life because it does not address questions of value at all.
The sound of a violin may be no more than the play of air waves caused by
the vibration of dried catgut. Yet this is simply irrelevant to the beauty or
cacophony of the music. What matters for value is not the causal dimension of process but the experiential dimension of product as it bears upon
the lives of sentient and intelligent beings. The issue of the meaningfulness of life is a value question, which is something that science does not
affect in any negative way. Science is not and cannot be at odds with value
because the questions of valuation are ones that it does not address at all.

In the final anaylsis, science as such has to leave the world's values as it
finds them—its mission is to characterize and explain the real, not to destroy it. In accounting for how it is that people go about valuing things, it
does not show that value is somehow unreal—any more than in explaining

color vision, science shows that color is somehow unreal. Value attributions like color attributions are rooted in experience. And while science can presumably explain experience, it does not and indeed cannot thereby show that it is somehow unreal or insignificant.

Explanation and evaluation are different and distinct matters. On the one hand, we deal with information; on the other, with appreciation. Different dimensions of experience are at issue. And it is this difference of thematic dimension that averts any prospect of a clash. There is no reason of principle why we cannot validate value judgments in a world constituted as the science of the day maintains—and this includes judgments about the value of life itself.

Activism

But value claims, if validatable at all, can be validated only with reference to experience. And how does experience bear on the vindication of values?

One can, in theory, see the crux of evaluation to lie in:

What pleases me?
What suits my purposes (ends, goals)?
What can I appropriately deem for the best with reference to:
    my own interests,
    the interests of others, and
    the good of "the great scheme of things"?

It is clear that an evaluative validation of life's meaningfulness will require moving well down the preceding list. The standard for proper valuation in this context will have to be something larger than oneself, one's wishes, one's interests. What makes one's life meaningful is not simply a matter of one's own egocentric benefits, wishes, or interests. More is involved than any merely subjective frame of reference; that "larger scheme of things" does indeed come into it.

Cosmic history is a process of development. Chemical elements and their properties and modes of behavior were not yet present in the first microseconds after the big bang. Astronomical objects (stars, planets, and the like) took much longer to develop. And life took longer yet. Intelligent beings with their goals, purposes, and values came even later. These last sorts of things are doubtless latercomers in the course of value's evolution. But the fact remains that with the emergence of intelligent agents, they are indeed there—not as given but as developed. And with their emergence purposeful action and rational evaluation came to be possible in a heretofore purposeless and value-free cosmos. Intelligent life

can and does have a meaning because value emerges with the emergence
of intelligence.

The meaningfulness of life lies in its affording us the opportunity of
making a difference—a positive contribution to the totality of realized
value. A life is rendered meaningful through the promotion of values, the
fostering of the good on however small a scale. Nothing grand need be at
issue; rather, even mundane things can in this context achieve the level of
grandeur: being a good friend or a good neighbor or a good companion, for
example. It becomes something positive through the furtherance to the
best of one's efforts—however ineffectual—of the values that people appropriately hold dear. What ultimately renders life meaningful is not the
"pursuit of happiness" but the "pursuit of value."

Some modicum of yearning for something "larger than life"—for transcendent goods and values to endow one's life with a value beyond itself—
is an essential aspect of the makeup of an intelligent agent. The central
thesis of Miguel de Unamuno's 1913 classic *Del sentimiento trágico de la
vida* was wrong. The ultimate evil for man is not the eventual death that
inheres our mortality—the inescapable prospect of the termination of
one's personal self. It is not death we fear as much as meaninglessness and
pointlessness. Death is merely the ending of our own lives, and this concerns itself with merely one value among others; meaninglessness, by
contrast, could spell the extinction of value as such. Bad though death may
be, there thus looms the threat of something far worse. The annihilation
of everything we value and prize and stand for is the ultimate evil. It is not
so much personal survival that we yearn for as vindication or validation—
the sense that our efforts need not be wholly in vain and all our endeavors
in life an exercise in futility. Precisely because true "self-actualization" is
a matter of striving for the best, what ultimately counts for us is not so
much the survival of our selves as the survival of our *values*.

Defeat does not come to the life of an individual through death. Things
being as they are, death is inevitable and itself forms an integral part of
human life. Nor does defeat come through a failure to achieve success—
for this, in large measure, is something fortuitous, something outside the
range of our control. Defeat and failure in life are always something self-
inflicted—the willful persistence in that most sorry of all human failings,
the failure to try to make something of ourselves through the endeavor to
contribute to the world's ever-insufficient stock of the good. And the price
of failure is the stark dilemma between inhumanity on the one side and
undergoing a deserved dissatisfaction with oneself on the other—the realization of some deeper level of thought that one has failed as a human
being, that one has conducted one's life in a way that the rational side of
one's being will not allow oneself to approve of. For we suffer a small
defeat in life with each failure to harmonize action and evaluation, each

time we do something we cannot in our heart of hearts approve of. A life in which such small defeats becomes massive, prevailing, and predominant is a life whose bearer stands self-condemned to utter failure.

Every person who is not totally incapacitated, who retains some capacity for agency at all, has the possibility of acting for the good in some small way at least—of doing the better instead of the worse. Every such life therefore is potentially of value as an agent for enlarging the world's stock of good. Human life *is* of value because it affords us the chance to promote value within the world's scheme of things.

At this point there is no reason for being intimidated by a sense of impotence. For the crucial issue here is that of what sorts of people we make of ourselves—an issue for which endeavor counts every bit as much as accomplishment—is something that lies wholly in our own control. The crux resides in this matter of striving to make the best of ourselves—of self-optimization. Value is self-engendering. Our lives become the bearers of value through the very fact of their affording us an opportunity to endeavor to make them valuable.

"Does life have meaning?" is thus not a question of the same sort as "Does Brazil have petroleum deposits?" We are not going to resolve it by some sort of observational search. It is going to take theoretical reflection. The issue ultimately comes down to this: "Can we make better sense than we otherwise could of the world and of our lives within it by proceeding on the supposition that human life can be a thing of value?" And interestingly enough, this issue of valuation is—in significant measure—a self-fulfilling one. We can endow life with meaning and value in the course of proceeding on the supposition that these things belong there. "Is life meaningful?" is a question somewhat like "Are people friendly?" Even as we can render people friendly only by viewing and treating them as friends, so we can render life meaningful only by and treating it as such.

Life can be *made* meaningful by living the sort of life that any sensible person would find meaningful through its involvement with the realization of values—a sort that will include many instances! The crux is that life has meaning because the human person is itself an item of value—a worth that in turn is determined by what people can do, namely: understand, act, and aspire. People can themselves assure the meaning of life through the cultivation of rationally merited self-respect. By living our lives in a certain way, we can manage to make them into things of value.[9]

---

[9] Note, however, that life is not made meaningful by mastering formulas, by learning and subscribing to claims on the order of "The meaning of life is . . ." It is one thing to recognize that a certain sort of life has value—a "full and productive" life, say, or a life "dedicated to the service of others." It is a very different sort of thing to *live* such a life.

The "humanistic existentialists" are right in this regard, at least, that the question of the meaning of life is ultimately not a matter of finding meaning in life but one of making life meaningful—of endeavoring to live our lives in such a way that a reasonable person can appropriately see them as meaningful. The question "Does life have meaning?" ultimately comes down to: "Do I have the possibility of living the sort of life that is meaningful in my own sight when I take the trouble to view the matter rationally?" The real issue is this: Can we make ourselves into the kind of person whose life can plausibly be deemed a bearer of value by anyone— ourselves included—who uses standards that reasonably qualify as appropriate?

Human life at large has a meaning precisely because individual lives can be of value in affording their bearers an opportunity for the achievement or furtherance of good results. Whether one succeeds or fails in one's efforts, one can at least *try* to promote the realization of values. And just herein—in the possiblity of effort, of aspiration and struggle, achievement and failure—lies the values and thus the meaningfulness of human existence. It is, ultimately, not in humanity's *achievements* that the value of life resides, but in its irrepressible determination to exert its *efforts* in the endeavor to avert nothingness.[10]

[10] It is impossible to write sensibly on this subject without sounding preachy. Contemporary philosophers seem to want to have it both ways. Witness David Wiggins, who informs us in the closing passage of his above-cited discussion that the account he advocates would accommodate "the insight that to see a point in living someone has to be such that he can like himself" and shortly thereafter quotes with enthusiam F. H. Bradley's obiter dictum: "If to show theoretical interest in morality and religion is taken as setting oneself up as a teacher or preacher, I would rather leave these subjects to whoever feels that such a role suits him." Philosophers, like other folk, like to have their cake and eat it too. (The theme of this chapter is also treated in the author's *Human Interests*.)

Part IV

VALUES AND MORALITY

Nine _____

Optimism and Pessimism

Modes of Optimism

One's evaluative stance regarding the position of humanity in the world's scheme of things is one of the most characteristic and informative aspects of a person's makeup. In this connection, the quarrel between optimism and pessimism has been raging since classical antiquity. Following the lead of the Socrates of Plato's *Timaeus*, the Stoics taught that the world's arrangements are designed for the best and promote the good of all.[1] The followers of Hegesias maintained to the contrary that nature is fundamentally unfriendly and so operates as to make the attainment of well-being (*eudaimonia*) impossible for us.[2] The two conflicting tendencies have opposed each other since the dawn of philosophical thought.

Optimism pivots on the contention that things are well with the world, that its arrangements are on balance for the good. But such a view can take very different specific forms, depending on whether it is maintained that the condition of things is

presently in good order; or

tending toward the good—that in the natural course of events, matters will continue to assume a better condition; or

movable toward the good—that matters can indeed be impelled in this direction, provided that we do the right things to bring this about.

Three quite different questions are at issue: how things are, whither they tend, and what opportunities are open. When these questions are answered favorably, we may call the three resultant positions *actuality* optimism, *tendency* optimism, and *prospect* optimism, respectively.

Actuality optimism takes the stance that things stand in good condition—that, on the whole, all is right with the world in the prevailing order of things. Such a position is usually (but not necessarily) bound up with commitment to the benevolence of a presiding deity. This view was

---

[1] For a compact account of the Stoic position, see P. P. Hallie, "Stoicism," in *The Encyclopedia of Philosophy*, ed. P. Edwards (New York: Free Press, 1967), 8:18–22. Regarding the Stoic metaphysics of nature, see S. Sambursky, *Physics of the Stoics* (London: Routledge, 1959).

[2] Diogenes Laertius, *Lives of the Philosophers* 2, sec. 94.

already voiced by Plato, who maintained, "Since he judged that order was in every way for the better, God brought it [the world] from disorder into order."[3]

Tendency optimism, also called *meliorism*, is something very different from actuality optimism. It does not necessarily hold that all is well with the world as is; it simply takes the stance that things are getting better.[4] It compares the present with the relevant future and envisions an improvement in the confident conviction that, whatever might be happening now, better times lie ahead. (However, since improvement as such is at issue, the amelioration at issue could in principle merely be a change from terrible to bad, rather than one from good to even better.)

Prospect optimism compares the present as it stands with the prospective future that our efforts and opportunities put at our disposal. It looks to the presumably realizable future and maintains that suitable actions on our part can pave the way to improvement. (By contrast, the belief that things will deteriorate despite our best efforts to the contrary, represents a tendency pessimism.) Both meliorism (tendency optimism) and prospect optimism are oriented toward the future. But tendency optimism holds matters *will* get better of their own accord, while prospect optimism holds they *can* get better if only we manage to do the right things.

Optimism in all its forms is indissolubly linked to the dimension of value. All the various modes of optimism are *evaluative* positions that contemplate some manner of goodness:

> Actuality optimism: things *are* in good condition.
> Tendency optimism: things *are moving* toward the better.
> Prospect optimism: things *are movable* toward the better.

Optimism is accordingly a general evaluative position about "the state of things" at large. To be sure, people also speak of "being optimistic" about the favorable outcome of a *particular* situation or episode—the expectation that all will turn out well in a particular case, such as the marriage of John and Mary. But optimism as such is a doctrine that operates at the level of generality, rather than restricting itself to such episodic expectations with respect to individual outcomes. The single-case "optimism" of the gambler who, presumably in the face of considerable counterevidence, thinks that he is bound to win *this* time, or of the drunkard who thinks that *this* bottle will engender no unfortunate results, lies outside the range of the present discussion.

---

[3] *Timaeus* 30A.

[4] Think, for example, of Immanuel Kant's discussion in the *Streit der Fakultäten* of the—as he sees it unsubstantiable—choice between the "eudaimonistic" hypothesis that humanity is continually improving, the "terroristic" hypothesis that it is constantly degenerating, and the "abderitic" hypothesis that it is oscillating randomly between these two conditions (see *Gesammelt Schriften*, vol. 8 [Berlin: George Reimer, 1917], pp. 81–82).

Parameters of Optimism

Four questions can be always raised with respect to any sort of optimism:

What things are being held to be good/improving/improvable?
What manner of "goodness" is at issue: *in what way* is something to be good or better?
Just *how* good, or *how much* better?
Good or better *for whom?*

These four basic questions reflect, respectively, the *range*, the *mode*, the *degree*, and the envisioned *beneficiaries* of the optimism at issue. By varying these factors, we can obtain, for example, such melioristic theses as "The life expectancy of infants is getting somewhat longer," "Hospital patients are receiving ever more effective care," or "The quality of life is improving for citizens of technically advanced societies."[5]

Different kinds of optimism thus arise from variation in the four basic parameters. With respect to range and mode this is clear enough. The issue of beneficiaries in particular opens up much scope. We have the prospect that those at issue are:

me – oneself (egocentric optimism),
we – our group (parochial optimism),
many or most people (general optimism),
everyone (universal optimism).

The relative inclusiveness of the group of contemplated beneficiaries will determine the scope or scale of the optimism at issue. Of course, the fact that we ourselves can plausibly see improved conditions in the light of *optimism* will hinge crucially on our stance toward the group of beneficiaries—in particular on the question of whether we can identify with them in taking their interests to heart. If the beneficiaries were people whom we wish ill, the prospect of improvement in their lot would hardly represent an optimistic view.

The degree-oriented question "*How much* good or better?" also leads to considerable variation. Let us suppose the following evaluation scale:

G*: as good as can be
G + : very good
G: good
0: indifferent

---

[5] A technological optimism to the effect that modern science and technology will create the conditions of a new social order became very popular in the Soviet Union under the influence of Friedrich Engels. Cf. Boris G. Kuznetsov, *Philosophy of Optimism* (Moscow: Progress Publishers, 1977), which, despite its title, offers little of philosophical substance.

B: bad
B–: very bad
B*: as bad as can be

Given such a spectrum, there are bound to be substantially different varieties of optimism—and, in particular, very different sorts of meliorism. A movement from G to G* is one thing, one from B* to B quite another. It is tempting to think that optimism is a matter of going "from good to better," and pessimism one of going "from bad to worse." But this is a grave oversimplification that takes one prominent case as representative of the whole.

Again, optimism is sometimes characterized as the view that "good will ultimately prevail over evil." But this too is a very special form of the doctrine. Consider a society populated by three groups of people, whose condition is viewed by a certain theory as subject to the course of change set out in display 9.1. This theory is surely optimistic, since things are getting substantially better for all three groups. All the same, we do not have a condition where the good ultimately predominates: in the end, the various groups still occupy a condition substantially less than good.

Display 9.1. A Hypothetical Course of Change

Group No.	Average Initial Condition	Average Final Condition
1	B	0
2	B–	B
3	B*	B–

Different Constructions of Actuality Optimism

Let us consider actuality optimism somewhat more closely. Markedly diverse versions result with varying positions regarding the status of negativity:

1. *Absolute optimism.* Everything is literally for the best. All negativity is only seemingly such. Anything bad is, even at worst, only a lack of imperfection—a shortfall of the good. Negativity (badness, evil) is in fact nothing substantial as such; everything there is, is good, though perhaps in varying degrees.

2. *Instrumentalistic optimism.* There is actual evil and negativity, but whenever present, it serves as a causal means to a greater good. There is always a chain of causes and effects through which any evil is ultimately productive of a

predominating good. All those clouds have silver linings: any item of negativity is in fact a causally productive means operating toward augmenting the good. The bads of the world are causally necessary conditions for the realization of greater goods.

3. *Compensatory optimism.* There indeed is evil and negativity, and it is not always causally productive of a predominating good—not in every case simply a means causally conducive to a greater good in just exactly that same causal locality. But at the overall, collective level, the good outweighs the bad. The world is a systematic whole of interlocking elements, and matters are so arranged that a preponderant good always compensates for the presence of evil. The good and the bad stand in a relationship of systemic interconnection: evil is an integral and irremovable part of a holistic world order that embodies a greater good.

Very different things are at issue here. With (1) we have a "blind" optimism that refuses to see negativity as something real. With (2) we have a theory of causal facilitation that acknowledges the reality of negativity but sees it as a means to greater good. With (3) we have a theory of compensation that sees negativity outweighed by a coordinated positivity in the world's overall systemic arrangements.

Some historical observations are in order. It would seem that (1) has not been squarely held by any (Western) philosopher since the Neoplatonism of classical antiquity—mystics and spiritualists aside.[6] The position is clearly at odds with the standard Christian view of the Fall of man, and to find its more common expression, we must turn to the Oriental religions, which see the phenomenal world with all its evils as maya, or illusion. Voltaire's Dr. Pangloss—that supposed parody of Leibniz—who sometimes talks in the manner of (1), comes closer to holding (2). But Leibniz himself, who sometimes talks in the instrumentalistic manner of (2) in his *Theodicy,* actually holds the compensatory version at issue in (3). Accordingly, Voltaire's parody of the bad-will-lead-to-good idea in *Candide* does not really hit its target, Leibniz.

A theory that denies the existence of the bad only because it also denies the existence of good within the context of a comprehensive denial of all value in the world's arrangements—in short, a Spinozistic negation of objective value—cannot be called a form of optimism. It falls outside the optimism-pessimism spectrum and is at odds with it in precluding any sort of evaluative stance toward the world's scheme of things. (This is, quite by design, a profoundly antihumanistic philosophy.)

---

[6] Mary Baker Eddy wrote that "evil is but an illusion, and it has no real basis. Evil is a false belief" (*Science and Health,* authorized ed. [Boston: Christian Science Publications, 1934], p. 480, secs. 23–24).

Tendency Optimism (Meliorism, or Progressivism)

Tendency optimism (meliorism) is not a single theory but a madding crowd of theories of the most diverse kinds, with little in common except their generic structure: things of some sort are getting better in some way or other for certain beneficiaries. In particular, when these beneficiaries are people in general, then a melioristic position represents a doctrine that sees the world's arrangements as fundamentally favorable to human interests generally.

Meliorism in all of its versions constitutes a substantive doctrine about the nature of the world and its course of events. Once a standard of good and bad is given, it represents a factual thesis to the effect that a course of change of a certain sort is under way and is, accordingly, matter-of-factly true or false. This is illustrated by what is perhaps the most usual and familiar form of meliorism, that based on the following parameter determinations:

range: conditions of life ("quality of life");
mode: qualitative improvement;
degree: from bad (B) to very good (G +);
beneficiaries: humankind at large.

The resulting melioristic thesis maintains that the quality of life is getting ever better for people at large and is moving toward a generally good condition. Once we are informed about how this matter of "quality of life" is to be assessed, the thesis becomes a straightforward factual one that turns on how matters actually stand on the world's stage.

But while such a melioristic view is clearly factual in character, the fact at issue is patently *evaluative*. Meliorative optimism stakes a claim that can be understood (and substantiated) only with respect to a suitable standard of value to provide the necessary yardstick of evaluation. It is a substantive doctrine that is predicated on an essentially normative basis.

With any mode of meliorism, the question of pace of improvement will always arise. When things are held to be getting better and better, the issue of velocity looms—a snail's pace versus an avalanchelike rush. Moreover, any meliorism that looks to a coming improvement leaves open the question of just when this transformation will come about—whether soon or in the impenetrable fog of a future "eventually." If we look optimistically with Peirce to a cognitive victory of science over nature or with Marx to the political triumph of proletarian power, there yet remains the crucial issue of just when this happy eventuation is to be realized. With eschatological meliorism, as with doomsday theologies, that all-important question of timing is always there.

Meliorism is indissolubly linked to the idea of progress: any theory of progress is a mode of meliorism, and, conversely, any meliorism a progressivism. For progress necessarily involves something more than mere change—namely, improvement—since progress is change in some positively evaluated direction, encompassing a sequence of events in whose course things are "getting better" in some fashion or other. Accordingly, there will be as many distinct types of meliorism as there are types of progress. Very different sorts of "courses of ongoing improvement" can be contemplated: material, intellectual, social, moral, and the like. The complexity and diversity of meliorism come to the fore in this connection. The same range of questions that apply to meliorism in general will apply to a progressivism of any sort: how fast, how far, how distributed, and so forth.

The distributional aspects of meliorism are of particular interest. Suppose an evaluative scale ranging from 0 to 100, a hedonic scale, say, or a scale of *quality of life*, or some such—the details do not matter as long as we are operating in a context where "bigger is better." Consider now two very different situations:

Case 1: The average gets bigger and bigger, but the minimum gets ever less.

Year 1: 90 percent of the time at 90, 10 percent at 20;

Year 2: 90 percent of the time at 95, 10 percent at 10;

Year n: 90 percent of the time at halfway between the preceding year's 90-percent value and 100; 10 percent of the time at halfway between the preceding year's 10-percent value and 0.

Case 2: The average gets less and less, but the minimum gets ever bigger.

Year 1: 90 percent of the time at 90, 10 percent at 10;

Year 2: 90 percent of the time at 70, 10 percent at 20;

Year n: 90 percent of the time at halfway between the preceding year's 90-percent value and 50; 10 percent of the time at halfway between the preceding year's 10-percent value and 30.

These examples show that we will get a very different sort of "course of ever-continuing improvement," depending on whether we focus on the situation *on the average* or on the situation *at the miminum*.[7] There is accordingly substantial room for disagreement and controversy with regard to just the question "Does improvement in a particular respect actually constitute an improvement on the whole?" With melioristic opti-

[7] Recall the comparably problematic position of John Rawls's *Theory of Justice*, with its demands that justice focus on the condition of those at the very bottom of the scale.

mism, it may not be all that clear exactly what sort of "course of improvement" should actually count as a meaningful or significant improvement.

It is illuminating to consider the historical example of Leibniz in this connection. Leibnizian optimism is a complex and many-sided theory—a combination of several distinct forms of optimism. It involves, as we have seen, an endorsement of the compensatory version of actuality optimism. But another important feature is the contention that this world of ours is "the best possible world"—with stress on *possible*. There is, no doubt, a good deal that is not right with the world, but all the attainable alternatives are even worse. (Voltaire's ironic plaint "Si c'est ici le meilleur des mondes possibles, que sont donc les autres?" implements rather than invalidates the Leibnizian approach.) Leibniz was not one of those rosy-visioned theologians who argue that all of the world's evils and imperfections are mere illusions—that if only we saw things more fully and deeply, we would come to realize our mistake and reclassify all those negativities as goods. As they see it, all imperfection is only seeming imperfection—evils are simply shadows needed to secure the painting's overall effectiveness, and any complaint about the badness of things reflects a misunderstanding arising from an incomplete understanding.[8] However, this possible (albeit problematic) line of absolutistic optimism just is not Leibniz's. Leibniz was quite prepared to recognize that much is wrong in the world. But he held the view that all the other possibilities are worse. And after all, even a half-full barrel can be fuller than all the rest. Leibniz recognized evil as real. But he saw it as a systemically necessary condition for the greater good—a negative but unavoidable aspect of optimization. The myth of Sextus at the end of the *Theodicée* illustrates this: "The crime of Sextus serves for great things: It renders Rome free; thence will arise a great empire, which will show noble examples to mankind."[9] The world's arrangements are systemically interconnected, and reality is a "package deal" where we must take the bad with the good. If we improved something here, even more would come unstruck over there—an "improvement" at one point of the system always has damaging repercussions at another.[10] (As with the harmony of a painting, however, those interconnections are matters of harmonization and systemic interlinkage, not of causal interaction.)

---

[8] This is essentially the doctrine of Plotinus: all existence roots in the divine One and is therefore good. Evil is not something positive and real as such, but only something negative, a mere lack or deficiency of good. See *Enneads*, esp. 3.2.3–18; 4.3.13–18; 4.4.45.

[9] G. W. Leibniz, *Theodicée*, sec. 416.

[10] One recent author writes: "It is of course common knowledge that Leibniz believed that the appearance of evil in the world was only a symptom of our defective or limited understanding" (Catherine Wilson, "Leibnizian Optimism," *Journal of Philosophy* 80 [1983]:767). But "common knowledge" is quite wrong here. Leibniz holds not that evil in the world is mere appearance but rather that it is compensated for by a preponderant good.

A further aspect of Leibnizian optimism is a meliorism with respect to the conditions of life for organic creatures in general and rational beings in particular. Of course, this is not to say that they are superbly good or (given the inherent imperfections of finite creatures) that they can ever become so. But things will improve on balance in the long run.

The salient feature of Leibniz's position lies in its commitment to a compensatory optimism that sees the world as good on the whole. It is *now and always* the case that, on balance, considering everything, the good outweighs the bad. Following in the footsteps of Christian Neoplatonism of thinkers like Augustine and Aquinas, Leibniz is deeply committed to the idea of a cosmic order that is essentially good: good predominates over evil at every stage of the world's history. Leibniz saw this position as essential to considering the world as the creation of a benevolent deity. (In this regard, Schopenhauer's pessimism is a flat-out denial of Leibnizian optimism. Unlike Voltaire, Schopenhauer identifies his target correctly.) In any case, the example of Leibniz shows that a meliorism of the tendency-optimism variety is perfectly compatible with the endorsement of an actuality optimism. Its improvability need not be seen as conflicting with the idea that the world is good as is.

Given this combination of views, there is no doubt that Leibniz's position is properly characterized as a version of optimism. But it is certainly not one of the facile ostrich-head-in-the-ground sort, which maintains that everything is just fine and dandy, seeing no evil simply because it refuses, in Pollyannaish fashion, to look evil in the face.

Is meliorism tenable at all? *Memento mori.* Does not the inevitability of death automatically preclude any possibility of being optimistic about the condition of man? Presumably not. The inexorability of death does indeed preclude the possibility of ever-continuing improvement at the level of the individual. But the general condition of the continuing group (clan, nation, species) may well improve, despite the merely transient presence of its particular members. ("I myself grow older," Caesar lamented, "yet the crowd in the Appian Way ever remains the same age.") Thus only egocentric persons who are concerned for themselves alone are denied a recourse to long-term optimism. Those whose wider range of concern embraces their posterity at large can in principle be optimistic about the human condition, ignoring for the moment such very remote eventualities as the "heat death" of the solar system.

In contrast, it is clear that mainstream Christianity is at odds with an unalloyed optimism regarding the condition of man as such. The kingdom it contemplates is not of this world, and it is not through their own powers and abilities that people can come to enter it. The progressivistic theory of the perfectability of man through the ministrations of science is a modern notion by which theorists of the Age of Enlightenment sought to supplant an older, less sanguine view of human prospects here on earth.

In any case, the melioristic thesis that things are tending toward the better is generally difficult to establish on any actually available basis. The best we can standardly claim on evidential grounds is that things are getting better *at present*. And this seldom affords a firm guarantee for the future. (Our most secure inductive conclusion is that the long-term projection of current tendencies is generally inappropriate.)

The fact that meliorism is hard to substantiate has its other side in the fact that it is also hard to refute. Even if things have not gone well of late, this may well be a matter of preparation for a strong spurt toward the better: reculer pour mieux sauter. Sometimes one must travel east to go west—via the Panama Canal, for example. Appearances can be deceiving; the circumstance that things do not look to be getting better does not really mean they are not. The fact that melioristic optimism is hard to refute on evidential grounds opens the door to contemplating its acceptance on a nonevidential basis through a pragmatic rather than probative route to validation. This idea has important ramifications.

Attitudinal Optimism

Optimism as we have so far considered it is a substantive and descriptive (albeit value-determined) position. But there is room for yet another version—an optimism whose character is attitudinal rather than strictly descriptive. It is represented by a policy of proceeding (when possible) in the confident hope that the tendency or prospect afforded by the future is auspicious—that things will work out well and matters continue to improve. Such attitudinal optimism is something very different from the descriptive, fact-oriented modes of optimism with which we have dealt so far. It does not presuppose the actuality of a meliorative tendency or prospect. Rather, it is an attitudinal disposition toward viewing things in a favorable light as a basis for action. Attitudinal optimism is not a matter of a cognitively well-based conviction regarding how things will comport themselves in the world but represents a praxis-geared posture of hopeful confidence. What is at issue is not a well-evidentiated thesis but a hopeful attitude one takes toward the future when this is not precluded by the state of our information. The assumption of such a position accordingly involves no actual prediction that the contemplated course of improvement will eventuate but only a confidently hopeful anticipation that this will occur; what is at issue is a point of practical policy rather than one of factual foreknowledge.

Consider an illustration. Hegel was an optimist, and the fundamental optimism of their master is shared alike by the Hegelian left and the Hegelian right, but in very different ways. On the left lies the tendency optimism represented by the eschatological posture of dialectical materialism—a melioristic view predicated on the historical inevitability of a better order of things (for the proletariat, at any rate). And on the right lies the attitudinal optimism of the German idealists—a position that is not comparably eschatological but represents an optimism of attitude and intellectual orientation rather than historical process. The former is an essentially predictive position, the latter an essentially attitudinal one.

Various expressions of attitudinal optimism are to be found in the pragmatic philosophy of William James, but its main theoretical exponent is the obscure Austrian philosopher Hieronymus Lorm.[11] With an eye on Kant's distinction between a phenomenal and a noumenal order, Lorm contrasts the order of experience (*Erfahrung*) with the order of sensibility (*Empfindung*). The bitter lessons of experience endorse pessimism, but the positive inclination of human sensibility calls for a life-enhancing optimism. Lorm accordingly endorses an attitudinal optimism (*Meinungs-Optimismus*) that is evidentially "groundless," because it flies in the face of our actual experience of how the world actually goes (our *Erfahrungs-Pessimismus*). But it is nevertheless seen as valid—experience to the contrary notwithstanding—as an expression of the inner spirit of man. Somewhat as in Kant, we are—as Lorm sees it—dual citizens belonging both to an empirical realm where optimism is inappropriate and to a noumenal realm where optimism is mandatory.

Attitudinal optimism is thus a matter of outlook and perception—of attitude or disposition rather than expectation or belief. The tendency optimist counsels *patience*: "Wait! Things will get better." The attitudinal optimist counsels *confidence*: "Hope! Don't let your spirit be crushed by present adversity. Spirit is something too valuable to be diminished by events whose overall worth in the larger scheme of things isn't all that big." Attitudinal optimism accordingly represents a fundamentally evaluative rather than a factually predictive posture.

Validating Attitudinal Optimism

But can these positions of personal attitude and factual belief be kept apart? Does attitudinal optimism not somehow require the support of melioristic convictions and thus stand in need of a grounding in scientific foreknowledge?

Not at all. It is perfectly possible for someone to adopt an optimistic attitude—quite reasonably and rationally—without being convinced of

---

[11] See Hieronymus Lorm, *Der grundlose Optimismus: Ein Buch der Betrachtung* (Vienna: Verlag der Literarischen Gesellschaft, 1894). Friedrich Ueberweg's *Grundriss der Geschichte der Philosophie*, pt. 4, 12th ed. (Berlin: E. S. Mittler & Sohn, 1923), provides some information about this author.

the factual thesis that a substantively optimistic trend or tendency indeed obtains. Even in situations where one cannot substantiate a melioristic tendency, one may well be able to validate an attitudinal optimism—not, to be sure, on evidential grounds, but on pragmatic ones. One can, that is, validate attitudinal optimism by maintaining (1) that factually *nihil obstat*, that the available evidence does not stand in its way, and (2) that positive consequences will (or are likely to) follow upon my proceeding in a tenor of hope and optimism. These considerations yield a pragmatic rather than an evidential justification—a justification on the basis of consequences rather than grounds. Accordingly, I can (quite reasonably) proceed to plan and conduct my actions in the firm hope that a favorable course of developments will unfold without first determining that this is actually (or indeed even probably) the case.

The principle at issue here is not that of the precept "Proceed in good hope, and you will (certainly or at least very likely) succeed," nor yet that of the precept "Proceed in good hope, since you have nothing to lose thereby," but rather that of the precept "Proceed in good hope, and you will improve the chances of success." If a policy for guiding one's actions can make even a small positive contribution to the probability that a desirable state of affairs will be realized, then its adoption can make good rational sense. When the balance of potential advantage is favorably adjusted, then those hopeful expectations are rationally defensible—albeit in the pragmatic rather than evidential mode of rationality.[12]

Yet how is one to reply to the objector who says: "Attitudinal optimism is not rationally justified in the absence of evidential support. In such cases one should not form anticipations at all but simply await developments." The response is straightforward. *Why not* adopt such a posture? Why simply wait with folded hands rather than act in hopeful expectation—particularly if such action can serve to improve the prospects of a favorable outcome? What is irrational about letting one's attitudes be shaped by the expectation of outcomes?

This decision-theoretic perspective carries us back to the position advocated by William James in *Pragmatism*. As long as I am appropriately convinced that a policy of hopeful action can make a positive difference, attitudinal optimism can make good decision-theoretic sense—even where factual determinations are infeasible. An optimistic attitude can manifest "the power of positive thinking," as per the example: "In the ordinary affairs of life, act (in the absence of evidence to the contrary) as if the people with whom you deal were reliable and honest." It certainly is not true that people in general are trustworthy. The justification of such a "pragmatic belief" can reside in the efficacy of the practical policy that it

---

[12] On the issues involved in the contrast between evidential and pragmatic justification, cf. the author's book *Pascal's Wager* (Notre Dame, Ind.: University of Notre Dame Press, 1985).

underwrites—its capacity to engender positive results—and need not call for preestablishing its substantive correctness as a factual thesis. It can, in principle, make perfectly good practical sense to proceed in a spirit of optimism even when the prospects of success are small. When we must play a stronger team, we do well to strive with an effort bolstered by sanguine hope, remembering that with luck even puny David can prevail over mighty Goliath and that victory is not invariably on the side of the big battalions.

Consider the objection:

> Surely it is not rational ever to let our attitudes be shaped in a way that outruns the reaches of our knowledge. To allow our outlook to be influenced by our values is just a matter of inappropriate wishful thinking.

This objection hits wide of the mark in its insistence in the name of "rationality" that attitudes must be shaped by knowledge alone. Rationality is a matter of the intelligent pursuit of appropriate objectives. And here knowledge does not have it all to itself. Man is not a *purely* cognitive creature—we do not live by information alone, and knowledge is not our only value. The sphere of our praxis must be allowed to play its part in the overall rational order of things. An optimistic attitude can thus be perfectly "rational" in appropriate circumstances.

The crux is simply this: There are two very different sorts of rationally valid expectations about the future—namely, *cognitively justified anticipations* based on evidence, and *pragmatically justified hopes* based on decision-theoretical considerations. The two can get out of step with one another. But there is nothing whatsoever irrational or unreasonable about this—when the decision-theoretical aspects of the issue are heeded, it makes perfectly good rational sense because quite different things are at issue. Cognitive rationality is not the only sort; practical rationality can also come into operation.

Acting so as to fly in the face of established facts is never rationally justified. But to fly in the face of mere probabilities can on occasion be justifiable. Indeed that is exactly what we standardly do in decision theory when we balance probabilities against prospective gains and losses, placing our bets on the side of the more favorable expectations. We can, quite appropriately, sometimes bet on long shots. Even if I am pessimistic and believe that the chances of realizing the good are low no matter what I do, the fact remains that when these chances are increased by my taking an optimistic attitude, then I am well advised to do so. And this is what matters for practical purposes. Even for a pessimist, an optimistic attitude may well pay off.

To be sure, the advantageousness, and thus the rational advisability of optimism or pessimism, will very much depend on conditions and circumstances. There are certainly situations in which optimism is unwarranted and where it is a matter of unrealistically inappropriate wishful thinking that verges on self-deception to persist in thinking that matters will eventuate favorably. It is clearly foolish to be optimistic in cases where a failure to cut one's losses is simply to throw good money after bad; attitudinal optimism would obviously be ill advised here. The sensible thing is to control our attitudes by a rational analysis of the objective situation, including a realistic appraisal of the likelihood both of possible outcomes and of their potential costs and benefits. The course of wisdom is a guarded optimism, chastened by a realistic appreciation of the determinable facts.

The rational optimist is accordingly one who adopts this policy not as a general rule but as a working presumption: "In the absence of sufficiently powerful indications to the contrary, act in the confident hope that your efforts will prove to good avail." (What is at issue is a presumption on the same order as that which underlies trusting other people and believing what they say.) The sensible thing is not to be optimistic always and everywhere, in season and out of season, but to be discriminating and allow the characteristics of particular cases and circumstances their just due. From the rational point of view, attitudinal optimism is a policy whose appropriateness is not universal but limited—and yet, within its proper limits, it has its place.

Pessimism

Much of what has here been said about optimism has its counterpart on the other side of the coin, the side of pessimism. In particular, pejorism is the reverse of meliorism, embodied in the claim that things are getting worse and worse. As such, it is not necessarily a matter of gloom and doom. In theory, the deterioration at issue may simply take us from superb to excellent.

Schopenhauerian pessimism, in contrast, is the doctrine that, on balance, the world's evils outweigh its benefits—that the condition of sentient beings in general and intelligent beings in particular is such that pain exceeds pleasure and suffering outweighs happiness.[13] As Schopenhauer put it in characteristically picturesque language: "If you try to imagine, as nearly as you can, how much of misery, pain, and suffering of every kind the sun shines upon in its course, you will admit that it would be much better if the sun had been as little able to call forth the phenomenon of life here on the earth as on the moon and if here, as there, the surface were still in a crystalline state."[14] Even in such a view, however, it does not

---

[13] Schopenhauer, of course, did not invent this view. It was already urged against Leibniz by Voltaire, by Maupertuis (*Oeuvres* [Lyons: Corbas, 1756], 1:202–5), and by Kant.

[14] A. Schopenhauer, "Nachträge zur Lehre vom Leiden der Welt," sec. 156.

necessarily follow that it would be better if the world did not exist at all. For it is possible to take the line that benefits in the nonaffective range (including, for example, knowledge or personal goodness) could redeem an overall negative balance in specifically affective regards—that suffering is the price we pay for the realization of other values such as wisdom or loving-kindness, and that it is worth it.

The fact that there are many different modes of optimism and pessimism means that it is possible to combine versions of the one with versions of the other in a perfectly coherent way. An interesting example is provided in the curious synthesis of Hegel and Schopenhauer (strange bedfellows!) that is presented in Eduard von Hartmann's *Philosophie des Unbewussten* (*Philosophy of the Unconscious*, 1869). He held, with Hegel, that there is indeed a spiritual dialectical progress in the evolution of consciousness and thought. But he also maintained, with Schopenhauer, that this is achieved at so great a cost in misery and suffering that it would be better if the world did not exist at all. (Similarly, Friedrich Engels was inspired by Malthus and Darwin to think of world history as the sphere of operation of a cruel force that exacts the sacrifice of millions of lives for the realization of every step of progress—a view that doubtless provided succeeding Communist rulers with aid and comfort.)[15]

Moreover, optimism and pessimism do not exhaust the field. There is, as we have seen, also room for a Spinozistic naturalism that sees the world's course of events as totally indifferent to human affairs, inclined neither positively nor negatively toward matters of human good and evil, and providing a value-free stage setting where matters of human well-being or ill-being are objectively irrelevant to the course of events as such but determined substantially by the subjective reaction of human minds.

And so, as display 9.2 indicates, every possible position in this domain has in fact been advocated by some thinker or other.[16] As is often the case

---

[15] John Stuart Mill too wondered whether evolutionary progress was "worth purchasing by the sufferings and wasted lives of entire geological periods" (Mill, *Three Essays on Religion*, ed. Helen Taylor [London, 1874; reprint, New York: Greenwood Press, 1969], pp. 192–93). He eventually came to abandon the utilitarians' faith in progress and hoped at best for a steady-state condition in regard to human well-being. See Lewis S. Feuer, "John Stuart Mill as a Sociologist," in *James and John Stuart Mill: Papers of the Centenary Conference*, ed. J. M. Robson and M. Laine (Toronto: University of Toronto Press, 1976), pp. 98–99.

[16] For the obscure German philosopher Julius Bahnsen, noted in (2e) in the display, see the article "Pessimismus," by Rudolf Eisler, in *Handwörterbuch der Philosophie*, 2d ed. (Berlin, 1922), pp. 473–74. Bahnsen's principal work is *Der Widerspruch im Wissen und Wesen der Welt*, 2 vols. (Leipzig: B. Franke, 1882). His bibliography is given in Ueberweg, *Grundriss der Geschichte der Philosophie*, 4:341–42, 701. For Bahnsen, the world is so designed as to frustrate every human hope and aspiration, and life is like a game of chance played against a diabolical house that is sure to win in the end. Death is not only the end of life but its telos as well. Life affirmation is the worst policy; the more we bet on life, the larger our losses are bound to be. The precept "Seek everywhere and choose the smallest evil, never the greatest good" represents the course of true wisdom (*Der Widerspruch*, 2:492).

Display 9.2. The Spectrum of Positions Regarding Value in Nature

1. Value (good and bad) does not apply to the world at all; it lies entirely in the imagination of its "beholders." (Spinoza, rigid materialism, positivism)
2. Value does indeed apply to the world and does so in such a way that:
   a. the world is maximally good—as good as it is possible for a world to be. (Leibniz)
   b. the world is predominantly (though not maximally) good. (Neoplatonism)
   c. the world is a (more or less) evenly balanced mixture of good and bad. (Manichaeanism)
   d. the world is predominantly (though not maximally) bad. (Schopenhauer)
   e. The world is maximally bad. (Julius Bahnsen)

with philosophical controversies, every feasible alternative has found its exponent. (Of course, to note that a case has been made for each of these diverse alternatives is not to say that all are equally good.)

Pessimism versus Optimism

Pessimism invites despair, optimism confidence. The former looks on the dark side, the latter on the bright. Common sense and "realism" alike require us to recognize both dimensions—holding two opposed factors in some sort of reasonable balance. The question is ultimately one of where we focus, of what aspect of a thoroughly mixed situation deserves to be accenuated.

Optimism takes a characteristic stance here. It is a policy that goes beyond realism to enclose a principle of hope. It views the human being as a creature of a Pascalian duality of mind and heart—of a binocular vision that sees with the body's eye what there is and with the mind's eye what there can and should be. It presses beyond fact to the impetus of value— not by failing to see things as they are but by appraising also what there might be. As optimists see it, the good outweighs the bad not in the balance of actuality but in the balance of importance. They do not shut their eyes to the imperfections of the real but work in cheerful hopefulness toward their amelioration.

The risk of disappointment is the unavoidable price for the potential advantages of attitudinal optimism. If one is erroneously optimistic during a course of deterioration, one is going to find one's hopes dashed, one's expectations disappointed. Pessimism manifests the other side of the coin here. If one is a pessimist during a course of improvement, one is going to be pleasantly surprised when those unhappy apprehensions turn out to be unwarranted. To say this is not, however, to say that pessimism is a wise policy during times of betterment, for it is bound to lead one to lose out on opportunities. Moreover, pessimists who resort to this "pleasant surprise" line of thought to support their position run into problems. For to justify taking a pessimistic stance on *this* basis—because one expects it to lead to pleasant surprises—is ultimately incoherent and inconsistent: it predicates pessimism on optimism. (The self-consistent line is for pessimists, expecting deterioration, to support their position on grounds of its averting disappointment.)

Optimists whose expectations are disappointed are bound to be dismayed and disillusioned; pessimists whose expectations are disappointed may well be pleased (after all, worst has not come to worst). But under what sorts of circumstances would an attitudinal pessimism that operates in the expectation that things are getting worse possibly be pragmatically justified as somehow useful or productive? Only if it actually helped us to prepare for the worst, to safeguard ourselves helpfully against difficulties that do indeed lie ahead. Thus attitudinal pessimsim might pay off as a practical policy in leading people to take sensible precautions in the face of impending misfortune. But, of course, this can prove to good avail only if (factually speaking) those pessimistic expectations correctly characterize the objective situation. For pessimism to prove advantageous, the expectation at issue must be correct—the deterioration we anticipate must in fact be en route.

In this regard, then, there is an interesting asymmetry between the two positions of attitudinal optimism and pessimism. A pessimistic attitude is of advantage only if pessimism is correct as a substantive position and things are indeed going downhill, while an optimistic attitude can also be useful when the reverse of its expectations is the case. The advantage of optimism is that it need not be predictively warranted to be pragmatically useful. Even if it eventuates as not justified in actual historical fact, attitudinal optimism can induce us to make things better than they otherwise would be. This sort of thing cannot happen with attitudinal pessimism.

Optimists hope; even when things look bleak, they anticipate a happy issue. Pessimists fear; even when there are good prospects of a favorable issue, they anticipate the worst and expect disaster. But fear is almost always a bad counselor. Hope is seldom so. (Though it sometimes can be: the investor who expects a current stock rally to last forever is a fool.)

An optimistic attitude impels its owner-operator to act with confidence—to run risks in hopeful expectancy that things will go well. It supports activity and enterprise. A pessimistic attitude tends to immobilize. If one confidently expects the worse (or worst), there is little point except in safeguards and insurance. And a sufficiently deep pessimism will dissuade one even from taking such measures because one expects that even they will prove unavailing. Insofar as these attitudinal matters lie within our control, we do well to favor the optimistic approach. Hope invites the penalty of disappointment but has the benefit of sustaining courage in the face of adversity. Pessimism invites inaction and, even worse, a despair that brings no benefits at all. We prefer optimism to pessimism in our companions because optimism is by its very nature life-enhancing.

The rational impetus to optimism lies in the fact that little is more bleak and more inhumane than a life not accentuated by some hope of better things to come—if not for oneself and one's posterity, then for one's successors at large. Concern for our fellows and our species is not altogether unselfish. By taking such a stance, we enlarge our stake in the world's affairs and broaden the basis of that hopefulness that endows our own life and labors with a significance it would otherwise lack. For us, at least, the extinction of hope is the ultimate evil—not least because a life without hope is thereby prevented in one significant respect from qualifying as authentically human.[17]

[17] The themes of this chapter are treated more fully in the author's *Ethical Idealism*.

Ten

Moral Objectivity (Are There Moral Facts?)

Is Morality Merely Subjective?

There are two distinct modes of moral egalitarianism. Both agree in holding that all moral codes are of equal validity-status, that each is as good as any other. But one mode—indifferentism—sees all as being alike *valid*; the other—nihilism—sees all as being alike *invalid*. The former, indifferentist approach takes the syncretistic line of an indiscriminate openness and acceptance; the latter, nihilistic approach takes the defeatist line of a total negativity and rejection. Either way, the prospect of a *reasoned* endorsement of one moral position over against others is excluded.

Both doctrines are deeply problematic, however. Moral indifferentism is caught up in the evident implausibility of holding that any and every moral code, any set of moral rules whatsoever, is actually as good as any other for us here and now, in the circumstances in which we actually find ourselves emplaced in our interactions with others. Moral nihilism, on its part, is caught up in the no less striking implausibility of the contention that no moral code whatsoever is cogent—that none can make good a claim to effectiveness in safeguarding the best interests of people. Both forms of egalitarianism are deeply enmeshed in difficulties.

However, even greater obstacles than those posed by the moral egalitarianism of validity equivalence arise with a subjectivism that maintains: "To each his own; such differences as there are between moral codes merely 'lie in the mind of the exponent.' While it is indeed that case that one moral code can be superior to others, this superiority is simply a matter of an inclination that varies with individuals and groups." As the subjectivist sees it, morality is a matter of customs, attitudes, or tastes—we have our moral code and they have theirs, period. Accordingly, the moral subjectivist insists that there simply is no real substance to a moral thesis like "Cheating people is wrong." The subjectivist insists: "That's just what people happen to accept in our set or our society." On this view, the sole reason why moral judgments ultimately matter for us is one of conformity through "keeping in step" with the rest of our group, averting the disapproval of our fellows though conforming our behavior to socially accepted norms.

This sort of subjectivist relativism has been popular among philosophers since classical antiquity.[1] And it is still going strong. In the present century, C. L. Stevenson's "attitudinal expression" theory is an influential instance of the general line of approach.[2] Stevenson holds that a moral evaluation characterizes merely the subject and not the object that is at issue. My contention "You acted wrongly in stealing that money" has two components: one factual (you stole that money) and the other a personal avowal: "I disapprove of your doing this and urge you not to do similar things in the future." The former component stakes an objective, descriptive claim; the latter expresses the assertor's attitude toward it. The point of making moral contentions, Stevenson insists, "is not [simply] to indicate facts but to *create an influence.* Instead of merely describing people's interests they [seek to] *change or intensify* them. They recommend an interest in an object, rather than state that the interest already exists."[3] Moral claims are primarily designed to exhort people to approved lines of action. Morality is accordingly a matter of the variable inclinations of individuals and groups, a matter of "the custom of the country," of what people just happen to approve—of fashion, if you will.

Such an approach denies that acts are ever actually wrong in themselves but insists that people merely think they are. Moral language is only "used to express feeling about certain objects, but not to make any assertion about them."[4] Moral judgments are only prescriptions—oblique injunctions designed to incite others to action.[5] In any event, they do not really express evaluations, which, as such, are right or wrong, appropriate or inappropriate. Rather, they reflect the circumstance that individuals and groups only attach or attribute value to human actions, ascriptions that are always made on an entirely variable basis reflecting the makers' feelings or wishes, attitudes or customs—always without any real foundation of warrant in the nature of the object. There is nothing more to moral praise or condemnation than the attachments of particular individuals or groups. Rightness or wrongness lies simply in the view of the individual (or the

---

[1] The most notable exponent of the position is David Hume. See his *Treatise of Human Nature* and sec. 1 of appendix 1 of *An Inquiry concerning the Principles of Morals* (London: A. Miller, 1752).

[2] See Charles L. Stevenson, "The Emotive Meaning of Ethical Terms," in his *Facts and Values* (New Haven: Yale University Press, 1963), and also his earlier *Ethics and Language* (New Haven: Yale University Press, 1944). Two works particularly useful on the "emotive theory" are G. J. Warnock, *Contemporary Moral Philosophy* (London: Allen & Unwyn, 1967), and J. O. Urmson, *The Emotive Theory of Ethics* (Oxford: Oxford University Press, 1968). The "norm expressivism" of Alan Gibbard's *Wise Choices, Apt Feelings* (Cambridge: Harvard University Press, 1990) affords a more recent example.

[3] Stevenson, *Facts and Values*, p. 16.

[4] Ayer, *Language, Truth, and Logic*, p. 108.

[5] Cf. Hare, *The Language of Morals*.

group) as a mere expression of personal (or social) disapproval. Evaluation on the basis of valid principles is simply not at issue.

Such an interpretation of moral judgment is quite untenable, however. Moral appraisal as we actually conduct it is something quite different—in the sight of its actual practitioners at any rate. No adequate paraphrase of a moral thesis can ever eliminate the element of (moral) *evaluation*. The "emotive" disapproval-recommendation theory reinterprets "Pointless deception is wrong" somewhat along the lines of "I/we disapprove of pointless deception; do so as well!" But this equation is untenable because the two locutions simply do not have the same force. "Doing *A* is wrong" entails that "it is wicked (bad, reprehensible) to do *A*"; merely disapproving of doing *A* does not. Contrariwise, a breach of the rules, even the moral rules, may on occasion plausibly gladden one's heart. (I need not withdraw my judgment that someone who upset Hitler by cheating him at cards did something morally improper when indicating that I am pleased by that one's having done so.) After all, merely expressing an attitude or declaring a preference does not state or claim anything; only contentions (assertions) manage to state or claim. (Expressing one's sentiments just does not come to claiming something to be the case—whether factually or evaluatively. Our disapproving says something about us, while an evaluative appraisal says something about the item.) The emotive theory runs very different things together in its identification of moral evaluation with a personal reaction. It lies in the very conception at issue that an act is immoral not because it is disapproved of but because it *deserves* disapproval on the part of duly sensitive observers.

The radically subjective view that "In moral matters there is only what people think; there just are no objective facts of the matter" is ultimately untenable for anyone who, rejecting nihilism, gives credence to some sort of morality or other. For one cannot consistently look on one's own moral convictions as "merely matters of opinion." In doing this, one would thereby ipso facto fail to accept them as such—that is, as *moral* convictions. In view of what can possibly qualify as such, it lies in the very nature of our moral judgments that we regard them as justified via a rationale regarding what is required by due heed of the interests of people. One is thus rationally constrained by considerations of mere self-consistency to see one's own moral position as rationally superior to the available alternatives. If one did not take this stance—did not deem one's moral position to be effectively optimal—then one could not see oneself as rationally justified in adopting it, so that it would, in consequence, fail to be one's own real moral position, contrary to hypothesis.[6]

[6] Cf. J. N. Findlay, *Language, Mind, and Value* (London: Allen & Unwyn, 1963), chaps. 4 and 9.

What renders morality objective is the fact that a moral evaluation can—and should—be validated as cogent when backed by good reasons that exhibit its appropriateness as such. To claim that someone ought (or ought not) to act in a certain way is thereby to commit oneself to the availability of a good reason why one should or should not do so, and a reason that is not only good but good in a certain mode, the moral mode, in showing that this sort of action is bound up with due care for the interest of others. And what sort of behavior constitutes due care for people's best interests is something open to general view—something that can be investigated by other people as readily as by the agent himself or herself.

Morality, after all, is an end-governed rational enterprise—one that is structured by a characteristic purposive mission of transparent appropriateness. For it is morality's object to equip people with a body of norms (rules and values) that make for peaceful and collectively satisfying coexistence by facilitating their living together and interacting in a way that is productive for the realization of the "general benefit"—the benefit probability of each and certainly of many. The pursuit of righteousness that constitutes morality is like the pursuit of health that constitutes medicine—both are projects with an inherent teleology of their own; specifically, the mission of morality is to promote patterns of action and interaction that promote the best interests of people in general.

The validity of most moral appraisals is accordingly something that is accordingly objectively determinable—and nowise lies in the eye of the beholder. To say "You acted wrongly in stealing that money" is not simply to assert that you stole the money and additionally to evince disapprobation and urge a different sort of future conduct but rather—and most important—to *indicate a reason* for acting differently. For the claim implies that your act instantiates a type of behavior (namely, stealing) that does injury to the legitimate interests of others. And this issue of human needs and benefits, of people's real interests, such as their physical and psychological well-being, is not a matter of subjective reaction. What is in our interest—what is advantageous for our long-term, overall physical and psychological well-being, given the sorts of creatures we are—in large measure is a factual issue capable of empirical inquiry that lies open to general, public investigation.

To be sure, various theorists are eager to subjectivize the issue of what is in a person's interest. They want to specify interests in terms of wants: in terms of people's wishes, preferences, and desires. But here they at once encounter the difficulty that people often want things (drink, drugs, revenge, etc.) that are patently destructive and run clean counter to anything that could *reasonably* be said to be in someone's interests. And so these subjective-interest theoreticians are led down the primrose path from actual to hypothetical desires and preferences, from what people actually want to what they would-want-if. They are, accordingly led to the equation:

a person's real interests – what he or she would prefer (wish, chose, etc.) if only he or she were operating in circumstances X.

And here that parameter X opens up a considerable spectrum of possibilities:

if the person was proceeding in a calm and unflustered state of mind, without any emotional stress;

if the person was proceeding in conditions of full information and plausible foresight;

if the person was proceeding with the benefit of ample hindsight;

if the decision was being made under ideal (optimal, wholly unproblematic) conditions.

But of course as we move along such a list, we are moving further and further away from the realistic situation of a person's own, actual and idiosyncratic wishes and desires. We do well, therefore, to shift from apparent interests (mere wants and desires) to real (true, "best," genuine) interests. That is, we arrive at something that is abstracted and idealized, namely:

what a benevolent, well-intentioned, well-informed, and ideally situated third-party chooser would select on behalf of the particular person at issue.

On such an approach the person's own makeup (tastes, modulations, preferences) still figure critically in the choice. But they do so in a substantially objective way—in a way that other people can be (and generally are) better judges of what is in someone's interests than the parties who are themselves at issue. And the interests that are at issue here are always general. If one has a liking for steak, then (other things equal) one should eat steak, but the principle at issue, namely, "Other things being equal, people should eat what they prefer" is one that altogether general, minimal, and "depersonalized." What is in a person's real (true, genuine) interests is not something strictly idiosyncratic but is always something that is "covered" by a universal principle of the indicated sort.

Physicians, parents, public officials, and others constantly concern themselves with issues of what is good for people, what enables them to thrive and lead satisfying lives. People themselves are by no means the definitive authorities regarding what is in their own interests—their doctor, lawyer, or financial adviser can know a good deal more about these interests than the individuals at issue. People are no doubt the definitive authorities regarding what *pleases* them, but certainly not regarding what *benefits* them. And this objectivity of people's interests carries in its wake also the objectivity of interest promotion—and thus of morality.

In the final analysis, the objectivity of *moral* evaluations thus resides in the very nature of the issue. Given the meaning of the word "dog" as characterizing objects of a certain description, it follows that *if* an object answers to this description, *then* it can appropriately be characterized as "a dog." Similarly, it follows from the very meaning of the expression "(morally) wrong" as something geared to the benefit of people that *if* an act is correctly described as "willfully causing needless suffering to a person," *then* it can correctly be characterized as "(morally) wrong." There can, of course, be argument over the linguistic/conceptual issue of whether a certain understanding of a term is correct—whether a particular characterization of what it means to say that something is a dog or a moral transgression is in fact correct or whether a linguistic misunderstanding has occurred. But once this terminological issue is resolved—a matter that itself is surely an objective one—then the question of whether a certain proposed instance of the phenomenon is or is not a correct instance becomes a perfectly objective matter.[7] In consequence, certain facts *within* morality (e.g., the wickedness of inflicting needless suffering) follow from certain facts *about* morality (specifically about how the characterization "[morally] wrong" is correctly employed).[8]

We thus cannot detach rational justification from objective validity in the moral sphere, because to say that someone is (rationally) justified in making a judgment is to say that that one is (rationally) entitled to take it to be objectively true or correct. Nor can we detach objective validity from factuality, for where there is no appropriate claim to objective factuality (no "fact of the matter"), there can be no justification of endorsement either—though, to be sure, the facts of the matter may happen to be *evaluative* facts.

Of course, the circumstance that morality is objective does not mean

[7] This does not mean that disagreements arising here are "merely linguistic"—there is nothing mere or trivial about disagreements about language use. Rather, the point—as just stated—is that there is no good reason to see such disputes as relating to anything other than an objective issue. What words mean depends not on what you or I think but on how the community uses them.

[8] We cannot move from the fact that certain actions are properly designated as "morally wrong" to the conclusion that people ought not to do them, without making use of a thesis to the effect that people ought to be moral. But since the "ought" at issue here is a moral one, this linkage is not hard to come by. To be sure, the question of whether people are prudentially well advised to be moral relative to their own best interests is a different and additional one. It can be answered affirmatively—but that is a longish story that will be dealt with in chapter 12.

that the subjective element has no place whatsoever in the moral domain. People's "feelings" unquestionably form an important part of what constitutes their interests, and thus deserve respect from the moral point of view. (It is clearly morally wrong to hurt someone's feelings unnecessarily.) And this consideration introduces a large element of personal variability into the moral domain. But there is nothing in this sort of variability that is at odds with the constancy of the fundamental principles at issue or with the objectivity of the factors invoked in them.

The morally crucial circumstance that certain modes of action are conducive and others deleterious to the best interests of people is something that can be investigated, evidentiated, and sensibly assessed by the standards generally prevalent in rational discussion and controversy. The matters are not questions of feeling or taste but represent something objective about which one can deliberate and argue in a sensible way on the basis of reasons whose cogency is, or should be, accessible to anyone. The modes of behavior of people that render life in their communities "nasty, brutish, and short" (or indeed even merely more difficult and less pleasant than need be) generally admit of straightforward and unproblematic discernment.

Reacting against Kant's moral objectivism, various nineteenth-century German thinkers (preeminently including Nietzsche and Marx) inclined to regard moral claims as simply masked or disguised expressions of subjective desires. But this subjectivistic deconstruction of moral discourse, which harkens back to the Greek Sophists, ultimately shatters on the realization—repeatedly stressed by "rationalistic" philosophers since classical antiquity—that people have not just desires but also actual needs, wants, and entitlements that (unlike mere desires as such) constitute "interests" that *deserve* the respect of others.

To be sure, some thinkers—Aristotle, for example—insist that there is no difference between the apparent good and the genuine article. But this very questionable contention has little to recommend it. If I desire something that, as such, is inherently bad (say, to injure someone simply out of dislike, or to drug myself to avoid boredom), then "getting what I desire" may, in the circumstances, be an apparent good for me but is certainly not a real one (i.e., is really good neither for me nor for people in general). Of course it could be said that I desire a bad thing (an injury to my rival, my own drugged condition) only under the guise of the good (pleasure through excelling, relief from boredom). But this, clearly, is simply the incidental aspect that makes that bad object of desire appear good and does not somehow make it over into a real good. It thus emphasizes rather than undermines the point at issue—that people can indeed desire the (objectively) bad.

Franz Brentano correctly insisted that the objectively good is not that
which we love or desire but that which is worthy or deserving of our love
or desire.[9] For the morally right is not made into such by the fact of being
something that we (or the king or God or anyone) actually approve of.
Rather, it is that which is worthy or deserving of the approval of rational
agents because of its (perfectly objective) bearing on promotion of the
interests of such agents. Such a judgment expresses a fact (a moral fact to
be sure), and it straightforwardly admits of characterization as correct or
incorrect in the light of objectively prevailing conditions.

The Functional Nature of Morality

There nowadays prevails a widespread but nevertheless unfortunate tendency to deny the possibility of rational controversy about moral matters—to relegate morality to the never-never land of matters of taste,
feeling, or otherwise unsupportable opinion. Such a view is profoundly
inappropriate. Once one recognizes the *functional* aspect of morality—as
inculcating actions that safeguard the real interest of people—then moral
issues become open to rational deliberation.[10] This functional aspect of
morality as in its very nature representing an inherently appropriate end-
oriented project blocks the prospect of indifferentism or of a relativisti-
cally detached view of morality as a mere matter of individual inclination
or of "the customs of the tribe."

A crucial flaw of the subjectivist position is its failure to recognize that
people—*reasonable* people at any rate—do not in general choose or endorse actions without good reason (which, to be sure, they need not necessarily articulate). They take positive views toward actions because they
recognize them to be beneficial—find something about them that conduces, on balance, to the advantage of people's interests. Underlying
moral objectivism is the recognition, cogently formulated by W. D. Ross,
that "it is surely a strange reversal of the natural order of thought to say
that our admiring an action either is, or is what necessitates, its being

---

[9] Franz Brentano, *The Origin of Our Knowledge of Right and Wrong*, trans. by R. M.
Chisholm and Elizabeth Schneewind (London: Routledge & Kegan Paul, 1969), p. 18; idem,
The Foundation and Construction of Ethics, trans. Elizabeth Schneewind (London: Routledge & Kegan Paul, 1973), p. 131; idem, *The True and the Evident*, trans. Roderick M.
Chisholm, Ilse Politzer, and Kurt Q. Fischer (London: Routledge & Kegan Paul, 1966), pp.
21–22. The point at issue had already been made by Kant, and indeed by Plato, though not
as explicitly and emphatically as by Brentano.

[10] It is to the credit of the utilitarian tradition that it has stressed this gearing of morality
to the benefit of people, for this clearly establishes the issues as subject to rational deliberation. But it is to its discredit that it has seen these benefits in terms of pleasure and mere
personal preference alone, so that the veneer of rationality is very thin indeed.

good. We think of its goodness as what we admire in it, and as something it would have even if no one admire it, something that it has in itself."[11] The fact that there are good (and poor) reasons for action from the moral point of view means that morality is not simply a matter of subjective taste or feeling. That it is morally right to act in a certain sort of way (to keep one's promises) and not right to act in another (to steal) is capable of being established through perfectly objective considerations regarding subsumption under universal moral principles. Moral subjectivism is precluded by the reality of good reasons for action.[12]

After all, moral subjectivism takes roughly the following line:

> In moral judgments, as in judgments of taste, it is impossible to be mistaken. Whatever people think to be right is thereby rendered right. In matters of moral obligation and permission, thinking something to be so makes it so (even as in matters of taste, thinking something to be pleasing means that it *is* pleasing).

But this view of the matter is altogether wrongheaded. It is very much mistaken to think that a certain practice is rendered morally acceptable simply because people chose to adopt and endorse it. For it lies in the very nature of the concept at issue that moral appropriateness has to hinge on how actions affect the real interests of people, and it is clear that an individual agent cannot be the decisive arbiter here. Morality turns on how actions affect people—on the negative side, for example, by doing them unwarranted harm, violating their rights, endangering their well-being, undermining their welfare, and the like. But that certain acts have such effects or tendencies is a perfectly objective matter—something that does not turn on the wishes, desires, tastes, or opinions of particular people. If causing someone needless suffering is morally wrong—which it indeed is—then this is so regardless of how people may think or feel about it. That you unwarrantedly did injury to another's interests is as objective a fact as that you absentmindedly forgot another's instructions. Accordingly, the moral quality of an act is emphatically not a matter of personal inclination, but one of rational evaluation.

To be sure, Hume and his congeners have denied that reason can guide action. But their denial of reasoned preferences involves a serious distortion of the actual facts. That the interests of a creature such as we humans are or claim to be can be advantaged (or disadvantaged) by doing A rather than B follows straightforwardly from the reason-establishable fact that A is more (or less) consonant than B is with our nature as at once rational and

[11] W. D. Ross, *The Right and the Good* (Oxford: Clarendon Press, 1930), p. 89.

[12] An interesting discussion of objectivity in ethics—albeit one that proceeds along lines rather different from those that figure in the present deliberations—is found in Thomas Nagel's book *The View from Nowhere* (Oxford: Oxford University Press, 1986).

embodied beings. Treating people's wounds serves their interests better than inflicting injuries, and lifting their spirits better than depressing them. Only an over-narrow conception of reason that blocks it off from any concern with evaluative matters can open the way to moral subjectivism.

The fact that morality (like medicine or speech or transportation) has an overarching characterizing aim or function makes for objectivity in appropriateness of moral judgments. Being thought to be morally appropriate no more makes a certain action so than being thought to be medically effective or transportationally efficient would render a certain practice so. The claim that a rule or practice is morally appropriate—that in the conditions prevailing in a society it is effective in serving and enhancing the real interests of people in general—is thoroughly objective and "factual." And so, when W. G. Sumner sensibly characterizes various practices as "socially harmful" (suttee, child marriages, and the destruction of a man's goods upon his death, for example),[13] he thereby squarely negates his own contention that customs are automatically right and that societies are immune from valid criticism by outsiders because "everything in the mores of a time and place must be regarded as justified with regard to that time and place."[14]

Morality is an inherently rational and objective enterprise. For to gain moral credit for an action, the agent must have objective and impersonally cogent *reasons* for doing it—reasons that relate to the impact of the sort of action at issue on the valid interests of others. What makes such reasons into morally good reasons has nothing to do with what I (or anyone) want or what I (or anyone) feel, but lies in the nature of morality itself, hinging on the fundamental issue of what the moral enterprise as such is all about—to wit, protesting the real interests of rational agents. Morality is by definition geared to the interests of people, even as refrigeration is by definition geared to cooling.

The functional nature of morality—its being geared to serving the interests of people—makes for a "moral realism" that maintains that there indeed are moral facts.[15] It does not, however, underwrite the mode of "realism" that maintains that moral rightness is a certain sort of *property* of acts (whether a "nonnatural" property or a "supervenient" property or the sort of preternatural property discernible only by some special power of moral intuition).[16] Rather, the functional approach indicates that what is at issue with "rightness" is not a property in the ordinary sense at all but a contextual feature of a *relational* sort that turns on the place of the act in

[13] William Graham Sumner, *Folkways* (Boston: Ginn, 1906), sec. 29.

[14] Ibid., sec. 65.

[15] A comprehensive bibliography of the subject appears in Geoffrey Sayre-McCord, "Moral Realism Bibliography," *Southern Journal of Philosophy* 24 (1986), supplement, pp. 143–59. Recall also the discussion of value realism in the final section of chap. 4 above.

[16] Critics of moral realism often suppose, quite wrongly, that ethical appraisals can reflect matters of fact only if ethical characteristics represent *supernatural properties* that are

question within a wider framework of relevant circumstances. Being "(morally) right," like being "average" in size or "inexpensive" in price, is a contextual and dispositional feature relating to the setting of one item within its embracing environment. While not a property of an isolated item, such a feature is nevertheless one whose possession is objectively discernible—albeit only within the setting of that larger context. The moral status of an act is not the sort of thing that is a property or quality at all, but a relational feature whose determination involves a wide variety of contextual issues: agents, circumstances, motives, alternatives, and the like. Moral evaluation does not deal in "properties" of the usual sorts at all, but in contextual relationships.

But this is a technical aside. The salient point is that morality is not something merely subjective—not a matter of people's feelings or tastes or wants that "lies in the eyes of the beholder." It consists in the pursuit, through variable and context-relative means, of invariant and objectively implementable ends that root in a commitment to the best interests of people in general. In consequence, it inheres in the very meaning of moral "right" and "wrong" that issues of morality admit of appropriate and inappropriate resolutions and can be deliberated about in sensible and foolish ways. A morality that is not objectively valid in this sense is no morality at all. And so, rational deliberation and controversy about moral judgments are possible precisely because claims about moral matters are, in their own way, preeminently objective and rational in nature.

Is Rational Controversy about Morality Possible?

From generation to generation, skeptically minded philosophers have been drawn to the following sort of argumentation:

> Moral contentions make claims about what ought (normatively) to be and not about what actually is the case with respect to descriptive matters of fact.
>
> Rational deliberation and controversy are possible only where matters of fact are at stake.

> *Therefore*: Rational deliberation and controversy about moral matters are impossible.

Accordingly, moral skeptics insist that judgments in this domain lie outside the pale of serious intellectual concern. The moral convictions of peo-

somehow discernible by a special faculty of moral intuition—a peculiar "moral sense," as it were. Only recently has this far-fetched view attracted the criticism it deserves. See Richard Boyd, "How to Be a Moral Realist," in *Essays on Moral Realism*, ed. Geoffrey Sayre-McCord (Ithaca, N.Y.: Cornell University Press, 1988), as well as some of the other essays of that anthology.

ple are reduced to a jumble of incompatible opinions held by different individuals or societies, and rational discussion of and adjudication among them become impossible. Claims that murder, torture, or anything else is wrong, wicked, or evil, are "merely subjective sentiments" that are no-wise matters of truth and have no basis in objective fact. Contentions about matters of morality are neither true nor false, and any idea of obtaining knowledge in moral matters is simply a delusion.

The flaw of this argumentation lies in the untenability of its initial premise. For moral contentions are indeed about matters of fact, but about evaluative rather than merely descriptive facts. They too can be correct or incorrect, well founded or inappropriate. Of course determining which is the case may be difficult here: the verification of morally evaluative facts is a complex matter—there is often no quick and easy way of settling the matter. But this difficulty and complexity does not mean that facts are not at issue (any more than it does in scientific matters).

There indeed are logically cogent arguments leading from factual premises to morally evaluative conclusions, but the "facts" at issue in those premises obviously have to be "morally laden" facts. Consider the following:

X did A deliberately and solely to inflict pain (harm, anguish) on Y.

Therefore: X acted wrongly.

Such an inference involves a perfectly valid move from matters of fact to a moral evaluation. (To be sure, an enthymematic premise about how the concept of "wrongdoing" works lies in the background here.) Once one acknowledges the existence of evaluative facts, the moral enterprise emerges as objective and fact-oriented.

Only if one subscribes to a mistakenly narrow view of "facts," one that focuses exclusively on descriptive matters and flatly excludes evaluative appraisals from the domain of factuality, can one maintain an unbridgeable divide that precludes the move from factual premises to evaluative conclusions. And this position is quite untenable. That certain items represent human advantages (by serving our needs, for example, as nourishment or companionship do) is a matter of empirical, determinable fact. That certain arrangements in regard to human action impede and others foster the satisfaction of people's interests is also a matter of empirically determinable fact. And such facts have straightforward moral implications—though, to be sure, indications mediated by moral principles.

"But moral objectivity is surely counterindicated by the circumstance that one cannot validly criticize the moral code of a society by any 'external' criteria." Rubbish! Whether a certain operational code is intended within the ambit of its social context to operate as a moral code may well be a proper subject of discussion and controversy. But once it is settled that it is indeed a moral code that is at issue, then one can certainly bring principles of critical evaluation to bear. For at this point the question becomes paramount whether—and how effectively—this code accomplishes for its society those functions for which moral codes are instituted among people—to canalize their interactions into lines that safeguard their best interests.

When we are evaluating a moral code in this way, we are not simply exercising a cultural imperialism by judging it against our own in asking how concordant or discordant it is with the prevailing moral standards of our environing group. We are judging it, rather, against those universal and, as it were, absolute standards in terms of which the adequacy of any code, our own included, must be appraised. What makes an action right or wrong (as the case may be) is just exactly the issue of whether doing the sort of thing at issue injures or protects the interests of all the agents concerned. (To reemphasize: morality is by definition geared to the benefit of rational agents, even as refrigeration is by definition geared to the cooling.)[17] This is part and parcel of the very meaning of "morally right" and "morally wrong." And it renders judgment in these matters factual, objective, and rationally disputable.

This means that arguments against moral verdicts from an absence of consensus simply do not work. Disagreement negates appropriateness no more in moral than in observational matters. It is notorious that people will disagree in eyewitness reports about the description of a perpetrator or about the size of a crowd in a public square. And different historical cultures have held very different views on the issue of whether the blood ebbs and flows in its channels or whether it circulates. The prospect (or even reality) of disagreement does not prevent such descriptive issues from being objective matters of correct and incorrect assertion. And there is no good reason to think the situation all that different with respect to moral matters. Here, as elsewhere, we must be prepared to face disagreement with comparative equanimity. (After all, we do not expect the natural science of other eras—of our remote predecessors, say, or even of our eventual successors—to agree with ours.) The existence of room for dissensus within it does not imply the subjectivity of a rational enterprise.

---

[17] Does this way of viewing the matter put subrational creatures altogether outside the pale of moral concern? By no means. We take an interest in many sorts of things. And it matters deeply to rational agents how other rational agents treat animals—or for that matter, any being that has interests capable of being injured. We have a substantial interest in how others comport themselves who also belong to the type to which we see ourselves belonging.

Morality is thus a matter of reason and not of arbitrary, ungrounded choice. Moral values (honesty, kindness, and so on) rest on a ruling principle—the value of the person and the (moral) requirement to take due account of the interest of others in our own actions. That a purported moral evaluation actually qualifies as such is and must be capable of rational explanation and justification. We do not choose or make moral values but learn about them by thinking through what is required for safeguarding the best interest of people.[18] If morality were a mere matter of taste or of custom or of arbitrary choice, then harming helpless people needlessly, for example, might, in some society's scheme of things, be seen as morally preferable to helping them, and this perverted "morality" would have claims to appropriateness just as good as those of practices based on kindness and considerateness. And this is patently absurd. The capacity of certain modes of conduct to meet, or fail to meet, the requirements of morality—to safeguard the best (real) interests of people in general—is clearly not a matter of "decision" or "perspective" but one of impersonal fact, so that the appropriateness of moral judgments can be supported in an intersubjectively cogent way.[19]

[18] Only by turning one's back upon morality altogether can an existentialist maintain, with Sartre, "that freedom is the unique foundation of values and that *nothing*, absolutely nothing, justifies one in adopting this or that particular value, this or that particular scale of values" (*Being and Nothingness*, trans. H. E. Barnes [New York: Pocket Books, 1953], p. 46). Morality is, as we have seen, inextricably bound up with rationality, since moral validity calls for a justification of a certain sort (in terms of protecting the interests of people). A "value" whose adoption one cannot justify with reference to cogent principles is no real value at all but merely an arbitrary preference.

[19] The issues of this chapter are also treated more fully in the author's *Moral Absolutes* (New York: Peter Lang, 1989).

Eleven _____

Moral Values as Immune to Relativism

Uniformity despite Diversity: The Role of Basic Principles

Moral pluralism is unavoidable: moral codes can appropriately differ from one society to another. Does this fact not entail an indifferentist relativism to the effect that, in the end, "anything goes," by making morality into what is ultimately just a matter of local custom?

Anthropologists and even, alas, philosophers often say things like "The Wazonga tribe deems it morally proper (or even mandatory) to sacrifice firstborn female children to the tribal gods." But there are big problems here. This way of talking betokens lamentably loose thinking. For compare:

(1) The Wazonga habitually (customarily) sacrifice. . . .
(2) The Wazonga think it acceptable (or perhaps even meritorious) to sacrifice. . . .
(3) The Wazonga think it *morally* acceptable (or mandatory) to sacrifice. . . .

It must be noted that, however true and incontestable the first two contentions may be, the third is just untenable. For compare (3) with:

(4) The Wazonga think it *mathematically* true that dogs have tails.

No matter how firmly convinced the Wazonga may be that dogs have tails, thesis (4)—taken as it stands, with its overt reference to mathematical truth—is firmly and squarely a thesis of ours, *not* one of theirs! That "mathematically" is clearly something that we ourselves have interjected into the picture. And for this very reason it is in deep difficulty unless the condition is realized—as in the circumstances seems highly implausible—that the Wazonga have an essentially correct conception of what mathematics is and, moreover, are convinced that the claim that dogs have tails belongs among the appropriate contentions of this particular realm. Analogously, one cannot appropriately maintain (3) unless one is prepared to claim both that the Wazonga have an essentially correct conception of what morality is (correct, that is, by *our* lights) and furthermore that they are convinced that the practice in question is acceptable within the framework of this (moral) project as so conceived. And this concatenation of conditions is not only implausible in the circumstances but even paradoxical, seeing that the first commitment powerfully counterindicates the second. The salient point is that the mere fact of seeing this practice as mandated by custom (as part of "what's expected of us and what we've always done") does not make it part of their morality. Only a morally cogent rationale can render a customary practice—however compulsory—into a moral one.

The anthropological route to moral relativism is, to say the least, eminently problematic. There is no difficulty whatever about the idea of different social *customs*, but the idea of different *moralities* faces insuperable difficulties. The case is much like that of saying that the tribe whose counting practices are based on the sequence "one, two, many" has a different arithmetic from ourselves. To do anything like justice to the facts one would have to say that they do not have arithmetic at all, but just a peculiar and very rudimentary way of counting.[1] And similarly with those exotic tribesmen of ours. On the given evidence, they do not have a different morality; rather, their culture just has not developed to a point where they have a morality at all. If they think that it is acceptable to engage in practices like the sacrifice of firstborn girl children, then their grasp of the conception of morality is—on the face of it—somewhere between inadequate and nonexistent. It is (just barely) conceivable that sense could be made of a locution like "The Wazonga believe that morality requires them to perform X," where X is suttee, say, or some other practice that we ourselves deem morally outrageous. But the story needed to implement this sense-making project would have to be complex and (to our ears) extremely implausible. (For example, that they believe that this practice affords the only way to prevent some evil demon from wreaking havoc on the community.) And of course the point of such a story must be a principle that (like saving the community from anguish, agony, and annihilation) envisions a patently moral purpose from our point of view and would thus (in the circumstances) serve as a moral motive for us as well.

It is, in the end, the controlling role of higher-level principles inherent in the very idea of what "morality" is all about that saves morality from a destructive fission that extends an open invitation to indifferentism. Such overarching moral principles provide for such "fixed" and "absolute" moral values as:

the value of the human person, grounding (inter alia) its rights of safety and security;

[1] The earliest Mesopotamian counting notation was a matter of context-variable numerical indicators, with one symbol indicating 10 when sheep were at issue, 6 when indicating containers of grain, and 18 when referring to fields or plots of arable land. Whatever these symbols were, they were not numbers, and such combinational manipulations as they admitted of do not constitute arithmetic. But this fact pivots on what *we* think—namely on how we understand what is at issue with "arithmetic," it being just this that is at issue in *our* discussion of the matter.

the dignity and respect of the individual;

liberty, individual freedom, the right to self-determination;

people's rights to consultation in matters affecting their well-being and interests.

We cannot at one and the same time remain within the moral purview and avoid acknowledging these fundamental desiderata as pivotal to the moral enterprise, seeing that they are constitutive of this enterprise as such. To abandon them is not to contemplate "a different morality" but to abandon the moral domain itself, to change the subject of discussion (e.g., to mores and customs). And when these rights are infringed or abrogated in a certain culture or society, it proclaims its moral failings in virtue of this very fact. There is simply no "room for negotiation" here.

Implementation Hierarchies

Morality is a particular, well-defined sort of project whose cohesive unity as such resides in its functional objective of molding the behavior of people through a care for one another's interests. Even as there are many ways to build houses, fuel automobiles, or skin cats, so there are various ways of being moral. But that surely does not mean that there is no overarching unity of goals, functions, principles, and values to lend a definitional cohesion to the enterprise. Moral variability is more apparent than real—an absolute uniformity does, and must, prevail at the level of fundamentals. "Act with due heed of the interests of others" is a universal and absolute moral principle whose working out in different contexts will, to be sure, very much depend on just exactly how the interests of people happen to be reciprocally intertwined. But despite the diversity of the substantive moral codes of different societies, the basic overarching principles of morality are uniform and invariant—inherent in the very idea of what morality is all about.

Accordingly, different "moralities" are simply diverse implementations of certain uniform, overarching moral principles. There is ample room for situational variation and pluralism in response to the question "What is the morally appropriate thing to do?" But there is no such room with respect to "What is morality—and what are the principles at issue here?" The concept of morality and its contents are fixed by the "questioner's prerogative" inherent in the principle that it is the inquirer's own conception of the matter that is determinative for what is at issue in his or her inquiries. In our deliberations about moral rights and wrongs it is thus our conception of "morality" and its governing principles that is conclusive for what is at issue. When *we* engage in deliberations about morality—whether our own or that of others—it is "morality" *as we understand it* that figures in this discussion.[2] And this circumstance of theoretic fixity engenders a fixity of those project-definitive moral principles.

All modes of morality have important elements in common simply in view of the fact that morality is at issue. Since (by hypothesis) they all qualify as "modes of morality," they are bound to encompass such fundamental considerations as the following:

1. What people do matters. Some actions are right, others wrong; some are acceptable, and some not. There is an important difference here.

2. This is not just a matter of convention, custom, and the done thing. Violations of moral principles are offenses not just against sensibility but against people's just claims in matters where people's actual well-being is at stake.

3. In violating the moral rules, we inflict injury on the life, welfare, or otherwise legitimate interests of others—either actually or by way of putting them unjustifiedly at risk.

Attunement to consideration of this sort is *by definition* essential to any system of "morality" and serves to provide the basis for imperatives like:

Do not simply ignore other people's rights and claims in your own deliberations.

Do not inflict needless pain on people.

Honor the legitimate interests of others.

Do not take what rightfully belongs to others without their appropriately secured consent.

Do not wantonly break promises.

Do not cause someone anguish simply for your own amusement.

In the context of morality, principles and rules of this sort are universal and absolute. They are of the very essence of morality; in abandoning them, we would withdraw from a discussion of morality and would in effect, be changing the subject. What we say might be interesting—and even true—but it would be dealing with another topic.

From the moral point of view, the *empirical* search for "cultural invariants" as pursued by some ethnologists is thus entirely beside the point.[3] When such investigations embark on a cross-cultural quest for "moral uni-

---

[2] But just who are the "we" at issue? Clearly, those who are members of our linguistic community—those who realize that when we speak of "morality," we mean *morality* (with the various things involved therein), and not, say, basket weaving.

[3] See Clyde Kluckhohn, *Culture and Behavior* (Glencoe, Ill.: Free Press, 1962); idem, "Ethical Relativity; Sic et Non," *Journal of Philosophy* 52 (1955): 663–77; R. Redfield, "The Universally Human and the Culturally Variable," *Journal of General Education* 10 (1957): 150–60; Ralph Linton, "Universal Ethical Principles: An Anthropological View," in *Moral Principles of Action*, ed. R. N. Anshen (New York: Harper & Row, 1952); idem, "The Problem of Universal Values," in *Method and Perspective in Anthropology*, ed. R. F. Spencer (Minneapolis: University of Minnesota Press, 1954).

versals" or "universal values" amid the variation of social customs, they are engaged in a search that, however interesting and instructive in its own way, has nothing whatever to do with the sort of normative universality at issue with morality as such. Moral universality is not a matter of cross-cultural commonality but of a *conceptually* constrained uniformity. (It would be just as pointless to investigate whether another culture's forks have *tines*.)

"But how can you pivot the issue on 'the very idea of what "morality" is all about'? After all, different people have different ideas about this?" Of course different people think differently about morality, even as they think differently about dogs or automobiles. But that is basically irrelevant. What is at issue with "morality" as such does not lie with you or with me but with all of us. What is relevantly at issue is how the word is actually used in the community—in the linguistic culture in which our discussion of the issue transpires. It is a matter not of what people think about the topic but of how they use the terminology that defines it.

Yet how can this fixity of the conception of morality and of the basic principles that are at issue within it—inherent in the monolithic uniformity of "what *morality* is"—be reconciled with the plain fact of a pluralistic diversity of (presumably cogent) answers to the question "What is it moral to do?" How can such an absolutism of morality's fundamentals coexist with the patent relativity of moral evaluations across different times and cultures?

The answer lies in the fact that several intermediate levels or strata inevitably separate those overarching "basic principles of morality" from any concrete judgments about what it is moral to do. We have, in fact, to deal with a descending hierarchy of characterizing aims, fundamental principles and values, governing rules, implementing directives, and (finally) particular rulings. (See display 11.1.)

At the topmost level we have the defining aims of morality, the objectives that identify the moral enterprise as such by determining its nature and specifying the aims and objectives that characterize what morality is all about. (Example: "Act with a view to safeguarding the valid interests of others.") These characterizing aims of morality represent the overarching "defining objectives" of the entire enterprise that characterize the project as such. They explicate what is at issue when it is with morality (rather than basket weaving) that we propose to concern ourselves. In spelling out the fundamental idea of what morality is all about, these top-level norms provide the ultimate reference points of moral deliberation. They are unalterably fixed—inherent in the very nature of the subject.

These fundamental "aims of the enterprise" also fix the basic principles and controlling values that delineate the moral virtues (honesty, trustworthiness, civility, probity, and the rest). Such values define the salient norms that link the abstract characterizing aims to an operational

---

Display 11.1. Illustrations of the Implementation Hierarchy for Moral Norms

Level 1: *Characterizing aims*
   To support the best interests of people and to avoid injuring them.

Level 2: *Governing principles and values*
   Do not cause people needless pain. (GENTLENESS)
   Do not endanger people's lives or their well-being unnecessarily. (CARE FOR SAFETY)
   Honor your genuine commitments to people; in dealing with people, give them their just due. (PROBITY)
   Help others when you reasonably can. (GENEROSITY)
   Don't take improper advantage of others. (FAIRNESS)

Level 3: *Governing rules*
   Don't hurt people unnecessarily.
   Don't lie; don't say what you believe not to be so.
   Don't cheat.

Level 4: *Operating directives*
   Be candid when replying to appropriate questions.
   Do not play with unfair dice.
   Where possible, use anesthetics when operating on people.

Level 5: *Particular rulings*
   Return the money you borrowed from Smith.
   Don't pollute this river; dispose of your sewage elsewhere.
   Don't let these children play with those matches.

---

morality of specific governing rules. The norms embodied in these basic principles and values are "universal" and "absolute," serving as parts of what makes morality the thing it is. (Examples: "Do not violate the duly established rights and claims of others." "Do not unjustly deprive others of life, liberty, or opportunity for self-development." "Do not tell self-serving falsehoods." "Do not deliberately aid and abet others in wrongdoing.") Accordingly, these high-level principles also lie fixedly in the very nature of the subject. At these two topmost levels, then, there is simply no room for any "disagreement about morality." Here disagreement betokens misunderstanding: if one does not recognize the fundamental aims, principles, and values that characterize the moral enterprise as such, then one is simply talking about something else altogether. In any discussion of morality, these things are simply givens. But this situation changes as one moves further down the list and takes additional steps in the descent to concreteness.

   At the next (third) level we encounter the governing rules and regulations that direct the specifically moral transaction of affairs. Here we have the generalities of the usual and accustomed sort: "Do not lie," "Do not

cheat," "Do not steal," and so forth. At this level we come to the imperatives that guide our deliberations and decisions. Like the Ten Command-
ments, they set out the controlling dos and don'ts of the moral practice of
a community, providing us with general guidance in moral conduct. Here
variability begins to set in. For these rules implement morality's ruling
principles at the concrete level of recommended practices in a way that
admits of adjustment to the changeable circumstances of local conditions.
   A generalized moral rule on the order of the injunction

Do not steal. = Do not take something that properly belongs to another.

is in itself still something abstract and schematic. It still requires the concrete fleshing out of substantive implementing specifications to tell us
what sorts of things make for "proper ownership." And so the next (fourth)
level presents us with the ground rules of procedure or implementing
directives that furnish our working guidelines and criteria for the moral
resolution of various types of cases. (Example: "Killing is wrong except in
cases of self-defense or under legal mandate as in war or executions.") At
this level of implementing standards and criteria, the variability of local
practice comes to the fore, so that there is further room for pluralistic
diversification here; we ourselves implement "Do not lie, avoid telling
falsehoods," by way of "Say what you believe (to be the case)," but a society of convinced skeptics could not do so. The operating ground rules of
level 4 thus incorporate the situation-relative standards and criteria
though which the more abstract, higher-level rules get their grip on concrete situations. Those general rules themselves are too abstract—too
loose or general to be applicable without further directions to give them
a purchase on concrete situations. They must be given concrete implementation with reference to local—and thus variable—arrangements.[4]
   Finally, at the lowest (fifth) level we come to the particular moral rulings, individual resolutions with respect to the specific issues arising in
concrete cases. (Example: "It was wicked of Lady Macbeth to incite her
husband to kill the king.")
   In such an "implementation hierarchy" we thus descend from what is
abstractly and fixedly universal to what is concrete and variable. Level 2
is contained in level 1 simply be way of exfoliative "explication." But as we

---

[4] The analogy of natural law is helpful: "Theft, murder, adultery and all injuries are forbidden by the laws of nature; but which is to be called theft, what murder, what adultery, what
injury in a citizen, this is not to be determined by the natural but by the civil law" (Thomas
Hobbes, *De Cive*, chap. 4, sec. 16). Thomas Aquinas holds that appropriate human law must
be subordinate to the natural law by way of "particular determination"; with different human
laws, varying from place to place, nevertheless representing appropriate concretizations
of the same underlying principle of natural law (see *Summa Theologica*, I of II, questions
95–96).

move downward past level 3 to the implementing specifications of level 4, there is increasingly a looseness or "slack" that makes room for the specific and variable ways of different groups for implementing the particular higher-level objective at issue.

The entire hierarchy comes to a head in a ruling imperative ("Support the interests of people") that stands correlative with an enterprise-determinative value ("the best interests of people"). This overarching concern does not itself stand subordinate to further moral rules. After all, only up to a certain point can we have rules for applying rules and principles for applying principles. The process of validating lower-level considerations in terms of higher-level ones must come to a stop somewhere. And with these implementation hierarchies it is the overarching controlling teleology of "the aim of the entire enterprise" that gives at once unity and determinatives to the justificatory venture.

Note that the element of abstract generality imposes the need for some suitable qualification above the bottom level of concrete particularity. Here some sort of qualification like "needless" or "unnecessary" or "inappropriate" (or their contraries) will be operative. The sorts of things that keep harms and so forth from being needless are clear enough. They include such qualifications as "merely for personal convenience," "for one's own gain," "for one's own pleasure," or "out of perversity or schadenfreude." To be sure, the list of inadequate reasons that render harms morally inappropriate is potentially endless, but the sort of thing at issue is clear enough to anyone but a moral imbecile.

Overall, then, we have to deal with a chain of subordination linkages that connect a concrete moral judgment—a recommendation or command for a particular moral act—with the ultimate defining aim of the moral enterprise. The long and short of it is that any appropriate moral injunction must derive its validity through being an appropriate instantiation or concretization of an overarching principle of universal (unrestricted) validity under which it is subsumed. It must, in short, represent a circumstantially appropriate implementation of the fixities of absolute morality. Thus even as in Roman Catholic theology there is a "hierarchy of truths" that places different teachings of the church at different levels of doctrinal essentiality or fundamentality, so in the present context there is a comparable hierarchy of imperatival strata that place different injunctions at different levels of fundamentality in the moral enterprise, with some (the basic principles) as, in this setting, absolute, and others as variable and relative to context and circumstance. Fundamentals are fixed as essential to the moral domain as such, but agreement on concrete issues is itself something more marginal.

To be sure, this sort of story holds not just for morality but for any inherently goal-oriented human project—medicine or dietetics or science or whatever. In every case, such a hierarchical series descends from the overarching defining objective of the enterprise at issue down to the specific resolutions of concrete cases. The same structure of practical reasoning by subordination under higher-level norms obtains throughout.

Medicine provides a helpful illustration. Here too there is an "implementation hierarchy" that leads from a fixed, "top-level" characterizing aim—health—through governing norms and values (like "well nourished," "well rested," "mentally balanced") to particular rules ("Eat and drink adequately"; "Get enough rest"; etc.). Finally, we move via moderating injunctions ("Three meals a day") down to the particular decisions and rulings of medical practice (particular diet plans or prescriptions). The top levels of such a normative hierarchy are "ultimate"—they define and specify what is at issue in the venture under condsideration. But variation arises at the lower levels of implementation. How a principle like "Do not drive in a way that needlessly endangers the lives of others" gets implemented will depend on a great many factors of situational variation (weather conditions, visibility conditions, the expectations of others as defined by local speed limits, and on and on). As one moves through the lower levels of such a hierarchy, there is a "slack" that leaves room for increasing variability and dissensus. Specific rules and guidelines will vary with situations and circumstances, with different experential contexts. "Maintaining an alert mind" is in everyone's medical interest, but "Getting eight hours regular sleep" is appropriate only for some.

The crucial fact is that one selfsame moral value—fairness, for example—can come into operation very differently in different contexts. In an economy of abundance it may militate for equality of shares, in an economy of scarcity for equality of opportunity. The particular circumstances that characterize a context of operation may importantly condition the way in which a moral value or principle can (appropriately) be applied. We cannot expect to encounter any universal consensus across cultural and temporal divides: physicians of different eras are (like moralists) bound to differ—and to some extent those of different cultures as well. There inevitably is substantial variability among particular groups, each with its own varying ideas conditioned by locally prevailing conditions and circumstances. But the impact of low-level variation is mitigated by the fact that justification at lower levels proceeds throughout with reference to superordinated standards in a way that makes for higher-level uniformity. Uniform high-level principles will have to be implemented differently in different circumstances. Medicine and morality alike are complex projects unified and integrated amid the welter of changing conditions and circumstances by the determinative predominance of high-level principles.

At the level of basic principles, then, morality is absolute; its strictures at this level hold good for everyone, for all rational agents. And lower-level rules and rulings must—if valid—preserve a "linkage of subsumption" to those highest-level abstractions, a linkage mediated by way of more-restrictive modes of implementation. These implementing rules involve contextual relativity—coordination with contingently variable (setting-dependent and era- and culture-variable) circumstances and situations. Thus while moral objectives and basic principles—those top levels of the hierarchy of moral norms—are absolute and universal, "slack" arises as we move further down the ladder, leaving room for (quite appropriate) contextual variability and differentiation. "Do not unjustifiably take the property of another for your own use" is an unquestionably valid principle of absolute morality. But it avails nothing until such time as there are means for determining what is "the property of another" and what constitutes "unjustified taking." "Don't break promises merely for your own convenience" is a universal moral rule; as such, it is global and absolute. But what sorts of practices constitute making a valid promise is something that is largely determined through localized social conventions. Local context—variable history, tradition, expectation-defining legal systems, and the like—thus makes for substantial variability at the level of operational rules and codes, of moral practices.

But a linkage of subordination is maintained throughout. The validity of concrete rulings is always a matter of their attuning global (and abstract) prescriptions to local (and concrete) conditions. Without that linkage to the fixed highest-level absolutes, the linkage to morality is severed. For a particular ruling to be a proper moral ruling at all, there must be a suitable moral rationale for the action—a pathway of subordination linkages that connects it in a continuous manner all the way up to the characterizing aims of the moral enterprise. Varying practices and codes of procedure possess moral validity only insofar as they are implementations of a fixed and determinate set of moral principles. Moral validity must always root in a moral universality that is constrained by a conceptual fixity.

Morality's characteristic universality is thus inevitably mediated through factors that are variable, conventional, and culturally relative. The rules of hospitality toward strangers, for example, do and cannot but differ drastically in European and in Bedouin culture. Still, the deeper moral principles that underlie the moral rules and practices of a society ("Even strangers have their due—they too are entitled to respect, to courtesy, and to assistance in need") transcend the customs of any particular community. As concerns morality, culture is indeed a localizing and differentiating agent—but one that merely conditions to local circumstances those fundamental invariants that are inherent in the very conception of morality as such. The local "moralities" of various communities merely canalize and implement such general principles by attuning them to the character of local conditions and circumstances. For the universality of fundamental moral principles does not mean that all moral agents must proceed in exactly the same way at the level of concrete detail. (To revert to the preceding example: medical competence too is also based on uniform and universal principles—conscientious care to provide the best available treatment for one's patients, but that does not mean that competent doctors must in all times, places, and circumstances administer the same treatments.)

The long and short of it is that the anthropological reduction of morality to mores just does not work. Some things are wrong in an absolute and universal way:

> murder (i.e., unjustifiedly killing another person);
> taking improper advantage of people;
> inflicting pointless harm;
> lying and deception for selfish advantage, betraying a trust for personal gain;
> breaking promises out of sheer perversity;
> misusing the institutions of one's society for one's own purposes.

The unacceptability (i.e., moral inappropriateness) of such actions lies in the very idea of what morality is all about. Local custom to the contrary notwithstanding, such things are morally wrong anytime, anywhere, and for anyone. Their prohibitions are moral universals—parts of morality as such. (And so they hold good not just for us humans but for all rational beings.)

To be sure, different societies operate with different moral ground rules at the procedural level. Some societies deem it outrageous for women to expose their faces, their breasts, their knees; others view this as altogether acceptable and perhaps even mandatory. But behind this variation stands a universal principle: "Respect people's sensibilities about the appropriate and acceptable appearance of fellow humans by conforming to the prevailing rules of proper modesty." This overarching principle is universal and absolute. Its implementation with respect to, say, elbows or belly buttons is of course something that varies with custom and the practices of the community. The rule itself is abstract and schematic—in need of implementing criteria as to what "proper modesty and due decorum" demand. The matter is one of a universal principle with variable implementations subject to "locally established standards and criteria" that are grounded in the particular customs and traditions of the community.

And so, while the concrete strictures of morality—its specific ordinances and procedural rules of thumb—will of course differ from age to age and culture to culture, nevertheless the ultimate principles that serve to define the project of "morality" as such are universal. The uniform governing conception of "what morality is" suffices to establish and standardize those ultimate and fixed principles that govern the moral enterprise as such. At the level of fundamentals the variability of moral codes is underpinned by an absolute uniformity of moral principles and values. At the highest levels alone is there absoluteness: here an impersonal cogency of acceptance prevails—the rejection of appropriate contentions at this level involves a lapse of rational cogency. But at the lower levels there is almost always some room for variation—and dispute as well. (How concern for the well-being of one's fellows can be brought to effective expression, for example, will very much depend on the institutions of one's society—and also, to some extent, on one's place within it.)

Against Relativism

Relativism proclaims: "We have *our* moral convictions (rules, standards, values), and they have *theirs*. One is every bit as good as the other. To each his own. Nobody is in a position to criticize or condemn the moral views of others."[5] But to take this line at every point as regards moral matters is simply to abandon the very idea of morality. Such a position does indeed hold good with respect to *mores*—we eat with cutlery, they with chopsticks; we sleep on beds, they in hammocks; we speak one language, they another; and each with equal propriety. But this indifference does not hold for matters of *moral principle*. "We treat strangers with respect; they (those cannibals) eat them. We treat the handicapped kindly; they drown them at sea. We treat darker-skinned humans as equals; they as inferiors. And the one way of proceeding is just as appropriate as the other. It's all just a matter of local custom." Rubbish! It is just not true from the moral standpoint. If crass selfishness, pointless maltreatment, wanton deceit, or the infliction of needless pain is wrong for us, it is wrong for them too—and conversely. At the level of fundamentals, matters of moral principle are the same for everyone. What holds good for us holds good for them too. A code that sees every mode of behavior as indifferent—every sort of action as equally acceptable—is by its very nature not a moral code (whatever else it may be).

To be sure, even people who class themselves as flat-out relativists usually incline to regard *some* modes of behavior (political torture, random violence, senseless vandalism) as improper and undesirable. How, then, must they appraise their own position on such matters? They incline to say

[5] After all, "the actual variations in the moral code [of different groups] are more readily explained by the hypothesis that they reflect different ways of life than by the hypothesis that they express perceptions, most of them seriously inadequate and badly distorted, of objective values" (Mackie, *Ethics*, p. 37).

something like this: "Of course we ourselves (civilized sophisticates that we are) deem this sort of thing to be wicked. But others could, with equal validity, think it to be acceptable—nay, even praiseworthy." The difficulty of course lies in the phrase "with equal validity." From whose point of view does this equality obtain? Ours? Certainly not! On our standards, our own position clearly prevails. From God's? But when did He become a party to our discussion? (And if He were a party to the discussion, then what price relativism?) In this matter as in any other, we must of course rely on *our own* basis of justificatory reflections to furnish a validation we can accept as satisfactory. We have no real choice but to proceed from where we are.

Relativists very mistakenly deem cultural variation to indicate that "it just doesn't make any real difference." But this slide from pluralistic variation to indifferentism roots in a grave error—a mistaken assimilation of morality to mere mores that are conventionally arbitrary and inherently indifferent. The fatal flaw of such radical relativism lies in its failure to distinguish sufficiently clearly between matters of custom and social approval on the one hand, and matters of principle and moral propriety on the other.

From the Thrasymachus of Plato's *Republic* to Nietzsche, Marx, Freud, and the existentialists, critics of "traditional morality" propose not to abolish morality as such but to put something different and better in its place—to provide a new set of "superior" moral values and principles. However, such revolutionism cannot be *altogether* revolutionary—at any rate, as long as its advocacy rests on a rational basis. For insofar as its proponents set out to *convince* us, they must somehow argue that their variant moral code somehow affords a better way of life. They must hold that it better achieves the aims and purposes at issue in morality—the safeguarding and enhancement of human well-being. And here, of course, "morality" is and must be "what people *mean* by 'morality'—that is, 'morality' as standardly understood." And that means that their arguments must ultimately pivot on the project of morality-as-we-understand-it— morality as action supportive of people's interests, with those fundamental values that characterize the entire project's reason for being left wholly intact. (Clearly, if we are to accept those putatively superior moral values as indeed better than ones that we endorse, this evaluative conclusion can only be *argued* with reference to values we already hold.)

The relativist thunders: "How can you justify accepting one set of practices and rejecting another?" This approval and condemnation is, of course, something one can validate only by *reasoning*, by reflective and judicious evaluative appraisal. But on what basis can this reasoning proceed, by whose standards and measures of morality? Why . . . by our own, of course! (Who else's would we use—or would we ever want to use?) Ultimately and at the highest level, the values at issue must be those that we ourselves envision as universal.

The relativist will of course ask: "But who are the *we* whose standards are at issue? Are we our family, our friends and relatives, our social confederates? Surely there is vast scope for variation here." The appropriate resolution is not all that difficult to come by. That standard-setting we-group consists of just exactly the same persons that determine the terms of reference in which our own deliberations proceed—the ones whose verbal behavior determines that "just" means *just* (and not *elm-tree*) and that "human" means *human* (and not *equine*). That is, the group at issue is simply the linguistic community within which our discussions about morality transpire, and the standards at issue are those that inhere in the very concept of morality as it is understood by us—and by anyone else who understands it.

But what, then, of moral variability—of interpersonal and cross-cultural disagreement regarding moral matters? It is tempting to indulge in a convenient impoverishment of the range of alternatives: throughout morality we have *either* mere mores, mere customs of the tribe, *or* unvarying and all-pervasive absolutes. Given this choice, the reduction of morality to matters of mere convention seems relatively plausible. But of course this particular range of alternatives is too narrow; it overlooks another possibility far more promising than either of those considered, namely, that moral norms can operate at very different levels and that morality accordingly involves the implementation of fundamental and invariant principles within diversified and variable situations.

The uniformity of the higher-level norms determinative of morality means that different families of (appropriate) moral rules—different moral codes—simply represent diverse routes to the same ultimate destination. And given the functional integrity of morality—as an endeavor geared to safeguarding and promoting the best or real interests of rational agents as such—this is exactly how it should be. The mere fact that a single enterprise—morality—is at issue means that, despite the plurality of moral codes, we have to deal with one single uniform family of fundamentals; the variability of moral rules is underpinned by an absolute uniformity of moral principles, the plurality of valid moral codes notwithstanding.

Relativism stands committed to the idea that morality is simply a matter of local convention. It loses sight of what is really at issue with morality— the proper heed of people's real interests. And thereby it makes a travesty of morality by restricting the idea of what people ought to do to what the particular customs of their society require. It confuses morality with mores. Mores indeed are simply matters of custom and convention, like table manners and dress codes. But morality involves the adaptation to local conditions of universal principles regarding the safeguarding of people's interests. A crucial divide thus separates morality from mores; a difference in kind is at issue. After all, moral choice is a matter of opting not for what people may happen to prefer but for what is (morally) preferable—or can reasonably be claimed to be so with a view to the determinitive aim of the whole enterprise, namely the safeguarding of the real interest of people in general. And this *normative* dimension means that the variability involved in the variation of moral rules is a mere surface phenomenon that does not reach down to the level of fundamentals.

Discussions of moral relativism by philosophers and social scientists alike are all too frequently vitiated by the oversimplification of seeing moral norms at all levels as being of a piece. They fail to distinguish between lower-level rules and standards, which indeed are variable and context dependent, and higher-level values and principles, which are fixed, universal, and unchanging. Recognition of the hierarchical stratification of moral norms is essential to a proper understanding of morality. The fact that there are uniform and unchanging principles at the top of the hierarchy—principles that inhere in the very conception of morality itself—is quite compatible with plurality, variation, and even some measure of conventionality in the moral norms of the lower levels. The multilevel structure of moral norms provides the key to reconciling the inherent absolutism of morality with the "cultural relativity" of moral codes by showing how the relativistic variation of such codes is perfectly compatible with the absolutism of moral fundamentals. Plurality and variability in regard to lower-level norms is nowise at odds with an absolutistic uniformity of higher-level principles.

An absolutistic one-morality doctrine at the level of the basic (abstract or "general") principles of morality is thus perfectly compatible with a circumstantially diversified plurality of moral codes at the level of concrete rules of operation. Morality has different levels. One is a parochial matter of particular practices—of locally conditioned concrete rules of operation relating to locally established claims, entitlements, obligations, and the like. But yet another is a universal matter of underlying principles that revolve about the governing factor of safeguarding people's real interests. Both are formative aspects of the overall enterprise. If one forgets about those overarching uniformities, the moral landscape assumes a kaleidoscopic variety. But appearances are misleading. There is a single overarching framework of *moral* principles that inhere fixedly in the very notion of what morality is all about. And so the transcultural variation of moral rules does not show that morality is something merely conventional and customary in nature. It illustrates rather than destroys the many-sided bearing of the uniform, context-transcendent, universal moral principles operative at the level of fundamentals.

The Claims of Our Own Community

But if the variability of its concrete procedural rules is a fact of life in morals—if different sorts of moral directives and rulings can (quite appropriately) obtain for different cultural groups—then how does one's own particular code secure its obligating hold upon oneself? Why should I see myself as duty-bound to follow "our established rules" rather than some others?

The answer to this question is straightforward. A certain (potentially variable) rule obtains its binding grip (its deontic hold, as it were) upon us precisely through representing the contextually appropriate way of implementing a certain fixed value or principle in the particular social context in which we are in fact emplaced. The mere fact of their being de facto part of the operational code of our social environment endows them with authority exactly because this society is (by hypothesis) our society.

The salient point is that the moral code of our own environing community is the one that is paramount *for us*. It is the one that defines and specifies the rights and expectations of those others with whom we are (ex hypothesi) cosituated in a context of mutual interaction. It makes little sense to say: "I concede that you have shown me I should be law abiding; but why abide by those laws of my environing community? Why not pick and choose one's laws?" The fact, however, is that being law abiding *consists* just exactly in respecting the laws of one's own community; to pick and choose one's own laws is not being law abiding at all. And the same holds for morality. People's real interests are largely canalized by their (justified) expectations, and these are determined and defined by the ground rules of the community in which they operate. To treat the people among whom one lives and acts according to the moral code of a community foreign to the environing one is simply to fail to honor the requisites of morality. As long as the local moral ground rules are indeed just that— the locally operative mode implementing the basic principles of morality—they deserve our respect and our allegiance. To engage in the moral project at all—to be moral agents—we have to "play it by the rules" of *our* community because it is (by hypothesis) just this community that delineates and canalizes the interests of its members in whose honoring morality consists.

After all, in morality, as elsewhere, the universal is available to us only through mediation of the specific: one can pursue a generalized desideratum only via its particularized (and variable) concretizations. Communication is universal, language is specific; eating is universal, cookery local; morality is universal, particular concrete moral codes are variable and diversified. But such variability does not undermine or abrogate validity;

it does no more than illustrate that, with morality as elsewhere, one must pursue generalized desiderata via their specific realizations—the "married state" via a particular spouse. The universals of morality not only permit but require adjustment to local conditions. And at that level we are concerned not with validation of morality as such but with the justification of a particular moral code for a particular group in particular circumstances. The concrete code of our community is the only way in which implementation to the higher-level demands of morality is available *to us*, given the realities of the particular context in which we live and labor.

No doubt there is a large measure of truth in Emile Durkheim's contention that morality is simply "a set of rules of conduct, of practical imperatives which have grown up historically under the influence of specific social necessities."[6] But the fact that people's moral views are historically and culturally conditioned—our own of course included—does not preclude their binding stringency for those to whom they appertain (ourselves preeminently included). In transacting our moral affairs in this world, as in conducting our physical movements within it, we have no choice but to go on from where we are.

Perhaps Leopold von Ranke was right in saying that every age and every civilization "is equal in the sight of God." But even if this is so, it does not mean that we, who surely lack all pretentions to divinity, can or should see the moral rules and guidelines of any one group as having equally good claims for our adherence as any other. For us, the moral ground rules of our local setting are paramount—and rightfully so. Our moral reflections have to proceed from the position that we ourselves occupy in relation to the issues. Here, as elsewhere, the sensible thing is to proceed from where we are.

To be sure, the behavioral practices of a society (ours included) are not above criticism—gift horses into whose mouths we must not presume to look. Anything that people do can be done badly—the shaping of a moral code included. Confronted by any set of purported "moral rules of behavior," we can and should ask: "How well do they implement the fundamental principles that articulate the aims of the moral enterprise as we do (and must) understand it?" Any system (for example) that authorizes the infliction of pain on people for no better reason than affording amusement to others deserves flat-out condemnation and rejection. It would be a decisive objection to any system of "morality" that it deems acceptable (let alone worthy of approbation) a mode of behavior that is immoral on the conscientious application of *our* fundamental standards—that it ap-

---

[6] From a discussion in *La Revue* 59 (1905): 306–8; trans. in W.S.F. Pickering and H. L. Sutliffe, eds., *Durkheim: Essays on Morals and Education* (London: Routledge & Kegan Paul, 1979), p. 34.

proves pointless lying, for example, or wanton cruelty, or any other practice that countervails against the legitimate interests of people. For these
fundamental standards of morality are, in virtue of being so, not just ours
but everyone's—if they indeed are fundamental, then they must apply
everywhere.

Accordingly, one's own moral code can also be subjected to moral criticism and reevaluation. For the question can always be pressed whether
the concrete moral practices and rules of one's own (potentially variable)
code do indeed implement effectively the definitive values of the moral
enterprise and—above all—whether they satisfactorily serve the best real
interest of people in general. The operational code of our community can
be found defective or deficient in point of morality. (Think of Nazi Ger-
many, for example.) Socially accepted principles of action are clearly not
beyond criticism. But this criticism can—if appropriate—be developed
only from the vantage point of those first and fundamental principles that
characterize the moral project as such. These are unavoidably part and
parcel of any morality worthy of the name.

Morality by its very nature as such consists in the project of acting so as
to safeguard the interests of others as best we can manage it in prevailing
circumstances. And people do not choose what is in their interests;[7] they
are set for them by the physical, social, and situational circumstances of
their lives. But certainly what advantages one (health, freedom of action,
etc.) is something objective and not something that one makes up as one
goes along. The fact that interests have a personal (individual and situa-
tion-variable) aspect does not make them subjective. (Even my mere preference of chocolate over vanilla ice cream is bound up with the impersonal
benefit of "getting the flavor we prefer in an item of such that we like to
eat." Even in matters of taste I do not *decide* that the one thing has a
better flavor than the other; I *find* it to be so.)

Of course, no belief system, no thought framework, no system of
norms—moral or other—is a world-detached absolute delivered to humankind in unchangeable perfection by the world spirit from on high. We
can do no more than make use of the local, particularized, diversified
instruments that we humans can manage to develop within the limitations
of our place and time. Thus far, relativism is both inevitable and correct.
But this emphatically does *not* engender an indifferentistic subjectivism.
For pluralism does not mean that there are no applicable standards—that
with morality one can throw things together any which way. An overarching function is operative in the very conception of what morality is all

---

[7] Their choices, however, do affect how these interests operate. Once you have chosen
Helen to be your future wife, her attitude toward you becomes a matter of substantial interest for you.

about, which prevents it from becoming unraveled as a rational enterprise through the pluralistic variability that relativists mistakenly see as somehow destructive of moral universality.

The crucial point, then, is that one can be a pluralist in matters of morality without being a relativist, let alone an indifferentist. Consider the following positions:

> *Moral pluralism.* There are different, yet in their own context appropriate, moral codes.
>
> *Moral relativism.* There are no fixed principles in moral matters. Everything hinges on contingent local options. Morality is wholly a matter of mores.
>
> *Moral indifferentism.* Moral issues are ultimately indifferent. There is no objective justification for one position rather than another, no rationale of good reasons through which a particular culture's resolution can be justified (not even for its particular conditions, let alone unconditionally).

Moral relativism is to be rejected because an absolute uniformity prevails at the level of fundamental principles and values. And moral indifferentism is to be rejected because the moral code of one's own community has a valid claim to our own allegiance. But moral pluralism does not fall with these objections; it is something we can and must accept—an absolutism of moral principles notwithstanding.

People must feed themselves and house themselves. Nature dictates no *single unique process for accomplishing such ends—we must proceed to* make the best use we can of the possibilities that place and time put at our disposal. And analogously with morality's requirements of due care for the interests of people. Here too one must simply do the best one can, striving within the conditions and circumstances of their setting for practices and rules that align human interactions in a productive harmony from which everyone can benefit. But the diversity of moral codes is not at odds with the fundamental demand of moral rationality: that we pursue our own ends *appropriately,* with a due recognition of the needs, rights, and claims of others. The stability of moral fundamentals is nowise destroyed or abrogated by the moral variability created by the changing circumstantial vagaries of the human condition.[8]

[8] Some of the issues of this chapter are developed in the author's *Moral Absolutes.*

Twelve _____

Moral Rationality: Why Be Moral?

The Problem of Convenient Exceptions

Two questions must be distinguished: (1) what does morality require of us; what must one do to count as a morally good person? and (2) why should we do that which morality requires; why be a morally good person at all? The former question is one that can (nay, must) be addressed by essentially linguistic/conceptual means deployed in the preceding chapter, the problem being one of determining whether an agent comforms to the specifications of "moral agency" in the light of the conception that is definitionally at issue here. The latter question, however, presses beyond this conceptual level to pose the substantive issue of why it is that people should act in this sort of way.

As the preceding discussion has already indicated, the answer to the first question is relatively straightforward. In briefest outline it is that the very nature of morality as such requires that we should always and everywhere heed and give due weight to the interests of others as significant factors in our practical deliberations regarding issues of action.[1] But the second issue as to just why one should proceed in this way wears a more substantive aspect: Does morality have a justificatory rationale that ensures that everyone has good reason to act on moral principles? We come to the sixty-four-dollar question of moral theory: Why should something's protecting *your* interests count as a reason for *me* to do it?

It might well seem that utility provides the key here. For each of us has a substantial practical stake in morality. The practices enjoined by the moral rules (truth telling, promise keeping, fair play, and the like) secure an immense social utility for us by mandating modes of operation from which everyone benefits (violators such as liars, promise breakers, and cheaters included).[2] Seeing that the welfare of people in human

---

[1] This does not mean that we must weigh the interests of others equally with our own. After all, our responsibility for ourselves and our own actions is of a different order from that toward others. But we must accord them a substantial weight in line with the inherent value of personhood and so must (morally) be prepared, in principle, to subordinate our interests to theirs if circumstances should so warrant.

[2] As one recent writer has sensibly noted, "Morality is another major item of background social capital, without which operating everything from credit cards to courts of law [and, he might have added, even more fundamental things like communication and cooperative activity of every kind] would be far more expensive—perhaps prohibitively so" (Thomas Sowell, *Knowledge and Decisions* [New York: Basic Books, 1980], p. 30).

communities is always systemically interrelated, it is generally in one's own interest to care for the interests of others. The boat that we build through our actions within the social context is one that we all sail in together.

In consequence, being a moral person—heeding the interests of others in one's own actions—is also, as the world goes, by and large very much in one's own best interests. Morality is indissolubly linked to prudence through the simple (Hobbesian) recognition that everyone—oneself specifically included—has a better chance of faring well in a society of moral agents where people treat one another in an honest and considerate way. Prudence (due heed of my own self-oriented interests) and morality (due heed of the interests of others) cooperate in fruitful symbiosis. Prudential self-interest accordingly exerts a strong impetus toward abiding by the precepts of morality.[3]

But this line of reflection, sensible and appropriate though it is, does not really suffice for the task that needs to be accomplished. For in particular (though presumably exceptional) cases, immorally secured advantages can seemingly outweigh the benefits that agents can secure for themselves by moral comportment. The connection between the moral life and the good life is—to all appearances—at most statistical. No doubt people will, on the whole, live happier, more satisfactory lives in a society of moral agents. But that does not alter the fact that individuals can sometimes gain advantages for themselves through immoral action in particular individual cases. And so, while we do indeed have a substantial prudential stake in morality at large, the question remains: Is this stake enough to provide a satisfactory justification for a morality that refuses to countenance convenient exceptions—as any *genuine* morality must do? After all, we can balance the benefits to be derived from the immoral act itself against the negativities that will ensue (overall and in the long run) from our violations in the present case of the (otherwise generally desirable) policy of abiding by the moral rules. It might well happen in theory—and seemingly does often happen in practice—that the magnitude of the former outweighs that of the latter. If advantage alone is the determinative factor, then morality must catch as catch can.

Contemplating situations in which one has to "pay a price" in terms of selfish advantage for doing the morally appropriate thing, opportunists through the ages have inclined to reason along the following lines: "To be sure, people stand to benefit by being part of a moral order. But that's beside the point. The most advantageous thing for oneself would clearly be for *others* to be moral, while one oneself is not always so. One could then seize opportunities to benefit as an unscrupulous 'freeloader,' taking advantage of those rule-abiding others whenever this can be done se-

---

[3] The case for this view is set out in substantial detail in Kurt Baier's *Moral Point of View.*

cretly—without undermining the otherwise advantageous social order."
Exactly this line of thought is at issue in Plato's "Ring of Gyges" story in
book 2 of the *Republic*, and the point was reformulated by David Hume
with his characteristic vigor. "And though it is allowed that, without a
regard to property, no society could subsist; yet according to the imperfect way in which human affairs are conducted, a sensible knave, in particular incidents, may think that an act of iniquity or infidelity will make a
considerable breach in the social union and confederacy. That *honesty is
the best policy*, may be a good general rule, but is liable to many exceptions; and he, it may perhaps be thought, conducts himself with most
wisdom, who observes the general rule, and takes advantage of all the
exceptions."[4] Any satisfactory validation of morality must provide for the
fact that a "morality" that admits of convenient exceptions for the sake of
personal advantage is no morality at all, having abandoned the indispens-
ably crucial element of universality. Any prudentialist theory of morality
seems destined to shipwreck at just this point.

After all, morally problematic practices can often redound to the advantage of the great majority of a group—feeding only the strongest survivors
among the stranded, to take a textbook example, or the Eskimo practice
of killing female babies by exposing them to the elements, or perhaps
even abortion as managed in contemporary advanced societies. Such practices may be deemed advantageous on grounds of public policy because
they "maximize social utility" through benefiting a statistical majority in
the community. But they certainly cannot be supported on *moral*
grounds. Since they overtly sacrifice the few for the advantage of the
many, they lack that inherent universality of concern that characterizes
authentic morality.

The fact of the matter is that morality and utility maximization go their
own separate ways. The utilitarian policy of providing for the greatest
good of the greatest number may perhaps afford a plausible political policy, but it just is not a plausible morality. The crux is that any morality
worthy of the name must leave no room for making exceptions to suit the
mere convenience of individuals, and no grounding of morality solely on
people's self-advantage can adequately fulfill this requirement.[5]

---

[4] *An Enquiry concerning the Principles of Morals* (London: A. Millar, 1752; reprint, ed.
L. A. Selby Bigge, Oxford: Clarendon Press, 1964), 2:282–83.

[5] Of particular relevance in this connection is the sustained attack on utilitarianism by the
British philosopher W. D. Ross. See his *The Right and the Good* and *Foundations of Ethics*
(Oxford: Clarendon Press, 1939). Useful anthologies of recent discussions of utilitarianism
include M. D. Bayles, ed., *Contemporary Utilitarianism* (Garden City, N.Y.: Anchor Books,
1968), Samuel Gorovitz, ed., *Mill: Utilitarianism—Text and Critical Essays* (Indianapolis:
Hackett, 1971), J.C.C. Smart and Bernard Williams, eds., *Utilitarianism: For and Against*
(Cambridge: Cambridge University Press, 1973).

The Problem of Deontic Force

Still another far-reaching difficulty inheres in basing the validation of morality on its derivative benefits. For it is part of the very idea of morality that one *ought* to be moral—that acting morally is a matter of duty or obligation. The core idea of morality is that someone who culpably fails to do the morally appropriate thing (wittingly and deliberately and without a good and sufficient excuse):

  1. does something *bad*—not just something unwise or counterproductive or unconventional, but actually something *wicked*;
  2. is *blameworthy* by way of deserving of the disapproval of others and the reproach of one's own conscience.

To default callously on one's moral obligations is to act in a way that by its very nature invites and deserves condemnation. The aspect of "requiredness" is something that is crucial to morality as the thing it is. Any adequate theory of morality must accordingly recognize the deontological aspect of moral judgments. It must account for the "deontic force" or duty-coordinated requiredness that is an ineliminable feature of such moral precepts as "Stealing is wrong." The sanctions of morality are thus stronger than those that mere considerations of self-interest can underwrite, seeing that they can ground not merely what makes people better off but what makes them better people.

To be sure, there are many different sorts of bases for obligation—many different sorts of grounds that a must/ought contention can have, such as self-interest, legality, religion, and social custom. But *morality* is yet another—different from and irreducible to these others. Moral judgments are normative in a characteristic way with respect to good-bad and right-wrong. A deliberately performed immoral act—the wanton infliction of needless pain on someone, for example, or hurting another's feelings simply for one's own pleasure of schadenfreude—is not just foolish or antisocial or prudentially ill advised, but *wicked*. Categories such as wise-foolish, customary-eccentric, prudent-imprudent, lawful-illegal simply do not capture what is at issue in moral-immoral. No theory of morality can lay claim to adequacy that fails to provide for this characteristic deontic force and somehow papers over the wickedness of moral transgressions.

It is important in this connection to distinguish the question of *motivation* ("what induces us to be moral—what considerations of personal advantage impel us in this direction?") from the question of *obligation* ("what obliges us to be moral—what considerations of impersonal advantage, of value enhancement, are at work here?"). Matters of the former, not irrational sort will doubtless hinge on our prudential concerns. But matters of the latter sort, of the compulsion of duty, must inhere in deontological considerations. Even if, contrary to fact, we actually did always and invariably have a stake of prudential interest in doing the morally right thing— say, because a benign "hidden hand" showered us with benefits for so acting—this would not accomplish adequately the job of accounting for the obligational, duty-bound aspect of morality. Advantageousness by itself only shows why we are well-advised to be moral (why we should be so), but cannot show that we are dutifully obligated to be so (why we ought to and indeed deontically "must" be so.) If morality rested wholly on self-interest and personal advantage, then "X ought to do A" would, in the final analysis, come to "X ought to do A *for prudential reasons.*" And then, try as we will, we could not validate the obligatoriness of moral duties. In the case of default we could not get beyond X's being *imprudent* to X's being actually *wicked.* Any strictly prudential validation of morality is thus inherently unsatisfactory because the problem of the ground of obligation remains untouched.

Without a satisfactory answer to this question of the basis of obligation, we lack an adequate account of morality. For such an account must provide satisfactory answers to questions like "Why *must* one be moral and heed the interests of others in one's actions and deliberations?" "What is the basis of the prescriptive impetus of moral injunctions as a matter of binding duty?" "Wherein does this obligatoriness of moral obligation lie?" And at this point, the resort to prudence leaves us in the lurch. Even granted that we have a prudential stake in morality—individually and collectively—this matter of mere interest cannot transmute into one of actual obligation.

At this point, someone might offer the following objection:

> You are quite right to insist that a prudential rationale for morality does not provide for the deontic force of moral claims. But what it can (and presumably does) accomplish is to establish that we are rationally well advised to deem ourselves (and others) to be morally obligated in the full-blooded, duty-oriented sense of the term. That is, it can show that we are prudentially bound *to believe in the deontic force of morality.*

By this sort of strategy, a prudentialist could maintain a mixed position that enjoins prudence and deontology through a recourse to (prudentially) rational belief.

However, this tactic still cannot provide a satisfactory rationale for authentic morality. It yields no more than a sham morality, because it does not go to show that we ever actually *are* obligated to moral action, but only that we are prudentially well advised to *think* ourselves (and others) to be so obligated. Accordingly, it does not provide for a real morality of actual obligation, but only for a playacting morality of "as if." (To be sure, its playacting morality is that of the "method actor" who endeavors to "live the role," but it remains playacting all the same.) Such a prudential impetus may perhaps take a step in the direction of morality but certainly does not reach morality itself. No explanation, analysis, or interpretation that conjures away the deontic aspect of morality can be adequate to this conception as we actually have it.

A different approach to the prudential validation of morality might also be attempted:

> Admittedly, a prudential validation of morality does not establish the deontic force of moral *obligation* all by itself. However, that duty itself inheres in a "social contract" or public agreement of some sort (presumably of an implicit or tacit nature). The prudential argument goes no further than to show that we are well advised to enter into this contract. But actual obligatoriness stems from the contract itself—the consideration that once we have entered into it, then we must see ourselves as bound by it, since this is what such entry consists in.

In this vein, one recent theorist maintains that "morality arises when a group of people reach an implicit agreement or come to a tacit understanding about their relations with one another."[6] Now this may well be part of the story, and perhaps even an important part, but it certainly cannot be the whole of it. For an "agreement" or an "understanding" (however tacit or implicit) cannot come to exist in vacuo—in a context where people have as yet no morality in place. It is the sort of commitment that by its very nature is possible only in a preexisting moral framework. Anything worthy of the name of "agreement" (compact, mutual understanding) can subsist only within a preexisting morality, where the binding force of agreements is accepted by those concerned. The very idea of an agreement involves a deontological relationship that cannot exist in a moral vacuum: "making an agreement," in the standard sense of the term, is already a moral act that can be performed only in a setting where the rule "Agreements should be honored" is accepted by those concerned. A mere alignment or coordination of action is no *agreement* in the absence of an acceptance of actual obligation by the parties involved; an "agreement" in which there is no acknowledgment (at least tacit) of the undertaking of an obligation is not even so much as an agreement in name only. A moral code can thus be *expanded* by agreements, but its moral aspect cannot altogether *originate* in them, because "agreement" as such already has a moral status.

Even if supplemented by the postscript of a "social contract," the prudential validation of morality cannot account satisfactorily for the deontic

---

[6] Gilbert Harman, "Moral Relativism Defended," *Philosophical Review* 84 (1975): 3. See also his *Nature of Morality* (New York: Oxford University Press, 1977).

force of moral obligation. The Hobbes-Rousseau approach of basing morality on a social contract—taking it to root in agreements or acquiescences based solely on mutual advantage for the interests of the parties involved[7]—has the crippling defect that it affords no way to explain why people should ever be *obligated* to be moral. For even if we are eminently *well advised* to honor contracts and agreements in this prudential mode, this does not show that we are *obliged* to do so. Morality as such accordingly cannot be validated on this basis.[8]

The long and short of it is that the proposed shifting of the burden of obligatoriness to a contract does not really solve the problem of explanation. It merely focuses the overall difficulty on one particular point, reducing the obligatoriness of morality in general to that of contracts (agreements, compacts, promises, and the like). The fundamental issue thus remains unresolved. For the question now arises as to just why we ought always to honor such agreements—as opposed to merely finding it prudentially advantageous to abide by them much of the time. The question has in fact been begged. What is so special about contracts? Why not just break an agreement in those particular cases where, all considered, it meets our selfish purposes to do so? In the context of the particular matter of agreements, we are now still left with just exactly that inital problem of accounting for the obligatoriness of morality.

This sort of argumentation also tells against a utilitarian morality that locates the impetus to moral conduct in considerations of *general* advantage. Such a position has no difficulty with the question why we are well advised to support morality. That is obvious enough, seeing that our own personal interest is in general inextricably interconnected with the general good. But when asked why we *ought* to do so—why this should be seen as a matter of actual *obligation*—the utilitarian runs into embarassing difficulties. Seeing morality as a matter of interest alone, the utilitarian has no satisfactory way to bring obligation into it. Utilitarianism lacks the machinery for building a bridge from motivation to obligation. Morality cannot be reduced to social utility. (Punishing the group for the transgressions of individuals may, in some circumstances, be a policy of great social utility—and thus be urged plausibly on political grounds—but it cannot appropriately be recommended on moral grounds. The urgings of Levia-

---

[7] The most recent and cogent articulation of this position is David Gauthier's *Morals by Agreement* (Oxford: Oxford University Press, 1985).

[8] To be sure, one can develop the idea of a hypothetical contract that it would (in idealized circumstances) be sensible to enter into as a device for assessing what is socially appropriate. But this would not afford a way of using wholly nonmoral factors (such as "prudentially advantageous contracts") to determine morality—let alone to validate it. One would still need to invoke moral considerations to validate this honoring of such a contract as more than a contrivance of self-advantage. Even a compact that advantages *all* participants (but only, say to the deteriment of their eventual descendants) is not ipso facto a morally appropriate one.

than are one thing, those of morality another—utilitarian *politics* makes sense in a way that utilitarian *morality* cannot.)

A reductionist moral theoretician, say of utilitarian or egoistic persuasion, may perhaps insist: "I am quite prepared to let moral deliberations rest on an appeal to values other than utilitarian (or egoistic) ones—provided those values are themselves in turn legitimated by utilitarian (or egoistic) considerations. My theory calls for the two-step approach of first adopting morality *en gros* as a general program that itself pivots ultimately on reasons of utility (or self-interest), and then proceeding to address all concrete issues on classical moral principles." But this line of approach will simply not do. It is like saying, "I'll sell my allegiance to the highest bidder, and from there on out I'll be a loyal follower." No *real* loyality (or *real* morality) is to be had along these lines. Where the foundations are unsatisfactory, the whole enterprise is vitiated. A validation of morality that rests its ultimate justificatory appeal upon any inherently amoral factor such as social solidarity or personal advantage cannot achieve a fully satisfactory result because its justificatory basis is insufficiently linked to the value system of morality itself. Accounting for the deontic force of moral judgments is a job that must be accomplished by other and very different means.

Ontological Obligation as the Source of the Deontic Force of Morality

In a classic paper of pre–World War I vintage, the Oxford philosopher H. A. Prichard argued that it makes no real sense to ask, "Why should I be moral?"[9] For once an act is recognized as being the morally appropriate thing to do, there is really no room for any further question about why it should be done. "Because it's the moral thing to do" is automatically, by its very nature, a satisfactorily reason-presenting response. The question, "Why do the right thing?" is akin to the question "Why believe the true thing?" On both sides the answer is simply: "Just exactly because it is, by hypothesis, right/true." When rightness or truth have once been conceded, the matter is closed. According to Prichard, then, the question "Why should one's duty be done?" is simply obtuse—or perverse. For duty as such constitutes a cogent moral imperative to action—automatically, as it were, of itself and by its very nature. To grant that it is one's duty to do something and then go on to ask why one should do it is simply to manifest one's failure to understand what the conception of "duty" involves. Duty as such constitutes a reason for action—albeit a *moral* reason.

[9] H. A. Prichard, "Does Moral Philosophy Rest on a Mistake?" *Mind* 21 (1912): 21–37.

This line of reflection, though quite correct, is probatively unhelpful. Self-support has its limitations as a justificatory rationale. The question still remains: "What makes reasons of moral appropriateness into good reasons?" or "Why should I be the sort of person who accepts moral grounds as validly compelling for his or her own deliberations?" If being moral indeed is the appropriate thing to do, there must be some sort of reason for it—that is, there must be some line of consideration, not wholly internal to morality itself, that renders it reasonable for people to be moral. We must probe yet further for a fully satisfactory resolution to the question "Why be moral?"—one that improves on the true but unhelpful answer, "Because it is the (morally) right thing to do." There has to be more to it than that. But where are we to look?

The most promising prospect is to look deep into the nature of personhood itself, to *the ontological duty of self-realization* that appertains to any rational agent whatsoever—the fundamental obligation of endeavoring to make the most of one's opportunities for realizing oneself as fully as possible, a duty that, insofar as one "owes" it to anyone at all, one owes no less to the world at large than to oneself. For any reason-endowed agent is thereby under an obligation to use its reason to capitalize on its potentialities for the good. The impetus of such an ontological obligation is predicated on the principle that one who systematically wastes one's opportunities for the realization of potential—say by having too low a self-image and too low a level of expectation for oneself—is being less than one can and should be and thus fails in that most fundamental of all duties, the ontological obligation to make the most of one's opportunities for the good. The dutifulness of obligation is inextricably connected with its rationality. To say that X ought (morally) to do A is to commit oneself to the claim that there are good reasons of the appropriate sort—namely, good *moral* reasons—for X to do A. The moral enterprise is an inherently rational one that pivots on reasons of a characteristic sort—those grounded in the inherent value of personhood. Such an ontological obligation is not an *ex officio* obligation (like that of the sea captain or husband) that one takes on in assuming a role but an *ex conditione* obligation (like that of the son or sister); it inheres in what one is rather than in what one has undertaken. It is an obligation that roots in personhood itself. And in deliberately violating this ontological obligation for self-development, one is doing something that is not just ill advised but somehow perverse and actually wicked.[10]

---

[10] Note that such an analysis is reductive but not eliminative. It does not, like utilitarianism, try to achieve the impossible fact of extracting duties from something other than duties (namely, considerations of advantage). Rather, it derives duties of one sort (moral duties) from those of another (those ontological duties of self-enhancement through the realization of positive potential).

What matters for us rational agents is not simply the sort of creature we are but the sort of creature we conceive and believe ourselves to be called upon to be—and thereby the sort of creature we purport ourselves to be. Now as Kant maintained, we *take ourselves to be* free rational agents and, in consequence, must assume the inherent commitments and obligations of such beings.[11] As intelligent beings, we rational agents have no adequate excuse for avoiding the questions: "What sort of creature am I?" "What possibilities and opportunities does this engender?" "What should I do to make of myself that which I ought to be?" "How can I realize my highest potential?" By its very nature as such, an intelligent agent who has the capacity and opportunity for value realization ought to realize it. The principle at issue is a conceptual one, implicit in the very idea of value. One could not appropriately call something a value if it were not of such a sort that a rational agent ought to opt for it whenever it is available at a reasonable cost.

We humans can, do, and should see ourselves as free rational agents. As such, we are in substantial measure self-made: we are the sort of creatures we are by virtue of the sorts of aspirations we have, the sort of creatures we see ourselves as ideally being. What we aspire to is, after all, an important aspect of what makes us what we are: in part we are what we are because of what we *claim* to be and what we *wish* to be. In particular, we class ourselves as members of the special category of persons—of rational agents. *Homo sapiens* is a creature capable of at least partial self-construction—one able to make itself into the being it ought (ontologically considered) to be, given the opportunities afforded it in the course of the world's events. And in this regard, wastefulness is wicked. If we are creatures who can realize certain goods, then we ought, for that reason, to work toward their realization, even when this involves forgoing even better opportunities elsewhere.[12]

An objector may well, at this point, remind us of Hegel's well-known complaint that a Kantian ethic of respect for persons is empty and contentless. But such an objection is not in fact well taken. For respecting people as free agents with wills of their own also involves respect for their interests and well-being, their aspirations and projects, and even their mere wants and preferences insofar as those do not conflict with larger desiderata. And in particular, the expectations that people form of one another in their reciprocal interactions within a social community give a rich substantive concretization to an otherwise schematic notion of the claims of personhood.

[11] Kant, *Critique of Pure Reason*, A814/B842.

[12] What is at issue here is not the "Mill's fallacy" inference from being valued to being valuable but the unproblematic move from being appropriately valued by a creature of a certain constitution to being something that objectively has value for this creature.

Our place in the world's scheme of things—our status as self-pro-claimed rational creatures—imposes on us the ontologically grounded ob-ligation to confront issues of self-definition and self-determination, to make the most of our opportunities for realizing the good. As rational agents, we "owe it to ourselves"—and derivatively to "the world at large" in virtue of our place within it—to achieve our positive potential: to real-ize ourselves as the sort of beings we indeed are and to take our proper place in the world's scheme of things. To stint one's ontological potential for the good through one's own deliberate action or inaction is fundamen-tally *wrong*. We have only one chance at life, and to let its opportunities for the good slip is a shameful waste—regrettable alike from the stand-point of the world's interests and our own. "Be the best you can be—become what you ought!"—so runs this ontological imperative for a ra-tional agent to make the most and best use of its opportunities in this world to cultivate its potential for the good.

Clearly, morality does not inhere in the realization of human potential as such, no questions asked. For every person has a potential for both good and evil—in principle, we each have it in ourselves to become a saint or a sinner. Discerning our specifically good potentialities requires more than a knowledge of human nature as such; it requires taking a view of the good of man—a normative philosophical anthropology. Clearly, other things being anything like equal, it is better to be healthy, to be happy, to understand what goes on, and the like. The pivotal question is what en-dows life with worth and value—what are the conditions that make for a rewarding and worthwhile life. This issue of human flourishing will inevi-tably involve such things as:

> using one's intelligence;
> developing (some of) one's productive talents and abilities;
> making a constructive contribution to the world's work;
> fostering the good potential of others;
> achieving and diffusing happiness;
> taking heed for the interests of others.

The good potentialities, in sum, are exactly those in whose cultivation and development a rational agent can take reflective self-satisfaction, those that help us most fully to realize ourselves as the sort of being we should ideally aspire to be. The crux is simply the matter of cultivating legitimate interests. And we cannot do this for ourselves without due care for culti-vating our specifically positive potentialities—those things that are inher-ently worthwhile.

This approach to deontology thus ultimately grounds the obligatoriness of moral injunctions in considerations of value. We are embarked here on a broadly economic approach, but one that proceeds in terms of a value theory that envisions a generalized "economy of values" and from whose standpoint the traditional economic values (the standard economic costs and benefits) are merely a rather special case. Such an axiological approach sees moral rationality as an integral component of the wider rationality that calls for the effective deployment of limited resources. (Observe that such a deontological approach contrasts starkly with a utilitarian morality, in that the latter pivots morality on happiness or "utility," but the former on value enhancement.)

Moral obligation ultimately inheres in this ontological obligation to the realization of values in one's own mode of life. Being a morally good person is part and parcel of a rational being's cultivation of the good. For us rational creatures morality (the due care for the interests of rational beings) is an integral component of reason's commitment to the enhancement of value. Reason's commitment to the value of rationality accordingly carries a commitment to morality in its wake. The obligatoriness of morality ultimately roots in an *ontological* imperative to value realization with respect to self and world that is incumbent on free agents as such. On this ontological perspective, the ultimate basis of moral duty roots in the obligation we have as rational agents (toward ourselves and the world at large) to make the most and best of our opportunities for self-development.

And so, in the final analysis, one ought to be moral for the same sort of reason for which one ought to make use of life's opportunities in general— one's intelligence, for example, or one's other constructive talents. For in failing to do this, we throw away chances to make something of ourselves by way of contributing to the world's good, thereby failing to realize our potential. The violation of moral principles thus stands coordinate with the sanctions attaching to wanton wastefulness of any sort. The crux is not so much self-realization as self-optimization. What is at issue with failure is throughout not merely a loss but a violation of duty as well. For to recognize something as valuable is, with the rational person, to enter into certain obligations in its regard (such as favoring it over contrary alternatives, other things being equal).

To be sure, it deserves stress that the obligation to morality—to conduct our interpersonal affairs appropriately by heeding the interests of others—is by no means our only ontological obligation. The epistemic obligation to conduct our cognitive affairs appropriately—to inquire, to broaden our knowledge, to pursue the truth by believing only those things that ought (epistemically deserve) to be believed in the circumstances—is another example, and the Kantian duty to develop (at least some of) one's talents yet another. The scope of ontological obligation is thus substantially broader than that of morality alone.

Morality thus ultimately hinges on axiology, the general theory of evaluation. For it is the metaphysics of value, and not moral theory per se, that teaches us that knowledge is better, other things equal, than ignorance, or pleasure than pain, or compassion than needless indifference. And what ultimately validates our moral concern for the interests of others is just exactly this ontological commitment to the enhancement of value, a commitment that is inseparably linked to our own value as free rational agents.

The obligation to morality, like the obligation to rationality, roots in considerations of ontology. If one is in a position to see oneself as in fact rational, then once one recognizes the value of this rationality, one must also acknowledge the obligation to make use of it. And if one is a rational free agent who recognizes and prizes this very fact, then one ought for that very reason to behave morally by taking the interests of other such agents into account. For if I am (rationally) to pride myself on being a rational agent, then I must stand ready to value in other rational agents what I value in myself—that is, I must deem them worthy of respect, care, and so forth in virtue of their status of rational agents. What is at issue is not so much a matter of reciprocity as one of rational coherence with claims that one does (and should) stake for oneself. For to see myself in a certain normative light I must, if rational, stand ready to view others in the same light. If we indeed are the sort of intelligent creature whose worth in its own sight is a matter of prizing something (reflective self-respect, for example), then this item by virtue of this very fact assumes the status of something we are bound to recognize as valuable, as deserving of being valued. In seeing ourselves as *persons*—as free and responsible rational agents—we thereby rationally bind ourselves to a care for one another's interests insofar as those others too are seen as having this status. [13]

In holding that something (life, liberty, opportunity) is of value—is not just something one wants but something one is rationally well advised to pursue—we rational agents must recognize its generic value and acknowledge that others too are well advised to pursue it. And if the capacity to be a rational agent—to act for reasons I myself think to be good and sufficient—is something I respect and value in me, then I am rationally bound, in simple consistency, to respect and value it in others as well. A rational creature values a condition that it finds in itself only insofar as it is valuable (period)—and thus of value in anyone.

---

[13] To be sure, someone may ask: "Why think ourselves in this way—why see ourselves as free rational agents?" To ask this is to ask for a good rational reason and is thus already to take a stance within the framework of rationality. In theory, one can "resign" from the community of rational beings, abandoning all claims to being more than "mere animals." But this is a step one cannot *justify*—there are no satisfactory rational grounds for taking it. And this is something most of us realize instinctively. The appropriateness of acknowledging others as responsible agents whenever possible holds in our own case as well.

Rational agents are accordingly bound by virtue of that very rationality to the view that valuing something commits one to seeing it as valuable, as worthy or deserving of being valued—by themselves or anyone like them in the relevant respects. One can, quite properly, *like* things without reasons, but for a rational agent to *value* them involves seeing them as having value by generalized standards. And thus to see value in my status and my actions as a rational agent I must be prepared to recognize this in others as well. For reason is inherently impersonal (objective) in the sense that what constitutes a good reason for X to believe or do or value something would automatically also constitute a good reason for anyone else who stands in X's shoes (in the relevant regards). So if I am to be justified in valuing my rationality (in prizing my status as a rational agent) and in seeing it as a basis for demanding the respect of other agents, then I must also—from simple rational self-consistency—stand prepared to value and respect rationality in others.

I may *desire* respect (whether self-respect or the respect of others) for all sorts of reasons, good, bad, or indifferent. But if I am to *deserve* respect, this has to be so for good reasons. Respect will certainly not come to me just because I am I, but only because I have a certain sort of respect-evoking feature (for example, being a free rational agent) whose possession (by me or, for that matter, anyone) provides a warrant for respect. And this means that all who have this feature (all rational agents) merit respect. Our self-worth hinges on the worth we attach to others like us: we can have worth only by virtue of possessing worth-engendering features that operate in the same way when others are at issue. To claim respect worthiness for myself I must concede it to all suitably constituted others as well. The first-person-plural idea of "we" and "us" that projects one's own identity into a wider affinity-community is a crucial basis of our sense of worth and self-esteem. In degrading other *persons* in thought or in treatment, we would automatically degrade ourselves, while in doing them honor, we thereby honor ourselves.

When people act immorally toward me—cheat me or deceive me or the like—I am not merely angry and upset because my personal interests have been impaired, but am also "righteously indignant." Not only have the offenders failed to acknowledge me as a person (a fellow rational being with personal rights and interests), but they have, by their very act, marked themselves as people who, though (to my mind) congeners of mine as rational agents, nevertheless do not give us rational agents their proper due, thereby degrading the entire group to which I too belong. They have added insult to injury. And this holds more generally. One is also indignant at witnessing someone act immorally toward a third party—being disturbed in a way akin to the annoyance one feels when some gaffe is committed by a member of one's own family. For one's own sense of self and self-worth is mediated by membership in such a group, and this can become compromised by their behavior. As rational agents, we are entitled and committed to be indignant at the wicked actions of our fellows who do not act as rational agents ought because our own self-respect is inextricably bound up with their behavior. They have "let down the side."

The upshot of such considerations is that to fail to be moral is to defeat our own proper purposes and to lose out on our ontological opportunities. It is only by acknowledging the worth of others—and thus the appropriateness of a due heed of their interests—that we ourselves can maintain our own claims to self-respect and self-worth. And so, we realize that we should act morally in each and every case, even where deviations are otherwise advantageous, because insofar as we do not, we can no longer look upon ourselves in a certain sort of light—one that is crucial to our own self-respect in the most fundamental way. Moral agency is an essential requisite for the proper self-esteem of a rational being. To fail in this regard is to injure oneself where it does and should hurt the most—in one's own sight.

Some theorists see the essence of morality as a matter of stepping entirely outside the framework of our self-oriented concerns. As one recent discussion puts it: "The subject matter of ethics is how to engage in practical reasoning and the justification of action once we expand our consciousness by occupying the objective standpoint."[14] However, the present deliberations view the matter in a much more personal and self-oriented light, namely that of the question "How must I behave if I am to make the most of my opportunities to make myself into the sort of person I ought to be—the sort of person I want to be in my better moments?" On this perspective, what lies at the core of morality is not an impersonal "one" but a very personal "I"—though, to be sure, this I projects out into *we*.[15] No one is closer to us than our own self (*egomet mihi sum proximus*, as Cicero put it). And what is perhaps the most fundamental and basic of the obligations (and interests) we have is that of being on good terms with ourselves, which demands being true to oneself as the sort of creature one deems it for the best to be. (And note the crucial link between "I" and "we" here, which prevents this *self-oriented* approach from degenerating into a purely *selfish* one.)

[14] Nagel, *The View from Nowhere*, p. 139.

[15] Nagel writes: "The basic question of practical reason from which ethics begins is not 'What shall I do?' but 'What should this person do?'" (ibid.). But while this may be so as regards the basic or beginning question, it is quite otherwise as regards the ultimate question, which is simply "What *should* I do?" And this combines the self-regard of Nagel's question no. 1 with the normativeness of his question no. 2. Ethical objectivity is indissolubly linked to people's self-perception—their vision of *themselves* as persons.

In basing the commitment to morality on such an ontological obligation, its ultimate rationale comes to be located outside the moral project itself—as we observed above that it would have to be. In this regard, the present ontological validation of morality indeed resembles that of the various theorists who pivot the rationale of morality on a morality-external factor such as custom, social utility, or individual advantage. But the crucial difference is that the ontological appeal to the value of personhood is itself altogether consonant with the inherent nature of moral concerns, whereas the alternatives are not so. There is no problem about locating the ultimate impetus to morality in an inherent obligation of responsible rational agents as such. There is a deep problem, however, in locating it in blind custom or social advantage or crass self-interest. For morality would be utterly compromised (nay, destroyed as the sort of thing it is) if its ultimate gounding were based on values that are wholly disjoint from those at issue in morality itself. Its "validation" would ultimately be incoherent. But this is clearly not the case with an account that sees the rationale of morality as rooted in the ontology of personhood and the rational commitment that it involves.

The ontological imperative to capitalize on our opportunities for the good carries us back to the salient issue of philosophical anthropology—the visualization of what man can and should be. "Be an authentic human being!" comes down to this: "Do your utmost to become the sort of rational and responsible creature that a human person, at best or most, is capable of being."[16] The moral project of treating of other people as we ourselves would be treated is part and parcel of this.[17] What we have here is in fact an evaluative metaphysic of morals.

Morality and Rationality

It deserves to be recognized that when one's commitment to morality is emplaced within an ontological obligation to achieve one's greatest potential as a free rational agent, then morality is also rendered consistent with a rational concern for one's prudential advantage—at any rate at the level

[16] Immanuel Kant portrayed the obligation at issue in the following terms: "First, it is one's duty to raise oneself more and more out of the crudity of one's nature—out of one's animality (*quoad actum*) to humanity, by which alone one is capable of setting oneself ends. It is man's prime duty to . . . supply by instruction what is lacking in one's knowledge, and to correct one's mistakes. . . . [T]his end is one's duty in order to . . . be worthy of the humanity dwelling within" (*Metaphysic of Morals*, p. 387, *Akad.*).

[17] A good treatment of relevant issues is given in Herbert Morris's essay "Persons and Punishment," *Monist* 52 (1968): 475–501. See also Elizabeth Telfer, *Respect for Persons* (London: Routledge & Kegan Paul, 1969).

of real or best interests. To see this clearly, one must consider the inherently ramified nature of rational action.

Every free act of an intelligent agent has wider ramifications. The issue with which we are confronted in our action choices is never just a matter of deciding what I want to do in this case: it is always also in part a matter of deciding *what sort of person I am to be*. The salient fact about a situation of apparent conflict between duty and advantage is that it is by deciding how to act here and now that we effectively also decide—in some measure, at least—what sort of person we are to be. Consider an illustration. In deliberately acting immorally—in deciding, say, to betray a trust merely for my own financial gain—I produce two sorts of results:

the *proximate*, local result of my action in the particular case at hand—whatever immediate gains and advantages it would secure for me; and

the *ulterior*, large-scale result of so acting as to make myself into a person of a certain sort—someone who would do *that* sort of thing to realize *that* sort of benefit.

This second, more far-reaching and systemic aspect is crucial—and unavoidable. For even if no one else knows it, the fact still remains that I myself am aware of what I deliberately do. And my self-respect is (or ought to be) of such great value to me that the advantages I could secure by immoral action cannot countervail against the loss that would be involved in this larger regard. For in acting in a way that I recognize to be wrong, I sustain a grave moral injury exactly where it should count the most—in my own sight.

In setting morality aside in the case at hand for the sake of selfish personal advantage, for example, we would shift our guiding principle of action from

(1) Always do the morally appropriate thing

to

(2) Always do the morally appropriate thing unless it is more beneficial in the prevailing circumstances for you not to do so.

Now in making this shift in the determinative rationale of our action, we ipso facto affect a change in our very nature, transforming ourselves from type (1) to type (2) agents. Such a shift is obviously not justifiable on *moral* grounds whenever a violation of moral principles is at issue. But—more surprisingly—it is, in general, not even justifiable on *prudential* grounds. For in becoming type (2) agents, we would exchange a limited and temporary advantage for a large and perduring loss. For the long and short of it is that we have a paramount stake (a real interest) in being moral agents, because this is needed to maintain proper self-respect. In this regard, morality is eminently rational and prudent—geared to the efficient achievement of appropriate ends.

"But what if I just don't happen to be the sort of person who attaches value to self-respect?" Then, alas, the rest of us have cause to feel sorry for you in your impoverishment, and, moreover, we are (normatively) justified in seeing your view of the matter as deeply mistaken. For your position is like that of someone who says: "Appropriate human values mean nothing to me." Such a stance is profoundly unintelligent—and irrational as well, since it runs afoul of the most basic of rational imperatives: to realize oneself as the sort of creature one can and should see oneself as being. (The crux is that of the injunction of Polonius: "To thine own self be true.") And this ontological obligation to self-development is the ground of the deontic force of the moral imperatives. It is the rope by which rationality pulls morality in its wake.

But how can there be such a thing as an *ontological* obligation, an objector may ask, complaining: "I can understand how it can be that our nature (our drives and needs) *motivates* us to act in a certain sort of way. But how can you say that our nature *obligates* us to act in a certain sort of way (namely, morally)?" The response is that the reasoning at issue is based on two considerations: (1) We are so constituted as to see ourselves as having at our disposal certain opportunities for the realization of value (opportunities from bringing about something of value for oneself and for the world at large), and (2) a creature that is situated in this way (one that sees itself as a free rational agent placed in a position to act for the good) in virtue of this very fact stands under a moral obligation to endeavor to realize this opportunity. ("Promote your good where you can do so without running afoul of countervailing interests" is effectively the operative principle here.) A rational agent that fails in endeavoring to realize its best or real interests is ipso facto failing to exercise that rationality to optimal effect. After all, working for the benefit of oneself and those with whom one's own interests are interconnected is of the very essence of rational competency.

The overall line of the preceding reasoning may thus be summarized as follows:

1. Since rationality commits us to the cultivation of value, every rational agent ought (ontologically) to make the best and most of his or her opportunities.

2. To be on good terms with oneself—having a proper sense of self-worth—is a crucial part of making the most of one's opportunities. (Indeed, without self-respect, rational agents cannot lead satisfying lives.)

3. Our self-worth is inevitably mediated through membership in a wider affinity group. To deem itself worthy as an individual, a *rational* creature must see itself as being of a type that is inherently worthy. Specifically, such beings must see themselves as *persons* (rational agents) and must value themselves as such.

4. Since our self-worth hinges on our membership in the category of persons, we must also recognize and acknowledge the inherent worth of the others who belong to this category.

5. But if in our thought and action we tread the interests of other persons underfoot, then we effectively deny that these interests should be duly respected. We degrade and devalue personhood as such. In denying or downgrading the claims of other persons to a due respect for their interests, we ipso facto downgrade or deny the claims of the entire type—a type to which we belong and should see ourselves as belonging, and claimed membership in which is essential to our sense of self-worth. In acting immorally, we deny ourselves the benefit of reflective self-respect.

This line of reflection shows how it is that our obligation to be moral agents derives from and is encompassed within the fundamental ontological duty to self-realization that is incumbent on rational agents. Our own best interests are deeply engaged via the requisites of our self-image as the sorts of beings we can and should be.

Such a position aligns closely with that which Plato attributes to Socrates in the *Republic*: that being unjust and immoral, regardless of what immediate benefits it may yield, is always ultimately disadvantageous because of the damage it does to our character (or *psychē*) by making us into the sort of person we ourselves cannot really respect.[18] ("What shall it profit a man if he shall gain the whole world, and lose his own soul?") On such a view, it is not the case that the rationale of morality consists in its rewards—either intrinsic ("virtue is its own reward") or prudential. The justificatory impetus at issue is of a very different sort. We should be moral not because of its benefits for what we *have* but because of its benc-

---

[18] Francis Hutcheson saw morality as a matter of so acting that we can reflectively approve of our own *character*. (See L. A. Selby-Bigge, ed., *The British Moralists*, vol. 1 [Oxford: Clarendon Press, 1897], which contains Hutcheson's *Inquiry concerning Moral Good and Evil* [London: L. Darby, 1725].) But even more fundamental is the matter of so acting that we can reflectively approve of our own *nature*, in prizing the kind of creatures we are—or see ourselves as being. And this requires acting in such a way that I need make no excuses for myself toward myself. (The linkage of morality to self-respect—the maintenance of a positive self-image and a proper sense of self-worth—shows why limiting the scope of "real persons" to an in-group of some sort is destructive of morality. The last refuge of the scoundrel who seeks to preserve his self-image in the face of immorality is to see slaves or barbarians or enemies in war not as being persons just like oneself, so that their maltreatment is nowise impeded by any threats to self-respect.)

fits for what we *are*—the sort of creature we can then appropriately see ourselves as being.[19]

And so prudential considerations do also come into play in the validation of morality. It is a crucial part of the rational cultivation of our own best interests not to deprive ourselves through our own actions of the self-esteem that goes with membership in a group to which we are pleased and proud to belong: indeed, belonging to which grounds our sense of identity as the sorts of beings we are. Injury to this sense of self-worth is one of the very worst things that can happen to a person, since it degrades one where it counts for the most—in one's own eyes. A feeling of self-worth as a rational being is crucial to one's sense of legitimacy—one's ability to see oneself as having a worthy place in the world's scheme of things. Self-interest is indeed at work here, but also something deeper than just that. An ontological obligation to morality is inextricably bound up with a fundamental ontological interest that we have, in virtue of our very nature, in being truly fulfilled as the sorts of creatrues that we see ourselves as being—as free rational agents.

Hume may well be right—perhaps the universe does not care about us.[20] But this, of course, is no reason why *we* should not care about ourselves—or about the universe, for that matter.

Accordingly, morality and rational self-interest can—and should—live in peaceful coexistence. For morality itself has a perfectly sound rationale, via the argument:

The intelligent cultivation of one's real self-interest is quintessentially rational.

Given that we are free rational agents, it is to our real self-interest to act morally—even when doing so goes against our immediate selfish desires.

Therefore: It is rational to be moral.

Rational persons will thus also be morally good—conscientious, compassionate, kind, and so on—because their own real and best interests are

---

[19] Even David Hume is drawn toward such a view. As he sees it, "sensible knaves," whom he imagines as taking improper advantage of their opportunities for selfish gains in a moral society, would, even "were they ever so secret and successful," nevertheless still themselves emerge as "in the end, the greatest dupes," because they have "sacrificed the invaluable enjoyment of a character, with themselves at least, for the acquisition of worthless toys and gewgaws" (*An Enquiry concerning the Principles of Morals*, 2:283). The sensible knave automatically forgoes the pleasure of "peaceful reflection on one's own conduct" (ibid.). Moreover, because he cannot then sustain even his own critical scrutiny, the knave also renders himself unable to enjoy membership in an organized society (which, as Hume sees it, is perhaps no lesser loss). Unfortunately, Hume thinks that prudence engenders rather than merely reinforces morality.

[20] See p. 142 above.

served thereby, seeing that they have a real and sizable personal stake in maintaining the worth and dignity of rational agents. For in trampling the just claims of other rational agents underfoot, we undermine the very factor on which our own claim to value and consideration is ultimately based.

Morality, in sum, is a part of rationality, but of practical and thus of judgmental/evaluative rationality. In failing to care for our real interests, we are being irrational, but by way of poor judgment rather than poor inferential reasoning. An immoral person errs not (necessarily) in calculation but certainly in evaluation, in failing to assess at their proper value the ends that people ought (metaphysically or otherwise) to set for themselves. And so whether or not we do care about our best interests, we ought (qua rational agent) to care about them as a matter of our ontological obligations. The point is best put in normative terms: every rational (reason-possessing) creature *should* and every fully reason-exercising creature *does* have such a tendency toward realizing its opportunities for the good. This normative impetus creates the bridge leading from rationality to morality and grounds the deontological force of appropriate moral injunctions in an ontological aspect of the human condition, namely, in our status—which is self-claimed and, as such, essential to our self-image—as free rational agents.[21]

The question "Why be moral?" can be asked from three perspectives:

1. from the standpoint of *morality* itself—of a due concern for the interests of others;
2. from the standpoint of *enlightened prudence*—of an intelligent heed of our own real interests; and
3. from the standpoint of *crass prudence*—of selfishness and egocentric desire-satisfaction.

Here (1) and (2) pose no real difficulties for the ontological validation of morality, as we have seen. But the case is very different with perspective (3). At this point we are indeed wholly at a loss. For there just is no earthly way to validate morality from the standpoint of the selfishness of a "self-interest" narrowly construed in terms of the satisfaction of people's mere (raw and unevaluated) desires. And this result is surely to be welcomed rather than lamented—at any rate from the moral point of view. For it lies in the very nature of morality to counterpose the stern call of duty against the siren call of strictly selfish gratification.

---

[21] The ontological-obligation response to the question "Why be moral?" exactly parallels the similar response given in chapter 1 to the question "Why be rational?" This is only fitting and proper, seeing that morality is simply one sector or subdomain of authentic rationality.

Yet the following objection remains:

Even if this assessment of morality's rationale is right in maintaining that an ontological obligation to self-realization is the ultimate *reason* for our being moral, this surely remains a relatively weak *motive*. Given the character of the temptations to immorality, the motivating impetus of so "abstract" an obligation is totally ineffectual, at any rate for those who, like so many of us, are predominately moved by considertions of narrow self-advantage.

This whole point must be conceded outright. It reflects the statistical realities of the human condition. That there is a good and altogether cogent reason for doing something does not, alas, automatically provide most of us humans with much of a motive for doing it. Motives are one thing and reasons another, and only with fully rational people will the two automatically coincide. All this must be granted. But it certainly does no damage to the import of our deliberations. For it is, of course, the *rationale* of morality that concerns us here, and not the variable motives of individual people for adhering to it. The objection is thus entirely beside the point of present purposes.

But what of the person who is not willing to operate on the plane of real interests, the person for whom the only acceptable rationale is that of selfish advantage—someone who simply refuses to be moved by impersonal reasons and will respond to motives of selfish advantage alone? Such a person will say: "But I just don't accept the ontological obligation at issue in morality. I propose to assert myself as a free rational agent by rejecting the validity of moral claims." So be it, if that is what one wants. The acknowledgment of a claim is up to each person. However, its appropriateness does not lie in its being accepted—any more than the validity of an argument does—but lies in the fact that it *ought* to be accepted. No obligation—whether moral or rational—is undermined by the fact that people are disinclined to accept it. The crux of the issue of moral appropriateness is not what we want or desire but what is in our best interest—not motivation but rationalization. "Even if being moral is in my best real interests, that means nothing to me. I don't care about my real interests—for me these just don't matter; wants are what counts." Given the inherent connection of rationality with enlightened self-interest, such a view—however widespread—is simply irrational. A position of this perverse sort may indeed explain why someone acts immorally, but it cannot even begin to justify that person in doing so.

But exactly why is something's being wrong (pointlessly deceiving or callously injuring others, for example) a cogent reason for us not to do it? Here again the distinction between motivational and rational reasons comes into play. Motives are personal; they depend on what people happen to want. (If, for example, somebody wants to be regarded as a "hard" person, so as to intimidate others, then such a person may have a perfectly good motive for immoral action.) Rational reasons, by contrast, hinge not on vagaries of people's actual wants but on appropriate wants, on what it makes good rational sense to want. And by definition, as if were, the rational person wants the sort of things that are in his or her best (real) interests, everything considered. (This, after all, is exactly what constitutes rationality at the level of volition.)

The commitment to rationality is itself an integral part of our best interests. No gain in goods or pleasures can outweigh its value for us rational beings. (The "happiness pill" hypothesis suffices to show that it is not pleasure of happiness per se that ultimately matters for us but rationally authorized pleasure of happiness.) The goods we gain through deception (or other sorts of immoral conduct) afford us a hollow benefit. This is so not because we are too high-minded to be able to enjoy illicit gains but because inasmuch as we are rational thinking beings—creatures committed by their very nature to strive for reflective contentment (as opposed to merely affective pleasure)—it is only by "doing the right thing" that we can maintain our reflectively based sense of self-worth or deserved merit.

The imperative "Act as a rational agent ought" does not come from without (from parents or from society or even from God). It roots in our own self-purported nature as rational beings. (In Kant's words, it is a *dictamen rationis*, a part of the "innere Gesetzgebung der Vernunft.") Its status as being rationally appropriate roots simply and directly in the fact of its being an integral part of what our reason demands of us. And because being moral is a part of being reasonable, morality too is part of this demand.

Morality is accordingly geared to rationality in a dual way: (1) morality is a matter *of* rationality—of acting for good reasons of a certain (characteristically moral) sort, and (2) morality is an enterprise that exists *for* rationality—for the sake of protecting the legitimate interests of rational agents. And it is precisely this gearing of morality to the interests of rational agents that renders an ontological validation of morality—in terms of the inherent requisites of rational agency—thoroughly consonant with the value structure of morality itself.

Morality is thus not at odds with rationality but is part and parcel of it. Only someone who mistakenly thinks that selfish reasons alone can qualify as good reasons can see an irreconcilable conflict between morality and rationality. And this would indeed be a gross mistake. For a rational commitment to morality inheres in the (ontologically mediated) circumstance that other-concerned reasons for action constitute perfectly good *rational* reasons because of their unseverable link to the real interests of agents themselves. The consonance of morality with rationality is established through the fact that the intelligent thing to do and the right thing to do will ultimately agree because acting morally *is* the intelligent thing to do for those who have a proper concern for their real self-interest. There is nothing irrational about being moral, and there is nothing imprudent about it either, as long as we understand "true prudence" aright. (To say this, however, is emphatically not to say that it is in its consonance with prudence that the *validation* of morality should be sought.)[22]

[22] The general line of these deliberations has been to ground morality in rationality, while at the same time denying that it is appropriate to ground morality in prudence. In simple self-consistency, then, a validation of rationality that proceeds wholly in terms of prudential self-interest alone is automatically denied us. Instead, consonance and consistency require a validation of rationality that is itself ultimately ontological and axiological (value oriented), validating rationality too in terms of its ontological fitness. And this is indeed the line of the author's book *Rationality*, as well as that of the first volume of the present trilogy. Relevant considerations are also presented in the author's *Moral Absolutes*, whose deliberations have been drawn upon here.

Part V _____

VALUES AND RATIONALITY

Thirteen _____

Rationality and Happiness

Are Rational People Happier?

Is rationality a good thing? The question has a rhetorical air about it. Rationality, after all, is a matter of the intelligent pursuit of appropriate ends.[1] And this is by its very nature a positive quality—a "perfection," in the philosophical terminology of an earlier day. Still, when everything is said and done, the question still remains: Are rational people happier? Does this key aspect of the human condition—the proper use of our intelligence—pay off for us in this regard? This theme harks back to deliberations that the thinkers of ancient Greece posed in the question "Is the wise man also happy?" a problem to which they dedicated much thought, concern, and controversy, one that has every bit as much interest today as it did in the first millennium B.C.

Two Modes of "Happiness"

As often happens with philosophical questions, the pivotal issue is not simply one of examining facts but predominantly one of clarifying concepts and issues. For the problem of the linkage between rationality and happiness hinges critically on just how we propose to understand the idea of "happiness." A closer look at the concept of happiness is thus in order. And here, distinctions must loom large. In particular, we face two crucially diverse alternatives, depending on whether we construe happiness in an *affective* or in a *reflective* sense—whether we conceive of it as a psychological state of subjective feeling and emotion, or as a judgmental matter of rational assessment and reflective evaluation. This distinction between affective happiness and reflective happiness—between euphoria of feeling and contentment of reflective appraisal, as it were—requires closer consideration.

---

[1] It is thus clear that rationality is here construed as involving more than a capacity to move efficiently to arbitrary (and themselves unexamined) ends. Someone who pursues (however effectively) an inherently absurd or inappropriate end is not being rational. To reemphasize: rationality overall involves both *inferential* rationality (valid reasoning) and *evaluative* rationality (appropriate appraisal)

As a psychological state, affective happiness is a matter of how one *feels* about things—a matter of mood or sentiment. Primarily, it turns on what would commonly be called enjoyment or pleasure. It is the sort of psychic state or condition that could, in theory, be measured by an euphoriometer and represents the sort of physiologically engendered condition that might—and indeed can—be induced by drugs or by drink. (Think of the "happy hour" at cocktail bars.)

By contrast, reflective happiness is a matter of how one *thinks* about things. It is embodied in appraisal and judgment—in how one assesses or evaluates the prevailing situation, how one sizes it up mentally rather than how one reacts to it emotionally or affectively or physically. It is not a psychological state of feeling at all but an intellectual stance of reflectively positive evaluation. It is a matter of being so circumstanced as to appraise one's condition with warranted judgmental approbation. The issue is one of rational satisfaction rather than pleasure, of what Aristotle called *eudaimonia* in contrast to *hēdonē*. Happiness in this second sense consists in the reflective contentment of those who "*think* themselves fortunate" for good and sufficient reason. Its pivot is not "pleasure" but "contentment of mind" on the basis of reflective appraisal.

Figuratively put, affective happiness depends on the viscera and reflective happiness on the mind. The difference turns on whether one responds to things positively by way of an emotive psychological reaction, some sort of warm, inner affective glow, or whether one responds to them by way of a rationalized pro-evaluation, a deliberate intellectual judgment of the condition of things. It is one thing to "be happy" about something by way of emotive response and another to "lead a happy life" in relation to a reflective appraisal as to how things manage to go as the whole.

The two sorts of happiness accordingly also have very different temporal aspects. Affective happiness (pleasure) is generally something fleeting and short-term—a thing of psychic moods and whims, of the feeling of the moment. By contrast, reflective happiness (rational contentment) is generally something deeper and less transient—a matter of understanding rather than feeling, of stable structure rather than transitory state. Its crux is not just a matter of feeling satisfied with one's life but of being rationally entitled to be so.

Very distinct issues are accordingly at stake with the sort of "happiness" that one has in view. People may well take reflective satisfaction (quite legitimately) in actions or occurrences that, like Kantian acts of duty, do not at all promote their happiness in any affective sense of that term— indeed, that may even impose a cost in this regard. It does not follow that people who prosper in happiness or "quality of life" thereby manage to realize a superior quality in their lives—or achieve happiness in its deepest sense. (We come back to the cutting edge of John Stuart Mill's obiter dictum: "Better to be Socrates dissatisfied than a pig satisfied.") Affective happiness is one thing, and reflective happiness another—substantially different from it.

Given these two very different ways of interpreting the idea of happiness, it should be stressed that which of them one adopts will make all the difference for the question of how rationality and happiness are interrelated. On the one hand, if happiness is construed in the reflective sense as rational satisfaction, then the use of rationality is a promising way to enhance one's happiness. For one thing, people who proceed rationally are, thanks to their rationality, going to improve the chances that things will eventuate favorably for the promotion of their real interests. And even when things do go wrong—as, life being what it is, they doubtless often will—the rational person has the consolation of rationality itself, of the recognition of having done one's best. For the rational person prizes reason itself and takes rational satisfaction in the very fact of having done what reason demands. Even when matters go awry because of "circumstances beyond one's control," the rational agent has the contenting consolation of "having done one's best in the face of the inevitable" that was so greatly prized by the ancient Stoics. Realizing the limits of human powers—one's own included—the rational person avoids pointless regrets and futile recriminations, achieving the self-respect and justified self-satisfaction that go with the realization that one has done all one can in a good cause. But the crux is this: reflective happiness pivots on the cultivation of our real or best interests—the realization of those conditions that are life enhancing and best enable us to realize our opportunities for the attainment of genuine goods. And only reason is able to provide us with sensible guidance about these matters. Accordingly, if happiness is construed in terms of one's reflective contentment with the condition of things by way of intellectual appraisal, then there is indeed good reason to think that the rational person will indeed fare better in the pursuit of happiness by virtue of that rationality.

On the other hand, if happiness is viewed as an affective psychic condition—a matter of point accumulation on the euphoriometer—then the thesis that rationality promotes happiness becomes very questionable. In the first place, there is the fact that we can gain ready access to euphoria through avenues not particularly endorsed by reason. For one thing there is the prospect of drugs and psychic manipulation. For another, the very fact that we can speak of "harmless pleasures" indicates that there are also harmful ones of which reason is bound to disapprove. By its very nature reason is geared not to our pleasure but to what is, all considered, in our best interests. And there is no basis for thinking that a heed of reason's dictates will advantage us in the pursuit of affective pleasure.[2]

But rationality can unquestionably help people to secure their objectives—to acquire wealth, cultivate friends, influence people, and generally improve their chances at acquiring the good things of the world. On this basis, somebody is likely to object: "Surely rational people are the happier for their rationality, even in the affective mode of happiness, because their intelligence is capable of benefiting them in this regard as well." Now it would doubtless be very nice if this were so. But alas it is not. For while intelligence can lead one to water, it cannot ensure that drinking produces any worthwhile effects. There is no reason to think that conducting their affairs intelligently benefits people in terms specifically of increased affective happiness. Even getting more than one's share of the world's good things does not lead to this objective. There are simply too many other factors involved.

To be sure, there is the fact that rational people will be the more "knowledgeable"—that they will (presumably) transact their cognitive and their practical affairs with greater success in the realization of their objectives. But this will not mean all that much for their specially hedonic happiness. For experience teaches that people are not generally made affectively happier by "getting what they want." This, after all, very much depends on the kind of thing that they are after. And even if people indeed are after the things of which reason approves, this will not help them all that much when affective or hedonic happiness is at issue. For affective happiness is something too ephemeral and capricious to lend itself to effective manipulation by rational means. (Even—and perhaps especially—people who "have everything" may yet fail to be happy; there is nothing all that paradoxical or even unusual about someone who says "I know that in these circumstances I *should* be happy, but I'm just not.")[3] Affective hap-

───────────

[2] It is useful to observe the close parallelism of these ideas to discussions in the post-Aristotelian schools of Greek philosophy. The distinction between affective happiness and reflective happiness runs parallel to their distinction between pleasure or enjoyment (*hēdonē*) on the one hand, and genuine well-being (*eudaimonia*) on the other. And if one identifies rationality with what those ancients called wisdom (*sophia*), then their insistence that wisdom was a necessary (though not necessarily sufficient) condition for the achievement of true happiness (well being = *eudaimonia* = human flourishing) parallels our present conclusion that rationality is a facilitating requisite of reflective happiness. The discussions of those classical moralists are intimately relevant to our present deliberations and point toward results of much the same general tendency. (Where human wisdom rather than "know-how" is concerned, there is no technological obsolescence.) For an informative and interesting treatment of the relevant issues, see J.C.B. Gosling and C.C.W. Taylor, *The Greeks on Pleasure* (Oxford: Clarendon Press, 1982).

[3] Recall Edward Arlington Robinson's somber poem entitled "Richard Cory," the man who had "everything to make us wish that we were in his place" and yet one night "went home and put a bullet through his head."

piness largely is a matter of moods and frames of mind—easily frustrated by boredom or predictability. It is an ironic aspect of the human condition that affective happiness is inherently resistant to rational management.

Of course, people who proceed rationally will be disappointed less often than they otherwise would be. Their rationality can plausibly be expected to spare them sundry unpleasant surprises. But by the same token, rationality may also possibly occasion its bearer some pain and dismay. For rational foresight and foreknowledge can also lead to painful apprehensions and gloomy forebodings with respect to things that will likely go wrong, of which life is bound to afford many instances. Rationality has far less bearing on affective happiness than we might ideally like.

Judge this from your own experience. Among the people you know, are the rational ones—the intelligent and sagacious and prudent ones—any happier, on balance, *affectively* speaking, than their more thoughtless and happy-go-lucky compatriots? Most likely not. On all indications, an easy-going disposition and good sense of humor count far more with affective happiness than intelligence and rationality. No doubt, matters here will hinge less on "savvy" than on "luck"—on the disposition one has inherited and on whether one lives amid circumstances and conditions where things by and large go well, or at any rate improve on what has gone before.

To be sure, it might seem on first thought that the single-mindedly efficient pursuit of affective happiness is bound to provide greater pleasure in the long run. But the facts of experience teach otherwise. John Stuart Mill's description of his own experience is instructive in this regard. In a striking passage in his *Autobiography* he wrote:

> It was in the autumn of 1826, I was in a dull state of nerves, such as everybody is occasionally liable to. . . . It occurred to me to put the question directly to myself: "Suppose that all your objects in life were realized; that all . . . could be completely effected at this very instant: would this be a great joy and happiness to you?" And an irrepressible self-consciousness distinctly answered, "No!" At this my heart sank within me: the whole foundation on which my life was constructed fell down.
>
> The experiences of this period had two very marked effects on my opinions and character. In the first place, they led me to adopt a theory of life, very unlike that on which I had before acted, and having much in common with what at that time I certainly had never heard of, the anti-self-consciousness theory of Carlyle. I never, indeed, wavered in the conviction that happiness is the test of all rules of conduct, and the end of life. But I now thought that this end was only to be attained by not making it the direct end. Those only are happy (I thought) who have their minds fixed on some object other than their own happiness; on the happiness of others, on the improvement of mankind, even on some art or

pursuit, followed not as a means, but as itself an ideal end. Aiming thus at something else, they find happiness by the way. The enjoyments of life (such was now my theory) are sufficient to make it a pleasant thing, when they are taken *en passant*, without being made a principal object.[4]

Getting what we naively and unevaluatedly want can be a hollow business. And ironically, when hedonically affective happiness is *pursued*, however rationally and intelligently, it inclines to flee away. (This is yet one more way in which the project of "the pursuit of happiness" faces substantial inherent difficulties.) For as Mill's ruminations indicate, rationality itself teaches us in the school of bitter experience about the ultimate emptiness of this sort of thing—its inherent incapacity to deliver on the crucial matter of real contentment by way of reflective happiness.

Considerations of this sort combine to indicate the implausibility of holding that the rational person is the happier for that rationality, when happiness is construed in the hedonic terms of affective euphoria or pleasure.[5]

More on the Affective Rewards of Rationality

There is, however, a further importantly relevant aspect to the issue of the bearing of rationality on happiness in its affective dimension. For our deliberations have to this point neglected an important distinction, in that the hedonic domain actually has two sides—the positive, which pivots on affective happiness or pleasure, and the negative, which pivots on affective unhappiness or pain.

A negatively oriented affective benefit is the removal or diminution of something bad. (It is illustrated in caricature by the story of the man who liked knocking his head against a wall because it felt so good when he stopped.) A positively oriented affective benefit, in contrast, is one that involves something that is pleasant in its own right rather than by way of contrast with a distressing alternative.

This distinction bears importantly on our problem. For there is no doubt that the state of human well-being has been, and still can be, greatly improved through the use of intelligence in science and technology to obtain the negatively oriented benefits of reduced human misery and suffering. Consider only a few instances: medicine (the prevention of child-

---

[4] Mill, *Autobiography*, ed. J. J. Coss (New York: Columbia University Press, 1929), pp. 94–101. Cf. the anticipation in *The Diary of George Templeton Strong*, Vol. 1, 1835–49 (New York: Macmillan, 1952), p. 289.

[5] To be sure, the fact remains that rational people will certainly be better off (reflectively speaking) on rationality's account, since they are bound to take satisfaction in rationality itself.

hood diseases through innoculation, anesthetics, plastic and restorative surgery, hygiene, dentistry), waste disposal and sanitation, temperature control (heating and air conditioning), transportation and communication, entertainment (films, TV, recorded music), and so on. It would be easy to multiply examples. Intelligence-devised technology can certainly stand us in good stead in averting causes of hunger, illness, discomfort, boredom, separation, and so forth. It can vastly improve the "quality of life."

But the unfortunate fact remains that, as the world turns, this diminution of the negative does not necessarily yield positive repercussions for affective happiness. Augmented well-being does not mean an increase in affective happiness; a lessening of suffering and discomfort does not produce a positive condition like pleasure or joy or happiness. For pleasure is not the mere absence of pain, nor joy the absence of sorrow. The removal of the affectively negative just does not of itself create a positive condition—though, to be sure, it abolishes an obstacle in the way of positivity. And so, the immense potential of modern science and technology for the alleviation of suffering and distress does not automatically qualify it as a fountain of affective happiness. The harsh fact of the matter is that technical rationality is ineffective as a promoter of ongoing hedonic happiness in its positive dimension.

To be sure, technical intelligence can indeed provide such enhancers of short-term affective positivity as alcoholic beverages or drugs. But there is a very big fly in this ointment. The affective pleasure of such euphoria inducers soon becomes eroded by routinization. Habituation swiftly undermines the pleasantness of these "pleasures," so that overall little if any real pleasure accrues from their merely nominal "enjoyment."[6] In the end, it is not the pleasure of indulgence but the discomfort of deprivation that comes to prevail. Natural psychological and physical mechanisms soon transmute the "benefits" at issue with these technically contrived euphoria-inducers from a positive to a negative character. Designed for the enhancement of pleasure, the contribution of these technical resources is soon reduced to the assuaging of appetite and diminution of pain.[7]

No doubt rationality pays. But the irony of the human condition is that as far as affective matters are concerned, the utility of reason is vastly more efficacious at averting unhappiness than at promoting happiness in its positive dimension.

[6] There is indeed some pleasure in familiarity, security, and routine of most any sort, but intelligence and the technology it supports are hardly needed for (or indeed particularly conducive to) the idealization of such desiderata.

[7] Means of transport and communication are perhaps an exception here, though their engendering the more hectic pace of modern life does render them something of a mixed blessing.

Is Rationality Inhumane?

It is sometimes said that a person's rationality can actually impede the realization of happiness. After all, man does not live by reason alone, and many rewarding human activities—family life, social interaction, sports and recreations, "light" reading, films and other amusements and entertainments, and so on—make little or no use of reason or reasoning. And so, people often say things like: "Rationality as such is cold, passionless, inhumane. It stands in the way of those many life-enhancing, unreflective spontaneous activities that have an appropriate place in a full, rewarding, happy human life." One frequently hears such claims made. But they are profoundly mistaken.

Admittedly, there is much more to humanity than rationality as such. Our natural makeup is complex and many-sided—a thing of many strains and aspects. We have interests over and above those at issue in the cultivation of reason. But there is no reason whatever why our reason should not be able to recognize this fact. To fail to do so would be simply unintelligent—and it would be flatly contrary to the very nature of rationality for reason to impede the pursuit of these positivities. The very fact that *Homo sapiens* is the rational *animal* means that there is a good deal more to us than reason alone—and nothing prevents reason from recognizing that this is so. For reason can and does acknowledge as wholly proper and legitimate a whole host of useful activities in whose conduct it itself plays little if any part—socializing, diversions, recreations, and so on. Reason itself is perfectly willing and able to give them the stamp of approval, fully recognizing their value and usefulness.

People can certainly neglect those various valuable arational activities in favor of overcalculation, overplanning, and an inflated overcommitment to reasoning. However, the salient fact is that rationality itself disrecommends this. In being "too rational," one would, strictly speaking, not be rational enough. It is perfectly rational sometimes to do heedless or even madcap things in this life—"to break the monotony" and inject an element of novelty and excitement into an otherwise prosaic existence. All work and no play makes life go stale. People can sometimes take quite understandable pleasure from "irrational" actions—climbing mountains, betting on the ponies, riding the rapids of a rushing river. To break the mold of a colorless rationalism is, within limits, not all that irrational: it is part and parcel of deeper rationality that goes beyond the superficial. After all, rationality aims at goods as well as goals. By its very nature, it is not stupid. It is clearly in a position to appreciate the value of enjoyment as well as those of achievement.

Accordingly, one really cannot be "too rational for one's own good." If, contrary to fact, there were such a defect—if this could be established at all—then reason itself could recognize and confront this circumstance. Intelligence does not stand as one limited faculty over against others (emotion, affection, and the like). It is an all-pervasive light that can shine through to every endeavor, even those in which reason itself is not directly involved, reflecting upon the merits and demerits of all our activities. Reason itself is in the end our only trustworthy guide to whatever human undertakings are valid and appropriate. It is the exercise of rationality in the cause of reflective evaluation that informs us about priorities. Reason itself thus takes top priority.

Several among the ancient philosophers—Aristotle preeminently—insisted on the primacy of the strictly intellectual pleasures inherent in the exercise of reason. They maintained that only the purely rational intellectual activities—learning, understanding, reasoning—yield satisfactions of a sort truly worthy of a rational being. Only in the pleasures of the mind did they see a prospect of genuine satisfaction for intelligent creatures. Accordingly they insisted that a truly rational being can take appropriate satisfaction only in the pleasures consequent upon the exercise of reason and that all else is a matter of dross and delusion.

But this line of thinking is deeply problematic. Rationality does not require us to take satisfaction in reason alone and view the pleasures of reason as solely and uniquely genuine. Far from it! Reason can and does acknowledge the need for diversity and variation; it can and does recognize the importance of activities that make little or no call on its own resources. The importance of a balance of varied goods within a complex "economy of values" is something that reason itself emphasizes, even though this complex must itself encompass various mundanely arational goods. To insist that rational satisfaction—reflective contentment—rather than mere "pleasure" is the pivot of genuine happiness does not mean that commonplace pleasures have no legitimate place in a truly happy life. There is no sound reason why rational people need be spoilsports.

A deep distrust of reason is a recurrent leitmotiv of Spanish philosophy that runs from Francisco Sanchez and Gracián y Morales in the seventeenth century to Miguel de Unamuno to José Ortega y Gasset in the twentieth. What the Spaniards have against reason is its not affording an adequate basis for a satisfying life. As they see it, reason directs people to specifically "reasonable" and paternalistically "sensible" ends that can be objectively validated through the approval of others (experts). But the pursuit of such ends does not make people happy. "Be reasonable!" is the ever-repeated cry of disillusioned middle age against the sanguine enthusiasms of youth. And this eternal cry is destined to be eternally unavailing because youth realizes instinctively—and rightly—that the way to happiness does not lie in this particular direction.

This Spanish perspective combines a commonsensical view of the many-sided fullness of a good life with a deep skepticism that reason can get us there. For the world—in particular the social world in which we humans live—is changeable, chaotic, and irrational. Here reason's "general principles" are of little help; the useful lessons of life are those people learn in the school of bitter experience. So urge the skeptically minded philosophers of Spain.

All of this has a certain surface plausibility. But even in a difficult and disorderly world, those who do not examine it rationally—and refuse to profit from a reason-guided exploitation of the experience of others—certainly create needless difficulties for themselves. To be sure, there are other guides to human decision than reason itself, including custom, instinct, experience, and spontaneous inclination. But only reasoned examination can teach us about their proper use and can instruct us about the extent to which it makes sense to rely upon them.

Yet does rationality not undermine the emotional and affective side of man—the uncalculating, unselfish, open, easygoing, relaxed side that is no less significant in the overall scheme of human affairs than the sterner enterprise of "pursuing our ends"? Is reason not deficient in one-sidedly emphasizing the "cold and calculating" aspect of human nature? Not at all! There are good grounds for reason *not* to deny the claims of our emotional and affective side. For life is infinitely fuller and richer that way. Reason, after all, is not our sole director in the conduct of life. Emotion, sentiment, and the affective side of our nature have a perfectly proper and highly important place in the human scheme of things—no less important than the active striving for ends and goals. Insofar as other valid human enterprises exist outside the range of reason-employing activities—and they certainly do—it is clear that reason can (and should) recognize and acknowledge them.

To say that reason is cold, inhumane, bloodless, and indifferent to human values is to misconceive it badly by misinterpreting it as purely a matter of means to arbitrary ends, committed to the approach of "let's get to the goal but never mind how, with no worry about who or what gets hurt along the way." Such an overly narrow, "mechanical" view of reason, regrettably widespread though it is, is totally inappropriate. It rests on that familiar fallacy of seeing reason as a limited-purpose instrument that is in no position to look critically at the goals toward whose realization it is employed. In taking this view, it refuses to grant reason that which is in fact its definitive characteristic—the use of intelligence.

There is little question that, as one recent author puts it, "one can do harm to important human values by overemphasizing the values of theorizing and cognition."[8] Yet acknowledging this nowise undermines the claims of reason. On the contrary! Reason itself demands that we recognize the limited place of the virtues of cognition, inquiry, and the cerebral side of life. An adequate account of rationality must rightly stress its importance and primacy and yet at the same time recognize that the intellectual virtues compose only limited component parts of the good life.

But is reason not defective because—as one hears it said—it generally counsels a prudent caution that is at odds with righteous indignation, courage, bravery, and other manifestations of the "spirited" side of human life? William Shakespeare's Troilus put this point as follows:

> You know a sword employed is perilous,
> And reason flies the object of all harm.
>
> . . . .
> . . . Nay, if we talk of reason,
> Let's shut our gates and sleep. Manhood and honor
> Should have hare-hearts, would they but fat their thoughts
> With this crammed reason. Reason and respect
> Make livers pale and lustihood deject.[9]

But here we have once more an overly narrow conception of reason. Reason is perfectly capable of acknowledging that "sweet reasonableness" is not called for everywhere and in all circumstances, recognizing (for example) that there may be occasion for indignation and outrage in a just cause.

What can and must be said on reason's behalf is that it is the very best guide that we have for the management of our life's doings and dealings. But it nevertheless still remains an imperfect and never altogether satisfactory guide. For in this regard those somber Spaniards are completely right. Reason's best-laid plans often go amiss. The role of chance and luck in human affairs means that our existence is always in large degree a riddle and a conundrum. In the end, the problems of life have no straightforwardly "purely rational" solution because the management of a satisfying life is a matter no less of the virtues of character than of those of the intellect.

As repeatedly indicated, reason urges the intelligent cultivation of appropriate ends. And insofar as those various arational activities do indeed have value for us, reason itself is prepared to recognize and approve this. The life of reason is not all calculating, planning, striving. For us humans, rest, recreation, and enjoyment are very much a part of it. Accordingly, reason is perfectly willing to delegate a proper share of authority to our

[8] Nathanson, *The Ideal of Rationality*, p. 157. This book is well worth reading on the subject of our present concerns.

[9] *Troilus and Cressida* 2.2.40–50.

inclinations and psychic needs. It goes against reason to say that rational calculation should pervade all facets of human life. Reason does not insist on running the whole show by itself, blind to its limitations in being simply one human resource among others. As has been stressed from the outset of this discussion, rationality is a matter of the intelligent pursuit of appropriate ends. It would be absurd to think that this is something that can be of doubtful propriety.

A feeling of self-worth is essential to one's sense of legitimacy—one's ability to feel at home in the world and secure in one's place in it. Rationality acquires its paramount worth for us precisely because of its determinative bearing on our self-image, in that we see ourselves as members of the community of rational beings. It is crucial for our self-definition.

None of this comes as news to reason. After all, it is of the essence of reason to insist upon the intelligent cultivation of appropriate ends. Rationality need not be unintelligent about it by insisting on the value of reasoning as predominating to the exclusion of all else, totally overlooking the importance for us of values outside the intellectual domain. What is counterproductive is not the reasonableness of rationality but the unreasonableness of an exaggerated rationalism.

In sum, it emerges that those who distrust reason do not properly understand what is at issue here. By misidentifying true rationality with cold calculation, they do grave injustice to the nature of intelligence. People who think that rationality is at odds with happiness have either a distorted notion of rationality or a distorted notion of happiness.

Reason as a Basis for Reflective Happiness

The upshot of these considerations regarding the bearing of rationality upon happiness is clear enough, even though subject to various complicating distinctions. If we construe happiness in the more reflective mode as an intellectual matter of rational contentment, then the rational person is bound to be the better off by way of improved chances for happiness. But if happiness is construed in the affective mode as a matter of pleasure or euphoria, then there are no good grounds for thinking that rationality is profitable for happiness in its positive aspect—though even here it does have the merit of being able to help in averting affective unhappiness. The outcome to the question of rationality's claim as a supporter of human happiness is accordingly indecisive. The answer will depend crucially on just which sort of conception of happiness we propose to adopt.

One further aspect of the matter also deserves stress. Rationality is inherently normative—by its very nature it looks to the guidance of values. But the values that are at stake in human affairs do not turn on personal happiness alone—they are something larger and deeper than that. Important though the pursuit of happiness may be for us, it is no be-all and end-all. For what does—and should—matter for us is not just the quest for happiness but something that is larger and weightier than just that, namely, the quest for meaning.

We arrive at a result that is not perhaps all that surprising. Given that rationality is a matter of intelligence—of the effective use of mind—it is only natural and to be expected that rationality should be congenial to and supportive of that reflective, judgmental mode of happiness over which mind itself is the final arbiter.[10]

[10] This chapter draws upon ideas developed more fully in the author's book *Rationality*.

Fourteen

Values, Pragmatism, and Idealism

The Scope of Values

The cognitive machinery at the disposal of us humans in our quest for factual knowledge has developed over the course of time owing to the utility of its application in the real world. Its origination has a profoundly pragmatic character, rooting in its capacity to satisfy a need of ours by enabling us to categorize, describe, and explain what goes on about us. It is a resource of operational adjustment to the real world, geared to orienting us cognitively in our existential environment. Insofar as our machinery of factual description is out of touch with reality—does not apply to the things we encounter in the world about us—it is so much useless baggage and would, for that reason, have been abandoned long ago.

But the matter stands rather differently as regards our machinery of normative evaluation. For valuation is geared not so much to what is actually real as to the merely possible. The reason for being of our evaluative machinery is to enable us to appraise not just actualities but possibilities as well: its orientation is not simply directed at the realities that exist about us but extends into the realm of hypothesis and imagination, seeing that value is concerned not only with what does happen but with what might happen, and not just "realistically" but even "by the wildest stretch of the imagination." The reason for being of the machinery of evaluation is, quite in general, to enable us to compare and contrast what is with what might be. Values are geared to mere possibilities to an extent that stretches our descriptive resources to and indeed beyond their natural limits. (Theologians generally hesitate to claim they can describe God, but seldom do they show reluctance to expatiate with unhesitating assurance on his evaluative aspects.)

Homo sapiens is *Homo valuens*. As the sort of creature we are, we are impelled by our nature to form for ourselves not just a cognitive picture of the real world but also a view of our own place within the order of things, preeminently including a value orientation that gives meaning and significance to our efforts in this realm. The human being is an amphibian: a creature that dwells not just through its body in the actual-world realm of reality but also through its mind in the thought-world realm of possibility. And from our human point of view, various diverse possibilities are avail-

able: the future is invariably seen as affording us a manifold of possible
eventuations, one or the other of which is a prospect for ultimate realization in a way that hinges, at least in part, on what we ourselves do about
it. We are confronted by a diversified range of choices embedded within
a manifold of contemplated possibilities.

At this point evaluation becomes necessary. We have to be in a position
to adjudge some possibilities as preferable—as better, more desirable, or
worthier than others. A mechanism for evaluation and the assessment of
preferability is an unavoidable requisite. For us, evaluation is the driving
power of purpose—the motive force of our effort to canalize the course of
the real in the endeavor to pursue our ends and thereby improve upon
what otherwise might be.

Whether we succeed in actually bringing our evaluatively selected desiderata to actual realization is something over which we feeble humans
have only partial and highly incomplete control. Whether we succeed or
not in our effect depends largely on the cooperation of reality itself. But
what we *want* to do and what we *try* to do depends on us. And values are
the pivotal instrumentality for this business of aim, effort, and aspiration.

Perhaps the place where our creative efforts are the most urgent—if not
always the most availing—is with respect to ourselves. Self-development
lies at the very core of human existence. The impetus "to make something
of oneself," *to make oneself into the sort of being one would like to be,*
represents a key characteristic constituent of *Homo sapiens.*

Human self-development is not simply a matter of self-aggrandizement
but one of self-improvement. Behind the impetus toward the "goods" that
represent our needs and wants in this world (ranging from food, shelter,
and clothing to wealth, power, and status), there also lies an impetus to
"the good"—to the cultivation of values and ideals. We want those we care
for to be not just well off but content and happy. And we desire for them
(and for ourselves) a contentment that is not just a matter of satiation but
one of reflective and rational satisfaction. Sensible people realize that
those who "have everything" are not on the path to true satisfaction but
well en route to boredom, vacuity, and disillusion.

Realizing the potential of human life to the fullest is not possible without a commitment to values and ideals in an endeavor to achieve some of
the positive possibilities at one's disposal. Regardless of the extent to
which it affords "enjoyment," a life of "enjoyment" devoid of the contribution of human potential—lacking all effort "to make something of oneself"
in the cultivation of one's talents and capacities for achievement—is a life
that is ultimately empty. Even when it offers pleasure, it affords no real
joy, no true reflective satisfaction.

We humans have an inherent commitment to endeavor to bring to realization something of value—a commitment if not to the world at large,

then at least to ourselves. To ignore this commitment is to default on an obligation to ourselves, to our fellows, and to the forces within the world at large that, in setting a place for us at the table of human life, have placed a unique opportunity at our disposal.

The Pragmatic Aspect of Values and the Idealistic Dimensions of Values

Values are practical instrumentalities, tools that aid us in conducting the business of life. The light of evaluation illuminates the prospects and possibilities that lie before us; without evaluation to guide us, we grope about blindly in the dark. Our information and our resources spread out before us a vast range of possibilities. At many junctures in life, diverse directions in which to move are available to us. Only through the evaluation of alternatives can we effect a sensible (rationally appropriate and acceptable) choice among them.

Values are accordingly instrumentalities that serve to make the satisfactory conduct of life possible. It is the prospect of intelligent choices that makes us humans into rational agents, but only through our having appropriate values does the prospect of intelligent choice become possible for us.

Values not only make our lives as human beings possible but also serve to make it meaningful. For the life of the human individual is brief: here today, gone tomorrow. Through living values, we can reach out beyond the drastic limits of the space and time at our disposal in this world toward the achievement of something large and more significant.

The pragmatic aspect of values lies in the fact that they provide a thought tool that we require in order to achieve a *satisfying* life. By contrast, the idealistic aspect of values lies in the fact that they alone enable us to achieve a *meaningful* life. And given our nature, these two aspects are inseparable. For we humans cannot be fully content with a life that we cannot regard as meaningful.

To be sure, sensible people cannot but recognize their finitude: the inevitable limits of their powers and of their life span. By and large, we humans accept with stoic resignation the fact of our incapacity at large and our mortality in particular. But we yearn for something greater, nobler, and more enduring than what we are or can be. For us the ultimate evil is not our own extinction but that of the values we hold dear—the principles and ideals to which we stand committed. Disaster absolute is not our death but the definitive destruction of what we value—the ultimate triumph of evil over good.

It is precisely because meaning is a matter of value that the idealistic aspect of evaluation is unavoidable—and indispensable for us. Values provide the requisite means for the orientation of our thought. And they accordingly make a crucial contribution to the formulation of our worldview, in particular, to our view of our own proper place within the scheme of things. Their role as indispensable thought-tools endows our values with an indelibly idealistic aspect. It is our dedication to values that ultimately gives meaning to our lives. In the final analysis, our yearning for transcendence is not a "selfish" yearning for something that appertains specifically to our own personal, individual selves—we have too "realistic" an appreciation of our finitude to demand the impossible. Our impetus to transcendence reflects a commitment to something abstract and time-less—to principles, ideals, and values. As we should and generally do real-ize, such factors are not just more durable but also something "higher" than ourselves.

Being human involves a commitment to ideality—a striving toward something larger and better than life. *Homo sapiens* is a creature that yearns for transcendence, for achieving value and meaning above and be-yond the buzzing confusion of the world's realities.

Closing the Circle: The Validity of Values

What is particularly ironic in the skeptical distrust of reason is its inevita-ble reliance on reason for its own validation. That reason may have its limits as a guide to the attainment of a satisfying life may well be true. But only reason itself can inform us about this—only rational scrutiny and rea-son-guided investigation of the matter can reliably inform us what these limits are. And so, in developing their case for the limitations of reason, the skeptics are (inevitably) constrained to make use of the resources of reason itself. And this is exactly as it should be. Any *reasoned* examination and critique of reason must rely on reason's own resources.

To be sure, various theorists mock reason as an exercise in futility. "Any defense of reason is predetermined to failure. For it must make use of the very instrument that is in question, and therefore commits the vicious circle fallacy." What nonsense! Whatever circularity is at issue is alto-gether virtuous. Reason is and must be self-endorsing; self-validation is the only thing that makes sense here. The only defense of reason worth having is of course a rational one. What more—or what else—could a sensible person ask for?

Even as the realm of reason should and does obtain the support of rea-son, so will the domain of valid values be substantiated through its own resources. The rational and the evaluative domains must in the end find their validation in their own normative terms.

The starting point of the book was set by considerations regarding the need of a rational agent for values to provide the guidance needed for its management of practical and cognitive affairs. This concluding chapter has brought us round full-circle to this theme that a value framework as an indispensable instrumentality of the thought orientation demanded by a rational creature. The intervening deliberations have sought to illustrate and emphasize how diversified and pervasive this role of values is and how intimately it is bound up with an idealized view of the human condition. To understand the real aright, in a way that enables the products of our intellectual efforts to satisfy the requirements for which these efforts were instituted in the first place, we must understand it is the light of value. Values are the instrumentalities by which we form a view of what we can and should be. As authentically rational creatures, it is the sort of view that we form regarding what can and should be in the world—ourselves included—that serves to make us what we actually are.

The validity of values accordingly roots in the fact that a recourse to values is a requisite to our being able to be the sorts of creatures we see ourselves as being (namely, free rational agents). To be sure, this consideration does not of itself validate a particular set of values—apart from speaking for such (very high level) value abstractions as freedom of agency, morality of mutual recognizance, and, of course, rationality itself. Many or most of our concrete values can be validated only in terms of some specific considerations about the situational context in which the free rational agent at issue will have to operate. But the salient fact remains that these abstract values that constitute the top level of the implementation hierarchy for the prospect of free rational agency are themselves rationally validatable through their determinative role relative to the prospect of free rational agency itself.

The decisive weakness of a philosophical relativism with respect to evaluation lies deep in the nature of the human condition. It emerges roughly as follows.

The characteristic stance of relativism is to insist on the *rational indifference* of alternatives. Be it contentions, doctrines, value-standards, practices, customs, or whatever that is at issue, the relativist insists that "it just doesn't matter" in point of rationality. People are led to adopt one alternative over another by *extrarational* considerations (custom, habituation, fashion, or whatever); from the rational point of view there is nothing to choose—all the alternatives stand on the same footing.

The difficulty with taking this position seriously roots in the fact that our commitments all belong to identifiable departments of purposive human endeavor—identifiable domains, disciplines, and the like. For all (or virtually all) human enterprises are at bottom teleological—conducted with some sort of end or objective in view. Even the moral enterprise is purposive, its mission being to define, teach, and encourage modes of action that bring the behavior of individuals into alignment with the best overall interests of the group. And art and sport also have various aims (to foster sensibility, to divert ourselves, etc.).

Homo sapiens is a pervasively purposive being. True, human life consists of more than goal-seeking alone. But goal-oriented comportment is a large and indispensable part of it. We are a being so extensively equipped with needs and wants that the adoption and pursuit of aims and objectives is a predominant feature of our lives. Even "play" and "mere diversion" satisfy some needs of ours. Our human aims and purposes are correlative with our needs and wants. And this means that they do not stand isolated and alone, but come in large groups, organized and coordinated with reference to the taxonomy of our needs and wants. (It is clear that we can thus classify people's aims and purposes in relation to our psychological, biological, intellectual needs, etc.). Such taxonomic groups of human needs and wants define our major projects and lines of purposive endeavor.

Now it is via their role in the large projects of cognition, sustenance, propagation, diversion, etc., that rationality gains its foothold in relation to all our various activities. And the crucial fact is that some claims, beliefs, doctrines, practices, customs, etc. are bound to serve the purposes of their domain better than others. It is pretty much inevitable that in any goal-oriented enterprise, some alternative ways of proceeding answer better than others with respect to the relevant range of purpose, proving themselves more efficient and effective in point of goal-realization. And in the teleological contexts they *thereby* establish themselves as rationally appropriate with respect to the issues. It is evident that the quintessentially rational thing to do is to give precedence and priority to those alternatives that are more effective with respect to the range of purposes at issue. Rationality, after all, is constituted through the intelligent pursuit of appropriate objectives. And in view of this, the appropriateness of our aims and objectives comes about through the smoothness of their fit within the comprehensive systematization of the sum total of our needs and wants. (Only wants duly coordinated with needs can qualify as rationally appropriate: the validation of our wants comes about through their means-ends coordination with our needs.)

There is no doubt that such a position qualifies as a version of "pragmatism." But it is crucially important to note that it is not a version of *practicalism*. It stands committed to the primacy of purpose but it certainly does not endorse the idea that the only possible (or only valid) sort of human purpose is that of the type traditionally characterized as "practical"—i.e., one that is geared to the physical and "material" well-being of people. Purposive enterprises can be as diverse and varied as is the whole spectrum of legitimate human purpose, and these can relate not only to the "material" but also to the "spiritual" side of people (their knowledge, artistic sensibility, social disposition, etc.). To signalize a step beyond the classical range of specifically *practical* purposes, such a pragmatism might perhaps better be characterized as *functionalism.*

This functionalist perspective is decisive in its impetus against relativism. For relativism is flatly indifferentistic; presented with alternatives of the sort at issue (cognitive, moral, etc.), the relativist of any stripe, be it cognitive, evaluative, or whatever, insists that it just does not matter—at any rate as far as the rationality of the issue is concerned. But once we see the issues in a purposive perspective, this line just doesn't work. In a purposive context, alternatives are not in general portrayable as rationally indifferent. Rationality not only permits but demands giving preference to purposively effectual alternatives over the rest (at any rate as long as other things are anything like equal). It is quintessentially rational to prefer what works within the relevant purposive context.

To the relativist one must concede *pluralism*—the absence of uniqueness and the availability of alternatives. But this does not underwrite irrationalistic indifferentism. On the contrary, two higher-level meta-norms—to wit, conformity to one's standards and conduciveness to one's goals and, above all, one's needs—operate so as to assure a purchase hold for rational appropriateness at the precedural level (even though they do not otherwise engender substantive uniformity.)

As this line of reflection indicates, relativism stubs its toe against the pervasively purposive nature of the human situation, the fact that all our proceedings—be they in inquiry, evaluation, or wherever—fall within the scope of various purposive ventures that have an end in view. This teleological aspect provides for rationality in a way that puts relativism into a thoroughly problematic and dubious light.

It is through the channel of considerations of this pragmatic/functionalistic sort, then, that the rational validation of our values can run its course.

A Pragmatic Idealism

Idealism as a philosophical doctrine insists upon the centrality of thought in the world's scheme of things. And values are essential instruments of rational thought. Hence insofar as values have a formative role alike in the constituting and the constitution of our world picture, they are mainstays of idealism.

To see *Homo sapiens* as *Homo valuens*—as committed to a value-informed view of the world and one's place within it—is one characteristic way of viewing humans in an idealistic perspective. And because this vision of ourselves as value-dedicated beings is something requisite to the achievement of a full and meaningful human life, it is, at the same time, an acknowledgment of values and idealization as the most quintessentially practical of human instrumentalities.

A pragmatic idealism that sees values in the light of indispensable thought instruments for beings involved in the processes of rational inquiry and decision is thus also a thoroughly "realistic" position—on one of the many senses of this versatile term. For values answer to a deep-seated need of ours. As ineradicably evaluative creatures, we humans need not only to have a workable explanatory view of the world and our place within it, but at the same time, we need an evaluative perspective that provides for a workable way of implementing a conception of the meaningfulness of our lives. Not only do we humans need some conception of how it is that we have managed to come by our place on nature's stage—and to understand how it has come about that matters have eventuated in the world so as to put a life at our disposal in the first place—but as rational creatures and members of *Homo sapiens*, we also very much need to have some idea as to what it makes sense for us to do with it.

Bibliography

Arrow, Kenneth J. *Social Choice and Individual Values*. New York: Cowles Commission Monograph no. 12, 1951; 2d ed., 1963.

Ayer, A. J. *Language, Truth, and Logic*. London: Macmillan, 1936; reprint, New York: Dover, 1952.

Bahnsen, Julius. *Der Widerspruch im Wissen und Wesen der Welt*. 2 vols. Leipzig: B. Franke, 1882.

Baier, Kurt. *The Meaning of Life*. Canberra: University of Canberra Press, 1957.
————. *The Moral Point of View*. Ithaca, N.Y.: Cornell University Press, 1958.

Ball, Stephen W. "Facts, Values, and Normative Supervenience." *Philosophical Studies* 55 (1989): 143–72.

Bayles, Michael D., ed. *Contemporary Utilitarianism*. Garden City, N.Y.: Anchor Books, 1968.

Benn, S. I., and G. W. Mortimore. *Rationality and the Social Sciences*. London: Routledge & Kegan Paul, 1976.

Bergström, Lars. "On the Logic of Imperatives and Deontic Logic." In *Mérites et limites des méthodes logiques en philosophie*. Paris: J. Vrin, 1885; reprint, Paris: Colloque de la Fondation Singer-Poliginac, 1984.

Black, Duncan. *The Theory of Committees and Elections*. Cambridge: Cambridge University Press, 1958.

Black, Max. "Making Intelligent Choices: How Useful Is Decision Theory?" *Dialectica* 30 (1985): 19–34.

Boyd, Richard. "How to Be a Moral Realist." In *Essays on Moral Realism*, ed. Geoffrey Sayre-McCord. Ithaca, N.Y.: Cornell University Press, 1988.

Brentano, Franz. *The Foundation and Construction of Ethics*. Trans. Elizabeth Schneewind. London: Routledge & Kegan Paul, 1973.
————. *The Origin of Our Knowledge of Right and Wrong*. Trans. R. M. Chisholm and Elizabeth Schneewind. London: Routledge & Kegan Paul, 1969.
————. *The True and the Evident*. Trans. Roderick M. Chisholm, Ilse Politzer, and Kurt Q. Fischer. London: Routledge & Kegan Paul, 1966.

Chisholm, R. M. "Brentano's Theory of Correct and Incorrect Emotion." *Révue Internationale de Philosophie* 78 (1966): 395–415.

Churchland, Paul. *Matter and Consciousness*. Cambridge: MIT Press, 1984.

Condorcet, Marquis de. *Essai sur l'application de l'analyse à la probabilité des décisions rendus à la pluralité des voix*. Paris: L'Imprimerie royale, 1785; reprint, New York: Barnes & Noble, 1970.

Dahl, Norman O. *Practical Reason, Aristotle, and Weakness of the Will*. Minneapolis: University of Minnesota Press, 1984.

Downie, R. S., and Elizabeth Telfer. *Respect for Persons*. London: Allen & Unwyn, 1969.

Durkheim, Emile. *Essays on Morals and Education*. Trans. W.S.F. Pickering and H. L. Sutliffe, London: Routledge & Kegan Paul, 1979.

Eddy, Mary Baker. *Science and Health*. Boston: Christian Science Publications, 1934.

Feuer, Lewis S. "John Stuart Mill as a Sociologist." In *James and John Stuart Mill: Papers of the Centenary Conference*, ed. J. M. Robson and M. Laine. Toronto: University of Toronto Press, 1976.

Feyerabend, Paul. *Against Method*. London: Verso, 1975.

——. "How to Defend Society against Science." *Radical Philosophy* 11 (1975): 1–22.

Findlay, J. N. *Language, Mind, and Value*. London: Allen & Unwyn, 1963.

Gauthier, David. *Morals by Agreement*. Oxford: Oxford University Press, 1985.

——. "Reason and Maximization," *Canadian Journal of Philosophy* 4 (1975): 411–33.

Gert, Bernard. *The Moral Rules*. New York: Harper & Row, 1973.

Gibbard, Allan. *Wise Choices, Apt Feelings*. Cambridge: Harvard University Press, 1990.

Gosling, J.C.B., and C.C.W. Taylor. *The Greeks on Pleasure*. Oxford: Clarendon Press, 1982.

Hallie, P. P. "Stoicism." In *The Encyclopedia of Philosophy*, ed. P. Edwards, vol. 8, pp. 18–22. New York: Free Press, 1967.

Hare, R. M. *The Language of Morals*. Oxford: Clarendon Press, 1952.

Harman, Gilbert. "Moral Relativism Defended." *Philosophical Review* 84 (1975): 3–22.

——. *The Nature of Morality*. New York: Oxford University Press, 1977.

Hegel, G.W.P. *Phänomenologie des Geistes*. Trans. A. V. Miller. Oxford: Oxford University Press, 1977.

Heidegger, Martin. *Being and Time*. Trans. and ed. J. Macquarrie and E. Robinson. London: Routledge & Kegan Paul, 1962.

Heyd, David. *Supererogation: Its Status in Ethical Theory*. Cambridge: Cambridge University Press, 1984.

Hume, David. *An Enquiry concerning the Principles of Morals*. London: A. Millar, 1752; reprint, ed. L. A. Selby-Bigge, Oxford: Clarendon Press, 1964.

——. "Of Suicide." In *Essays Moral, Political, and Literary*, ed. E. F. Miller. Indianapolis: Liberty Fund, 1985.

——. *A Treatise of Human Nature*. London: A. Millar, 1738; reprint, ed. L. A. Selby-Bigge, Oxford: Clarendon Press, 1964.

Huntford, Roland. *The Last Place on Earth*. New York: Atheneum, 1985.

Hutcheson, Francis. *Inquiry concerning Moral Good and Evil*. London: L. Darby, 1725.

Huxley, Aldous. "Inquiry into the Nature of Ideals and the Methods Employed for Their Realization." In his *Ends and Means*. London: Macmillan, 1937.

James, William. "The Sentiment of Rationality." In his *The Will to Believe and Other Essays in Popular Philosophy*. New York: Longmans, Green, 1897.

Kant, Immanuel. *Critique of Pure Reason*. Trans. Norman Kemp Smith. New York: St. Martin's Press, 1965.

Keeney, Ralph L., and Howard Raiffa. *Decisions with Multiple Objectives: Preferences and Value Tradeoffs*. New York: Macmillan, 1976.

Kluckhohn, Clyde. *Culture and Behavior*. Glencoe, Ill.: Free Press, 1962.

Kolakowski, Leszek. *The Alienation of Reason*. Trans. N. Guterman. Garden City, N.Y.: Doubleday, 1968.

Kuznetsov, Boris G. *Philosophy of Optimism*. Moscow: Progress Publishers, 1977.

Leibniz, G. W. *Theodicy*. Trans. E. M. Haggard. New Haven, Conn.: Yale University Press, 1952.

Linton, Ralph. "Universal Ethical Principles: An Anthropological View." In *Moral Principles of Action*, ed. R. N. Anshen. New York: Harper & Row, 1952.

Lorm, Hieronymus (pseud. of Heinrich Landesmann). *Der grundlose Optimismus: Ein Buch der Betrachtung*. Vienna: Verlag der Literarischen Gesellschaft, 1894.

Luce, R. D., and H. Raiffa. *Games and Decisions*. New York: John Wiley & Sons, 1957.

Mackie, John L. *Ethics: Inventing Right and Wrong*. Harmondsworth: Penguin Books, 1977.

Mavrodes, George. "On Deriving the Normative from the Non-Normative." *Papers of the Michigan Academy of Arts and Sciences* 53 (1968): 353–65.

Mill, John Stuart. *Autobiography*. Ed. J. J. Cose. New York: Columbia University Press, 1929.

———. *Three Essays on Religion*. Ed. Helen Taylor. New York: Greenwood Press, 1969; reprint of 1874 ed.

———. *Utilitarianism*. In *Mill: Utilitarianism—Text and Critical Essays*, ed. Samuel Gorovitz. Indianapolis: Hackett, 1971.

Moore, G. E. *Principia Ethica*. Cambridge: Cambridge University Press, 1903.

Morris, Herbert. "Persons and Punishment." *Monist* 52 (1968): 475–501.

Nagel, Thomas. *Mortal Questions*. Cambridge: Cambridge University Press, 1979.

———. *The View from Nowhere*. Oxford: Oxford University Press, 1986.

Nathanson, Stephen. *The Idea of Rationality*. Atlantic Highlands, N.J.: Humanities Press, 1985.

Neumann, John von, and Oskar Morgenstern. *Theory of Games and Economic Behavior*. 2d ed. Princeton: Princeton University Press, 1947.

Neurath, Otto. "Das Problem des Lustmaximums." *Jahrbücher der Philosophischen Gesellschaft der Universtät Wien* 18 (1912): 182–96.

Nozick, Robert. *Philosophical Explanations*. Cambridge: Harvard University Press, 1981.

Popper, K. R. *The Open Universe: An Argument for Indeterminism*. Totowa, N.J.: Rowman & Littlefield, 1982.

Prichard, H. A. "Does Moral Philosophy Rest on a Mistake?" *Mind* 21 (1912): 21–37.

Prior, A. N. "The Autonomy of Ethics." *Australian Journal of Philosophy* 38 (1960): 202 ff.; reprinted in his *Papers on Logic and Ethics*. Amherst: University of Massachusetts Press, 1976.

Putnam, Hilary. *Reason, Truth, and History*. Cambridge: Cambridge University Press, 1981.

Rawls, John. *A Theory of Justice*. Cambridge: Harvard University Press, 1971.

Redfield, Robert. "The Universally Human and the Culturally Variable." *Journal of General Education* 10 (1957): 150–60.

Rescher, Nicholas. *The Coherence Theory of Truth.* Oxford: Clarendon Press, 1973.

———. *Conceptual Idealism.* Oxford: Blackwell, 1973.

———. *Ethical Idealism.* Berkeley and Los Angeles: University of California Press, 1987.

———. *Forbidden Knowledge.* Dordrecht: Van Gorcum, 1987.

———. *Human Interests.* Stanford: Stanford University Press, 1990.

———. *Introduction to Value Theory.* Englewood Cliffs, N.J.: Prentice-Hall, 1969; reprint, Lanham, Md.: University Press of America, 1980.

———. *The Limits of Science.* Berkeley and Los Angeles: University of California Press, 1984.

———. *Moral Absolutes.* New York: Peter Lang, 1989.

———. *Pascal's Wager.* Notre Dame, Ind.: University of Notre Dame Press, 1985.

———. *The Primacy of Practice.* Oxford: Basil Blackwell, 1973.

———. *Rationality.* Oxford: Clarendon Press, 1988.

———. *A Useful Inheritance.* Savage, Md.: Rowman & Littlefield, 1989.

———. *Welfare.* Pittsburgh: University of Pittsburgh Press, 1972.

Ross, W. D. *Foundations of Ethics.* Oxford: Clarendon Press, 1939.

———. *The Right and the Good.* Oxford: Clarendon Press, 1930.

Russell, Bertrand. *Our Knowledge of the External World.* London: Allen & Unwyn, 1923.

Sambursky, S. *Physics of the Stoics.* London: Routledge, 1959.

Sartre, J. P. *Being and Nothingness.* Trans. H. E. Barnes. New York: Pocket Books, 1953.

Sayre-McCord, Geoffrey, ed. *Essays in Moral Realism.* Ithaca, N.Y.: Cornell University Press, 1988.

Schick, Frederick. *Having Reasons: An Essay in Rationality and Sociality.* Princeton: Princeton University Press, 1984.

Schiller, F.C.S. *Must Philosophers Disagree?* London: Macmillan, 1934.

Selby-Bigge, L. A., ed. *The British Moralists.* Vol. 1. Oxford: Clarendon Press, 1897.

Sidgwick, Henry. *A Method of Ethics.* 7th ed. London: Macmillan, 1928.

Simon, Herbert A. *Reason in Human Affairs.* Stanford: Stanford University Press, 1983.

Smart, J.C.C., and Bernard Williams, eds. *Utilitariansim: For and Against.* Cambridge: Cambridge University Press, 1973.

Sowell, Thomas. *Knowledge and Decisions.* New York: Basic Books, 1980.

Stebbing, L. Susan. *Ideals and Illusions.* London: Routledge & Kegan Paul, 1948.

Stevenson, Charles L. *Ethics and Language.* New Haven: Yale University Press, 1944.

———. *Facts and Values.* New Haven: Yale University Press, 1963.

Sumner, William Graham. *Folkways.* Boston: Ginn, 1906.

Telfer, Elizabeth. *Respect for Persons.* London: Routledge & Kegan Paul, 1969.

Thomson, Judith Jarvis. *The Realm of Rights*. Cambridge: Harvard University Press, 1990.

Todhunter, Isaac. *A History of the Mathematical Theory of Probability*. London, 1865; reprint, New York: Chelsea Publishing, 1949.

Ueberweg, Friedrich. *Grundriss der Geschichte der Philosophie*. Berlin: E. S. Mittler & Sohn, 1923.

Unamuno, Miguel de. *Del sentimiento trágico de la vida*. Ed. Felix Garcia. Madrid: Espasa-Calpa, 1976.

Urmson, J. O. *The Emotive Theory of Ethics*. Oxford: Oxford University Press, 1968.

———. "Saints and Heroes." In *Essays in Moral Philosophy*, ed. A. I. Melden, Seattle: University of Washington Press, 1958.

Warnock, G. J. *Contemporary Moral Philosophy*. London: Allen & Unwyn, 1967.

Weber, Max. "Der Sinn der 'Wertfreiheit' in den soziologischen und ökonomischen Wissenschaften." *Logos* 7 (1917): 63; reprinted in *Gesammelte Aufsätze zur Wissenschaftslehre*, Tubingen: Mohr, 1922, p. 476.

Wiggins, David. *Needs, Values, Truth*. Oxford: Clarendon Press, 1987.

Wilson, Catherine. "Leibnizian Optimism." *Journal of Philosophy* 80 (1983): 765–83.

Winch, D. M. *Analytical Welfare Economics*. Harmondsworth: Penguin Books, 1971.

Wittgenstein, Ludwig. *Tractatus Logico-Philosophicus*. London: Routledge & Kegan Paul, 1933.

Name Index

Aristotle, 42, 45n, 56, 56n, 57, 58, 113, 122, 179, 234, 241
Arrow, Kenneth J., 26n, 30n
Ayer, A. J., 78n, 174n

Bahnsen, Julius, 169n, 170
Baier, Kurt, 26n, 50n, 141n, 207n
Ball, Stephen W., 65n
Benn, S. I., 46n
Bentham, Jeremy, 38
Bergström, Lars, 68n, 70n
Black, Duncan, 35n
Black, Max, 31n
Boethius, 115
Boyd, Richard, 182n
Bradley, F. H., 152n
Brentano, Franz, 58, 180, 180n

Chisholm, R. M., 58n
Churchland, Paul, 97n
Cicero, 53n

Dahl, Norman O., 45n
de Condorcet, M. S. A., 35n
de la Mettrie, Julien Offray, 144
Descartes, René, 124
Diogenes Laertius, 155n
Dostoevsky, F. M., 141n
Durkheim, Emile, 203

Eddy, Mary Baker, 159n
Eisler, Rudolf, 169n
Engels, Friedrich, 157n, 169

Feuer, Lewis S., 169n
Feyerabend, Paul, 108, 108n
Findlay, J. N., 175n
Freud, Sigmund, 199

Galen, 4
Gauthier, David, 31n, 212n
Gert, Bernard, 50n
Gibbard, Alan, 174n
Gosling, J. C. B., 236n
Gracián y Morales, 241

Haldane, J. B. S., 98
Hallie, P. P., 155n
Hare, R. M., 90, 90n, 174n
Harman, Gilbert, 211n
Hartmann, Eduard von, 169
Hegel, G. W. F., 106, 109, 109n, 164, 169, 215
Heidegger, Martin, 106, 106n
Heyd, David, 129n
Hobbes, Thomas, 193n
Hume, David, 16, 46, 47, 47n, 48, 65, 78, 123, 123n, 142, 142n, 174n, 181, 208, 225, 225n
Huntford, Roland, 100n
Hutcheson, Francis, 127, 224n
Huxley, Aldous, 133, 134, 134n

Jacobs, W. W., 39
James, William, 101, 101n, 120, 165, 166

Kant, Immanuel, 124, 125, 126n, 156n, 165, 168n, 179, 180n, 215, 215n, 221n, 228
Keeney, Ralph L., 30n
Kluckhohn, Clyde, 190n
Kolakowski, Lasek, 108n
Kuznetsov, Boris G., 157n

Leibniz, G. W., 159, 162, 162n, 163, 168n, 170
Linton, Ralph, 190n
Lorm, Hieronymus, 165, 165n
Luce, R. D., 26n

Mackie, John M., 90n, 198n
Marx, Karl, 130, 133, 160, 179, 199
Maupertuis, P. L. M. de, 168n
Mavrodes, George, 68n
Mill, John Stuart, 26n, 74, 169n, 235, 237, 238, 238n
Moore, G. E., 78, 90, 90n, 91
Morgenstern, Oskar, 29n
Morris, Herbert, 221n
Mortimore, G. W., 46n
Mott, T. H., 68n
Mozart, Wolfgang Amadeus, 141

Nagel, Thomas, 27n, 140n, 181n, 220n
Nansen, Fijthof, 100
Nathanson, Stephen, 46n, 243n
Neumann, John von, 29, 29n
Neurath, Otto, 30n
Nietzsche, Friedrich, 48, 118, 179, 199
Nozick, Robert, 126n, 141n

Ortega y Gasset, José, 241

Pascal, Blaise, 125
Peirce, C. S., 160
Plato, 42, 155, 156, 199, 208, 224
Popper, K. R., 98n
Prichard, H. A., 213, 213n
Prior, A. N., 68n
Putnam, Hilary, 102n

Raiffa, Howard, 26n, 30n
Ranke, Leopold von, 203
Rawls, John, 55n, 161n
Redfield, Robert, 190n
Robespierre, Maximilien, 130
Robinson, Edward Arlington, 236n
Ross, W. D., 180, 181n, 208n
Russell, Bertrand, 142, 142n

Sambursky, Samuel, 155n
Sanchez, Francisco, 241
Sartre, J. P., 53, 122, 122n, 186n
Sayre-McCord, Geoffrey, 182n
Schick, Frederick, 52n
Schiller, F. C. S., 104, 104n

Schopenhauer, Arthur, 163, 168, 168n, 169, 170
Sidgwick, Henry, 49, 49n, 55n
Simon, Herbert, 26n, 47n
Socrates, 155, 224, 235
Sowell, Thomas, 206n
Spinoza, Benedict, 126, 170
Stalin, Josef, 130
Stebbing, Susan, 134, 134n
Stevenson, C. L., 174, 174n
Sumner, William Graham, 182, 182n

Taylor, C. C. W., 236n
Telfer, Elizabeth, 221n
Thomas Aquinas, Saint, 20, 20n, 193n
Thomson, Judith Jarvis, 79n
Todhunter, Isaac, 35n

Ueberweg, Friedrich, 165n
Unamuno, Miguel de, 117, 117n, 124, 124n, 150, 241
Urmson, J. O., 129, 129n, 174n

Voltaire, F. M. A. de, 159, 162, 163, 168n

Walpole, Robert, 30
Warnock, G. J., 174n
Weber, Max, 46n, 133
Wiggins, David, 140, 140n, 141n, 152n
Wilson, Catherine, 162
Winch, D. M., 26n
Wittgenstein, Ludwig, 107, 107n

Xenophanes, 57

Subject Index

absolutism, 11–12
activism, 149–52
actuality optimism, 158–59
affective happiness, 233–34, 238–40
anthropology and relativism, 187–89, 196–97
attitudinal optimism, 164–68
autonomy of persons, 113
autonomy of science, 108–10

circumstantial universality, 4–5
cognitive rationality, 12–20
coherence, 83–84
commensurability, 27–31
community and persons, 120–22, 202–5
conflicting ideals, 133–35
consequence principle, 68–69
consequentialism, 75–76
control: internal vs. external, 147–48
convenient exceptions, 206–8
cultivation hierarchies, 7–12

Darwinism, 93–100
deontic force, 209–13
desires, 71–74
dichotomy assumption, 69
domestic impetus, 137

economy of values, 60–62
ends: rational economy of, 43–44
eudaimonia, 234
evaluative rationality, 12–20, 45–62
ex conditione obligations, 214
existentialism, 152
ex officio obligations, 214

fact statements, 66–71
factuality of fact denial, 69
finalities, 9
flourishing (eudaimonia), 56–57, 234
free will, 146–48
functionalism, 180–83, 252

goods: homogeneity of, 42
grandeur of ideals, 136–39
Gyges, ring of, 224–25

happiness: affective vs. reflective, 233–34, 238–40, 244–45; and rationality, 233–45
heroic impetus, 137
hierarchies of cultivation, 7–12
hierarchies of implementation, 189–98
hierarchy of truths, 194
homogeneity of goods, 42
homo valuens, 246, 252–53
human insignificance, 139–42
humanity and reason, 240–44

idealism, 24–25, 106, 139, 246–53
ideals: conflicting, 129–39, 133–35; grandeur of, 136–39; unrealism of, 136; utility of, 132–33
identity: personal, 122–25
implementation hierarchies, 189–98
incommensurable goods, 27–31
indifferentism, 12
informative rationality, 48
insignificance of humans, 139–42
intelligence, 23–24
interests, 50–57
internal vs. external control, 147–48
irrationalism, 12

knowledge and values, 93–109

legitimacy of wants, 56
life: meaning and/or purpose of, 140–52

man as machine, 144–46
maximization vs. optimization, 27–49
maximizing (of utility), 32–36
meaning of life, 140–52
mechanical view of man, 144–46
meliorism, 160–64
"Mill's fallacy," 74
modes of optimism, 155–72
morality and rationality, 183–86, 221–29
moral objectivity, 173–86
moral pluralism, 187
moral rationality, 206–29
moral relativism, 187–205
motivation vs. obligation, 209–10

motive vs. reason, 227–29
mutual recognizance, 114

natural qualities, 90–91
non-natural qualities, 90–91
norms of rationality, 8

objectivity: in morals, 173–86; and value, 57–60
obligation: vs. motivation, 209–10; ontological, 20–24, 213–29
obligations: *ex officio* vs. *ex conditione*, 214; of personhood, 125–28
optimism, 155–72
optimization vs. maximization, 27–49

parameters of optimism, 157–58
personal autonomy, 113
personal identity, 122–25
personhood and obligation, 113–28
persons and community, 120–22
pessimism, 155–72
pluralism, moral, 187
practical rationality, 12–20
pragmatism, 166–67, 246–53
preferences, 34–36, 50–57, 71–74
primary qualities, 91
prudence, 226
purpose of life, 140–42
purposiveness, 93–100

qualities: natural vs. non-natural, 90–91; primary, secondary, tertiary, 91

rational economy of ends, 43–44
rational evaluation, 81–85
rational inquiry, 81–85
rationality: cognitive, 12–20; evaluative, 12–20, 45–62; and happiness, 233–45; and maximization, 22–44; moral, 183–86, 221–29, of morality, 206–29; norms of, 8; and optimization, 22–44; practical, 12–20
realism: of evaluation, 85–92
reason: and humanity, 240–44; vs. motive, 227–29; systemic unity of, 19–20; universality of, 3–6
reflective happiness, 233–34, 238–40, 244–45

relativism: anthropological, 196–97; moral, 187–205
ring of Gyges, 208, 224–25

science: autonomy of, 108–10; and values, 93–110, 148–52
secondary qualities, 91
selfishness, 249
self-realization, 214
social contract, 211–12
Spanish moralists, 241–44
standards, communal, 202–5
statements of fact vs. value, 66–71
subjectivism, 173–86
supervenience of values, 90
systemic unity of reason, 19–20

tendency optimism, 160–64
tertiary qualities, 91
truths: hierarchy of, 194

universality: circumstantial, 4–5; of reason, 3–6
unrealism of ideals, 136
utilitarianism, 31–38, 212–13
utility: of ideals, 132–33
utility maximizing, 32–36
utility theory, 36–38
utopias, 129

validation of values, 249–53
value: and knowledge, 100–108
value consequentialism, 75–76
value economy, 60–62
value naturalism, 65–66
value objectivity, 57–60
value realism, 85–92
value reductionism, 65–66
value statements, 66–71
value subjectivism, 65–66
value supervenience, 90
values: and Darwinism, 93–100; and science, 93–110, 148–52; validation of, 249–53

wants, 50–57
Wazonga tribe, 187–88
will: freedom of, 146–48